POSTCARD HISTORY SERIES

Malden

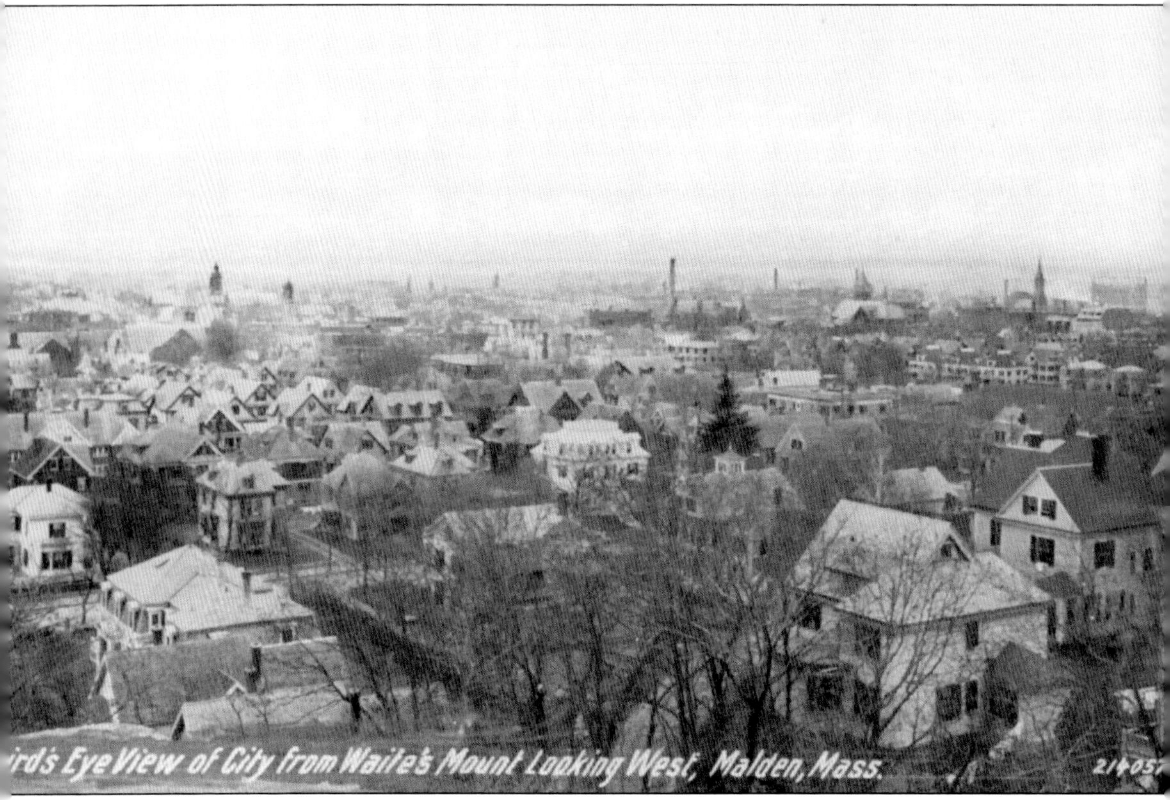

This bird's-eye view of Malden is taken from Waitt's Mount, the highest point in Malden. Once called Mount Prospect or Captain's Hill, Malden residents watched the Battle of Bunker Hill from its crest. In the fall of 1778, during the Revolutionary War, a campsite and an alarm beacon were located atop this hill. Searchlights and antiaircraft batteries were stationed here during the early months of World War II. It has variously been spelled "Wayte's Mount" or "Waite's Mount." It takes its name from Capt. John Wayte (1618–1698), who resided in a house at a northeast corner of Main Street and Mountain Avenue. Wayte was the son-in-law of Joseph Hills, who came from Maldon, England, in 1638. Hills named Malden after his hometown in England. (Courtesy of the Malden Historical Society.)

On the Front Cover: This c. 1900 photograph of Pleasant Street is looking west from Main Street in Malden Square. This intersection was once called Central Square. (Courtesy of the Malden Historical Society.)

On the Back Cover: This view of city hall shows the facade facing Main Street. Note the horse-drawn merchant cart to the right. City hall was built in 1857 and originally called the town house. (Courtesy of the Malden Historical Society.)

POSTCARD HISTORY SERIES

Malden

Malden Historical Society

ARCADIA PUBLISHING

ISBN 978-1-4671-2342-6

Published by Arcadia Publishing
Charleston, South Carolina

Printed in the United States of America

Library of Congress Control Number: 2014954867

For all general information contact Arcadia Publishing at:
Telephone 843-853-2070
Fax 843-853-0044
E-mail sales@arcadiapublishing.com
For customer service and orders:
Toll-Free 1-888-313-2665

Visit us on the Internet at www.arcadiapublishing.com

This book is dedicated to all who have helped preserve the record of Malden's past, to those who use this past as a guide for the present, and to those who may use what is recorded here as a plan for future action and preservation. We particularly wish to acknowledge those of recent memory who instilled in us our love for the city and its history and are no longer with us—especially Dorathy Rothe, Robert Graham, and Marion Baxter. We hope to carry on their labors.

Contents

Acknowledgments

The Malden Historical Society wishes to thank its publication committee for the preparation of this work: Edward Flaherty, Frank Russell, Barbara Tolstrup, and John Tramondozzi.

The society also wishes to thank the librarians and staff of the Malden Public Library for their help, especially Judy Weaver, library administrative assistant; Jack Ryan for his invaluable computer skills; families and friends of the beleaguered committee for putting up with them; and especially the board of directors of the Malden Historical Society for its encouragement. These images are from the collection of the Malden Historical Society and some of its members who have allowed them to be used in this book.

The Malden Historical Society is located in the Converse Memorial Building of the Malden Public Library. Donations to the society of photographs, artifacts, and other memorabilia are greatly appreciated and help to preserve Malden's history for future generations. You may contact us by writing to the Malden Historical Society, 36 Salem Street, Malden, Massachusetts, 02148; by telephoning (781-338-9365); or at www.maldenhistoricalsociety.org.

Introduction

Malden is one of the oldest communities in Massachusetts. Originally a part of Charlestown in the Massachusetts Bay Colony, Malden was in a section north of the Mystic River known as "Mystic Side." Settled in 1640, it was made a town when its first church and minister were established in 1648. Much of it was rural farmland, but a good deal of flowing water made the area ideal for mill works. In the mid-19th century, industry and manufacture became the main endeavors. The area known as Malden was considerably larger than it is today. It abutted Chelsea and Lynn and included what later became the cities of Melrose and Everett. Today, those abutting areas are Revere and Saugus.

In the 19th century, industry flourished, and Malden became a town populated with businesses and businessmen. This was further strengthened by Malden's position at the crossing of two main roads—the Salem-Medford Road and the Reading-Charlestown Road—one going north-south, and the other, east-west. When public transportation appeared, Malden Center became the hub for trolley, train, and bus transportation.

One of the earliest businesses was the Odiorne Mill, which manufactured nails. Barrett's Dye House made a "Turkey Red" pigment that was shipped throughout the country. Elisha Converse, Malden's greatest benefactor, founded the Boston Rubber Shoe Company and made a fortune, which he used to fund many philanthropic endeavors in the town, including the library, the hospital, YMCA, and the Baptist church, and he also donated land for a public park, Pine Banks. A.H. Davenport Company produced furniture for a broad market, including the Iolani Palace in Honolulu, the US Department of State in Washington, and the United Nations Building in New York. Malden became a center of pewter production, and David Morey and his family did very well in the business. A number of smaller companies were also visible on Malden's main streets. Main Street and Pleasant Street became the center of town, and retail business flourished with Woolworth, Kresge, and Grant department stores.

Malden always was and continues to be an active and progressive community. The Reverend Peter Thacher's Malden declaration of May 27, 1776, preceded the Declaration of Independence. The antislavery movement was embraced by a number of Malden abolitionists, including David and Almira Morey, whose home served as a central meeting place for the group. There were at least four Malden stops on the Underground Railroad: the Morey House on Hillside Avenue, the Redpath House on Maple Street, the Parsonage on Main Street, and the Cox-Haven House on Clifton Street. Although these houses still stand today, only the Parsonage has appeared on a postcard. Malden resident Harriet Robinson and Mayor Converse's daughter-in-law Mary Parker Converse were early woman activists.

The town became a city in 1882. Grand residences were built by the businessmen, and "nice" residences were constructed by the middle class. Since very little remains of Malden's 17th- and 18th-century roots, most of its oldest buildings date from the late 19th century.

Being progressive, Malden tore down buildings as they got old and replaced them with more modern ones or ones more adapted to newer uses. In the 1960s, Malden became one of the first communities in the commonwealth to undertake urban renewal. This resulted in whole areas and neighborhoods being razed and put to new use. Suffolk Square and the Commercial Street factory area were transformed at this time.

During the 19th century, Malden became a center for the arts and artists. The earliest ones were probably Cyrus and Darius Cobb, the sons of minister Sylvanus Cobb, who left Malden in the 1820s. The Frenchman Joseph Morviller and native Albion Bicknell painted numerous Malden scenes. When Elisha Converse provided funds for a library, he made sure it contained art galleries. Bicknell's *Lincoln at Gettysburg* has a prominent permanent spot in the Malden Public Library art galleries. Ernest Ipsen, a society portraitist, was born in Malden, as was Frank Stella, a modernist. One of the enduring forces of art in Malden was the presence of Horace Burdick, the nonagenarian resident and artist whose Malden home became a meeting place for many of the Boston artists. Malden continues as a center for the arts today.

Malden was the home to many well-known authors, including Eliot Paul, author of *Linden on the Saugus Branch*; Erle Stanly Gardner, creator of the Perry Mason series; Henry Morton Robinson, author of *The Cardinal*; and Kenneth Roberts, author of *Northwest Passage*.

At one time, Malden could also boast of at least three stage companies and seven theaters. Many of these have appeared on postcards and are shown in this book.

By the early 1900s, when postcards came into common use, Malden had developed into a large prosperous city. Immigrants from Europe and elsewhere—especially the Irish, Jewish, and Italians—brought a change to the city. A working middle class had different needs, and the city's development reflected this. Various religious congregations erected houses of worship, and numerous schools were built to accommodate the children. Proud inhabitants used postcards to send quick messages and to show friends and relatives where they lived or had visited.

Many of the cards were selected to show what was there. Over the years since then, many of these sights have been greatly modified, and some have entirely disappeared. Moreover, the postcards for this book also reflect the fact that many important sites were never recorded as postcards. Those selected for this book were chosen with the purpose of showing Malden's proud past leading to its strong future.

One

CHURCHES

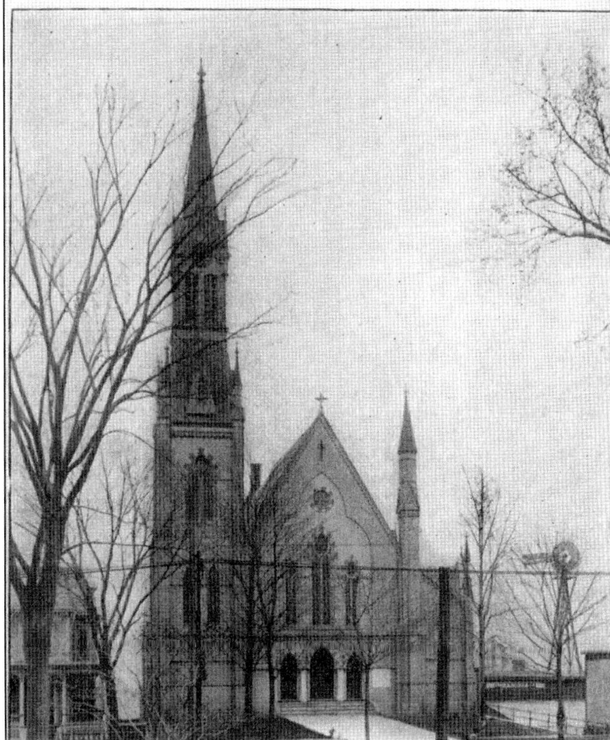

FIRST CONGREGATIONAL CHURCH, MALDEN, MASS.

The First Congregational Church (Trinitarian) is seen on Pleasant Street. Built in 1870, it was destroyed by fire on December 13, 1933. The present church was dedicated on the same site on April 7, 1935. In the early 1820s, a dispute arose with some of the towns becoming Unitarian and others Trinitarian, thus establishing a First Church and a First Parish in each. Malden chose to become Trinitarian and Universalist; the former becoming First Church and the latter, First Parish. By the turn of the 20th century, Malden also had multiple Episcopal, Catholic, and other Protestant denominational churches. Postcards of Jewish houses of worship are rare or nonexistent.

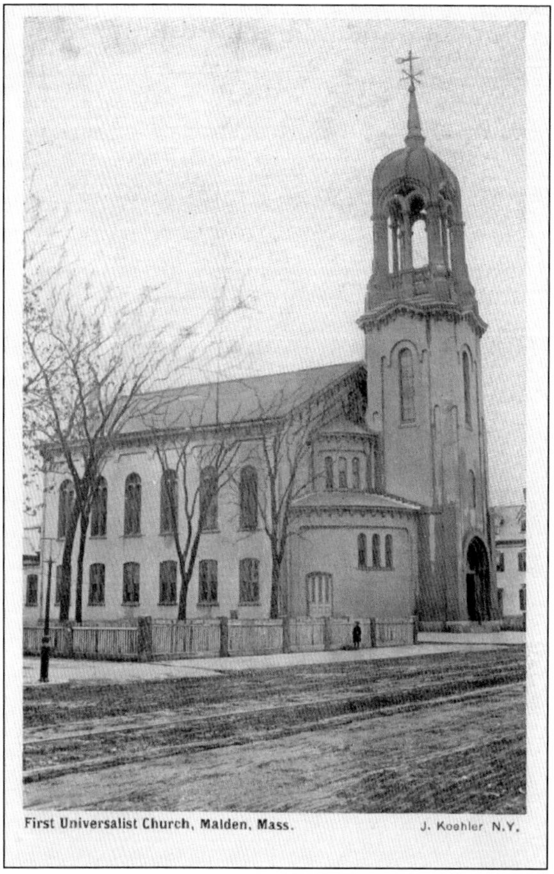

The First Parish Church was built in 1802 on the site of the present Walgreens, opposite Sacred Hearts Church. It also served as the town's meeting hall until the erection of the old city hall in 1857. It originally housed the Malden Church and, after 1828, the First Parish Universalist Church. It was demolished in 1911.

The First Parish (Universalist) Church is located at the intersection of Elm and Pleasant Streets.

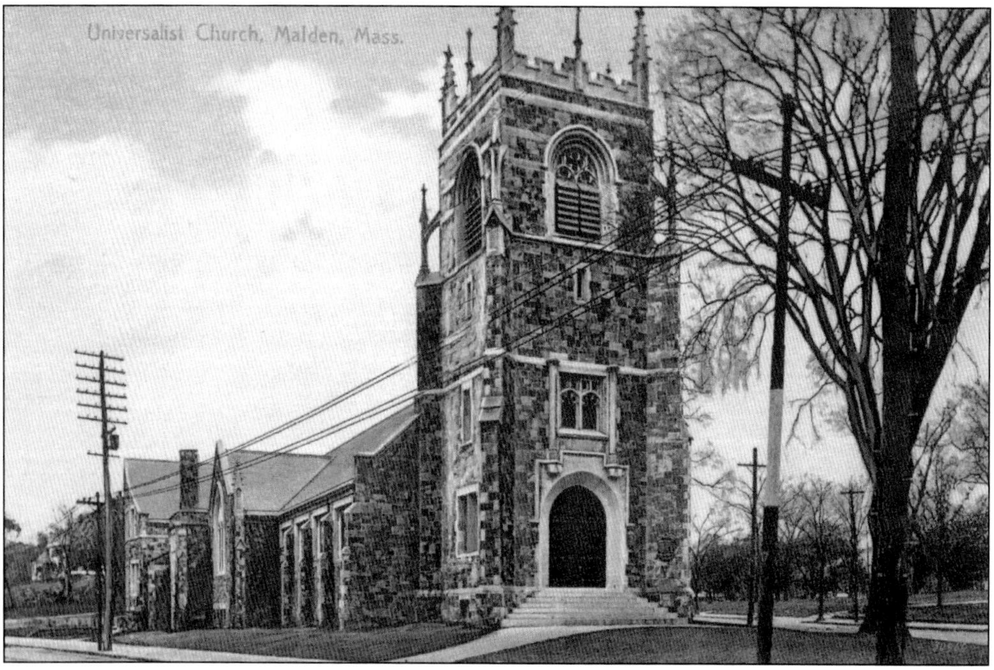

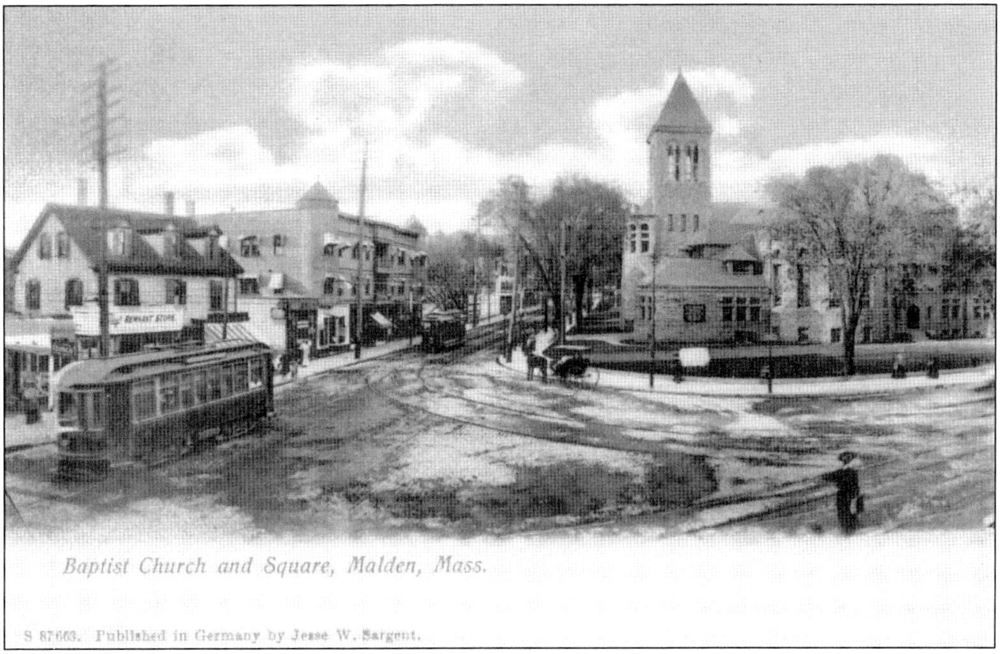

The First Baptist Church is seen in this panorama of Converse Square looking north. On the left, opposite the church, is Barrett's Opera House. The very first Baptist meetinghouse was located at the site of the Salem Street Cemetery. The second meetinghouse was located on this site on land donated by Joseph Hills.

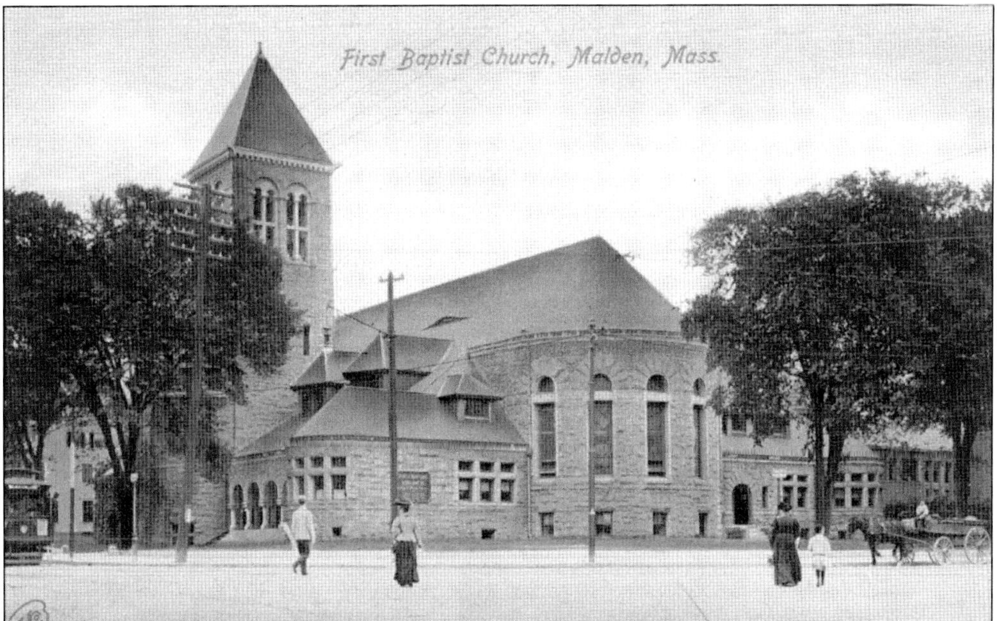

The First Baptist Church sat at the corner of Salem and Main Streets in Converse Square. This church was built in 1891 through the beneficence of Elisha Converse and replaced an earlier Baptist church at this site. Two earlier edifices were destroyed by fire in 1855 and 1862.

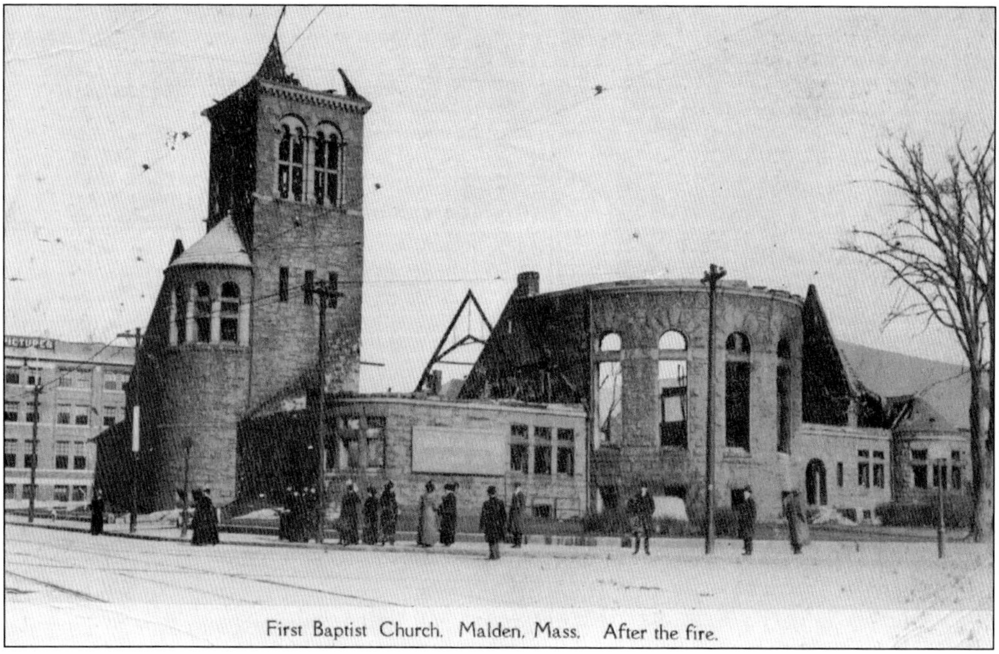

First Baptist Church. Malden, Mass. After the fire.

The First Baptist Church is seen after the ruins of a fire in February 1915. The church was rebuilt and dedicated in 1916. Its rose windows were the gift of Gov. Alvan T. Fuller in memory of his parents.

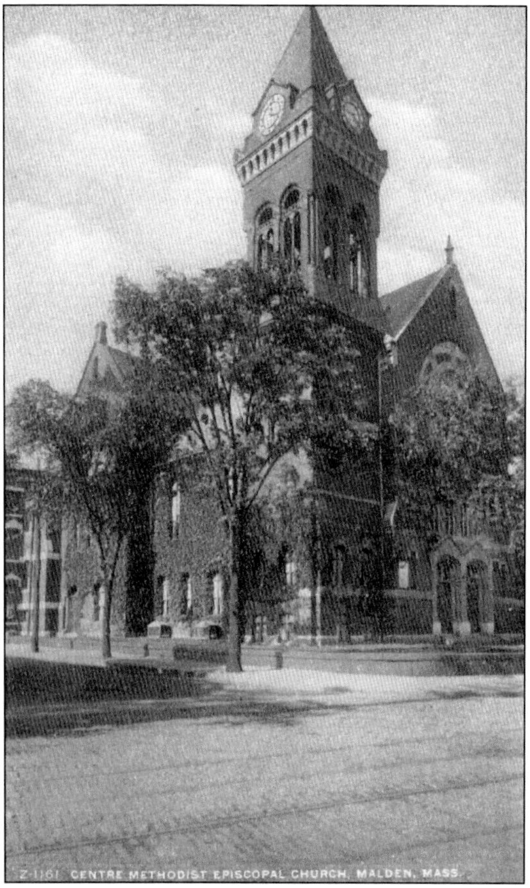

Z-1161 CENTRE METHODIST EPISCOPAL CHURCH, MALDEN, MASS.

The Centre Methodist Episcopal Church was located at the corner of Pleasant Street and Washington Street. Construction on it began in 1871; it was dedicated 1874. It was destroyed by fire in May 1971.

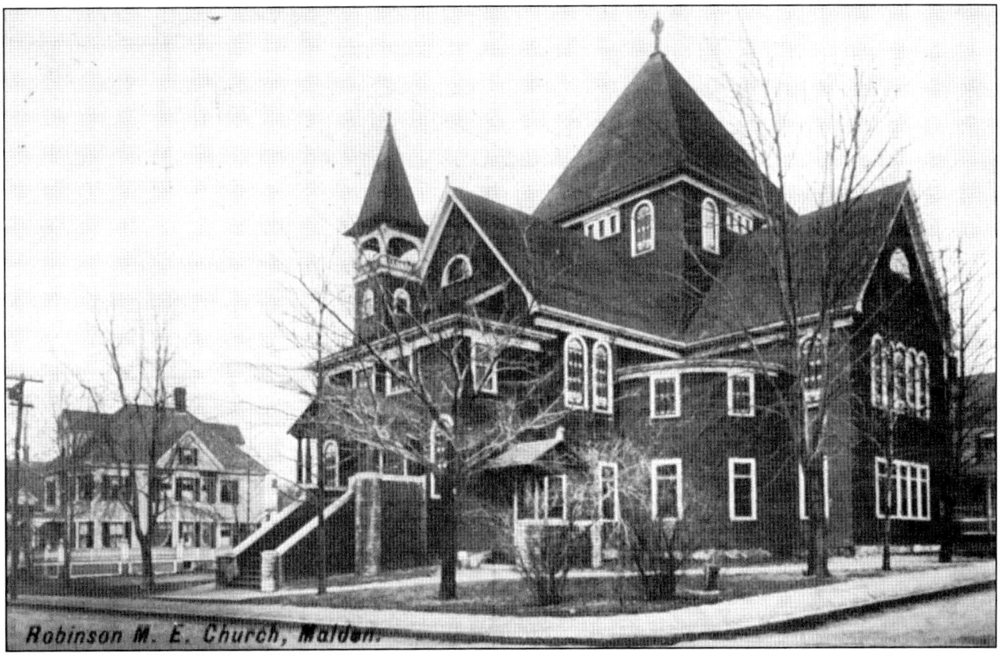

The Robinson Methodist Episcopal Church was located on the corner of Boston and Fairmont Streets in the Belmont Hill section of the city. It was built in 1888. Originally called the Belmont Methodist Episcopal Church, it was renamed after Roswell R. Robinson, who heavily endowed the church. When attendance dwindled, it joined with the Centre Methodist Episcopal Church to become the Centre United Methodist Episcopal Church.

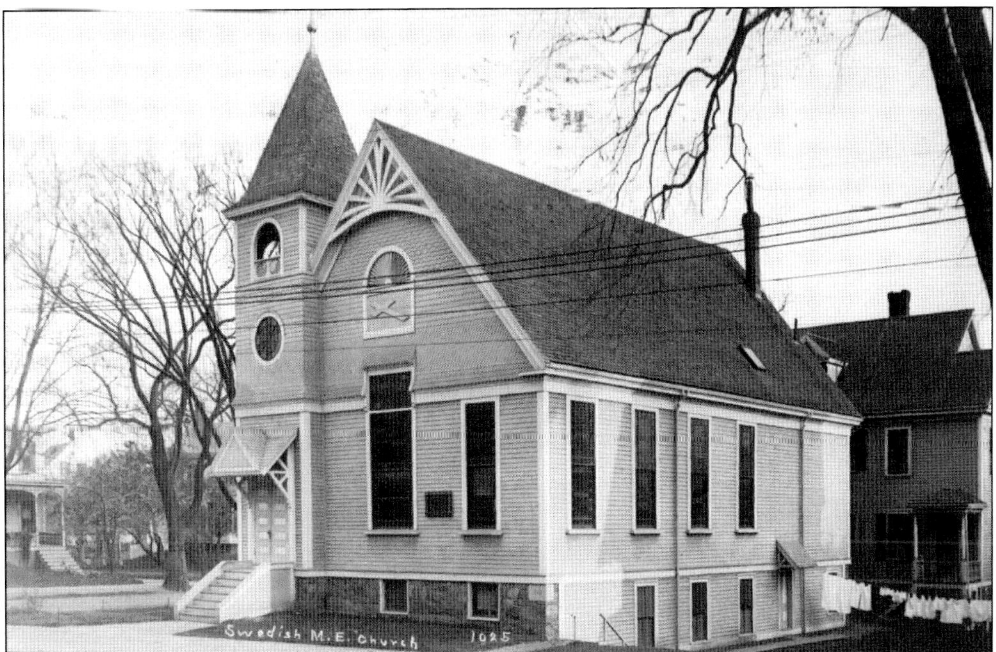

The Swedish Methodist Episcopal Church was located on Waite Street at the corner of Church Street. Today, it is the First Lutheran Church.

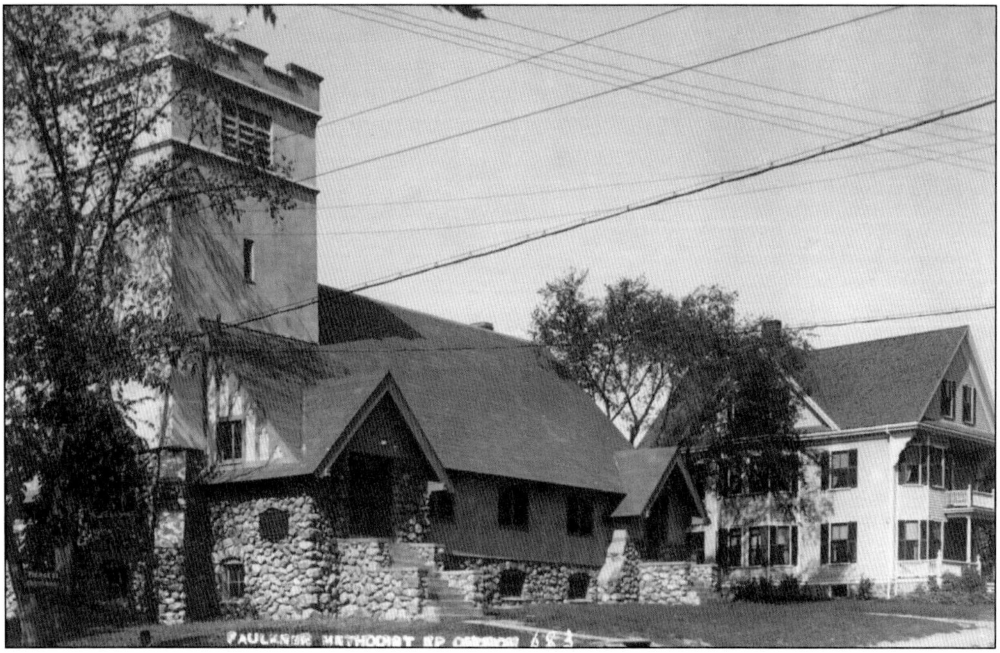

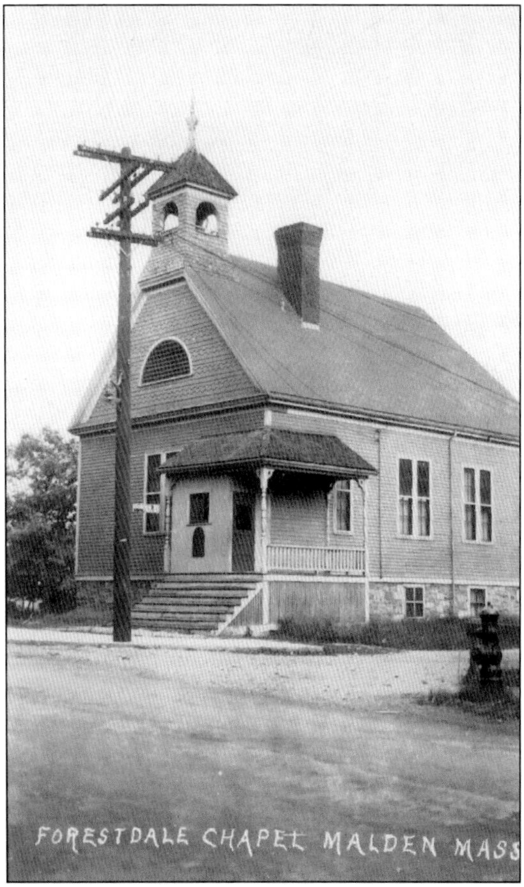

The Faulkner Methodist Episcopal Church at the corner of Salem Street and Pierce Street was built on land donated in 1883 by Mr. and Mrs. John B. Faulkner. After church use ceased in the 1960s, it became the Square and Compass Club of Masonic affiliation. It presently houses the Imani Temple.

The Forestdale Chapel was built in 1892 on Forest Street at the corner of Gordon Street and was a mission church of the First Congregational Church. Today, it is the Forestdale Community Church.

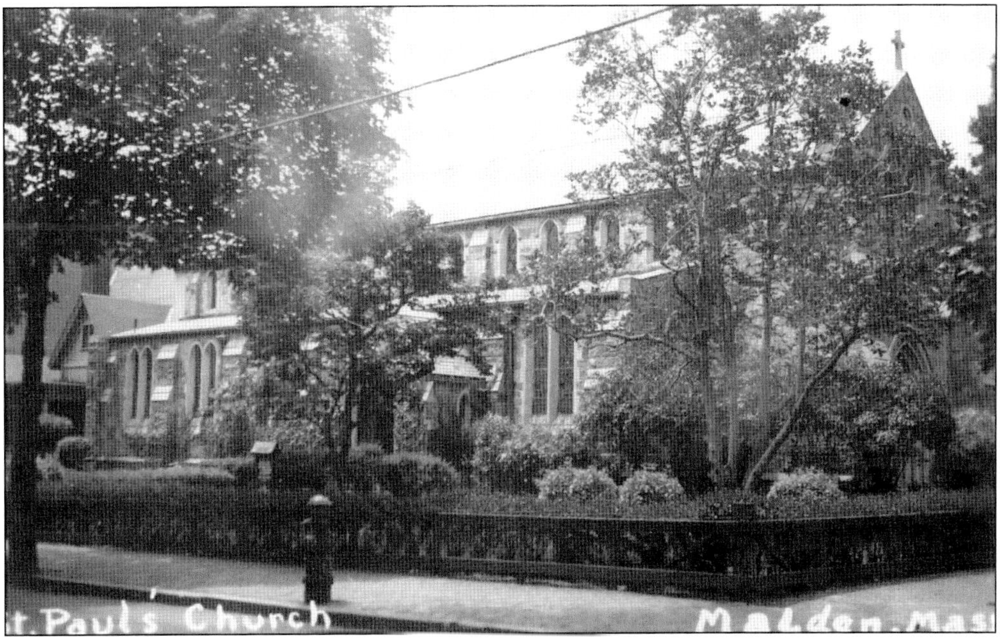

Originally called Grace Church, St. Paul's Parish, Episcopal is located at the corner of Washington Street and Florence Street. The church was designed by noted architect Ralph Adams Cram and is listed in the National Register of Historic Places.

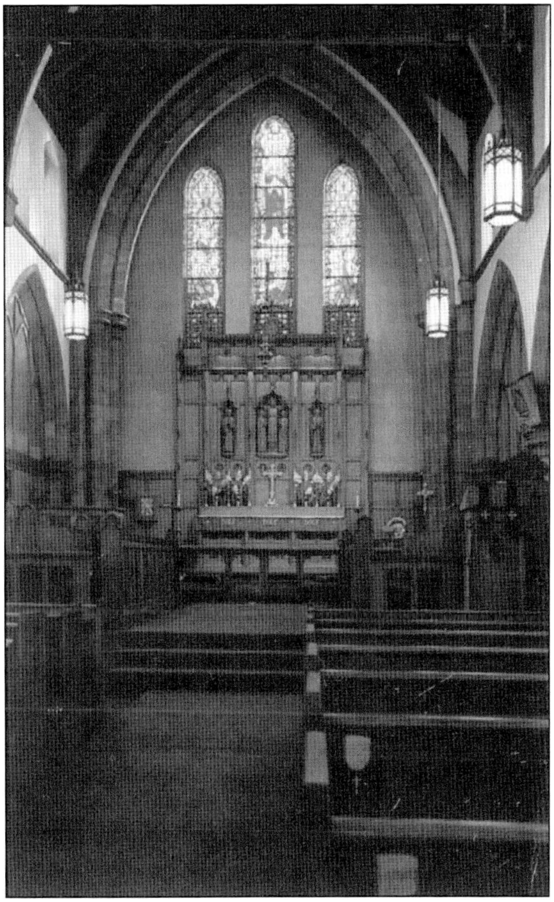

The beautiful Gothic interior of St. Paul's Parish, Episcopal is seen in this view and shows the high altar and hand-carved reredos. The church was built in 1913.

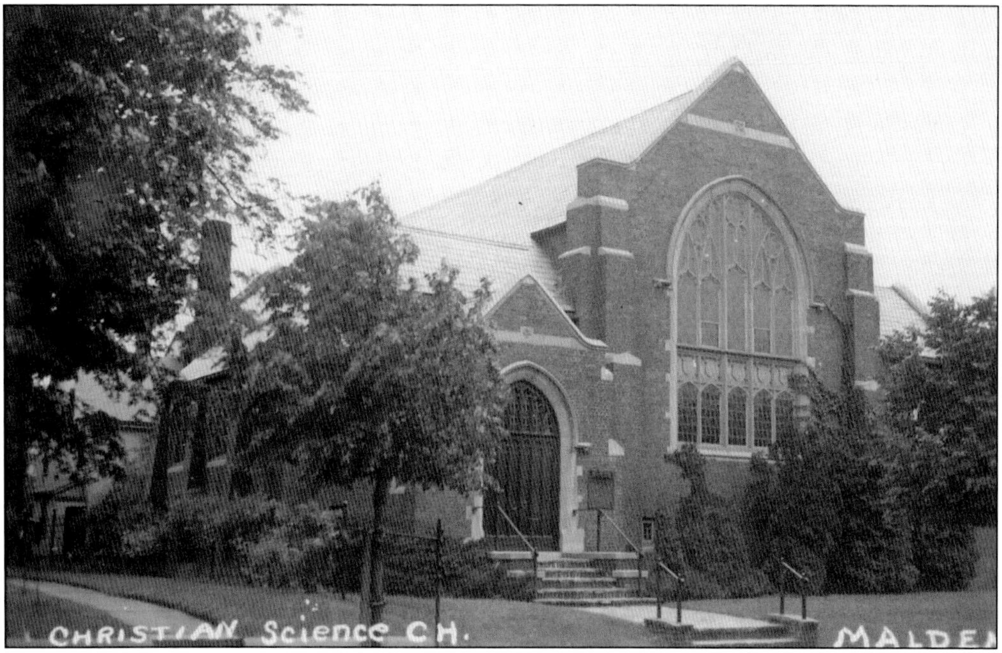

The Christian Science Church was on Main Street at the corner of Spring Street. Today, it is the home of the Philadelphie Seventh-day Adventist Church serving a predominately Haitian congregation.

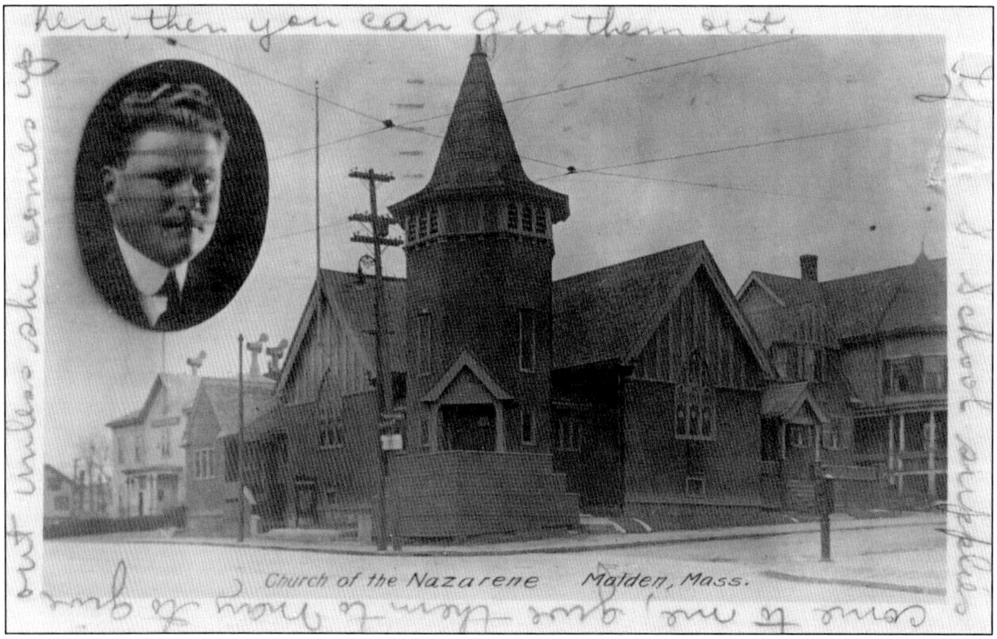

The Church of the Nazarene was located in Judson Square at the corner of Walnut and High Streets. It was razed in the 1970s. Note the Judson School to the left of the church.

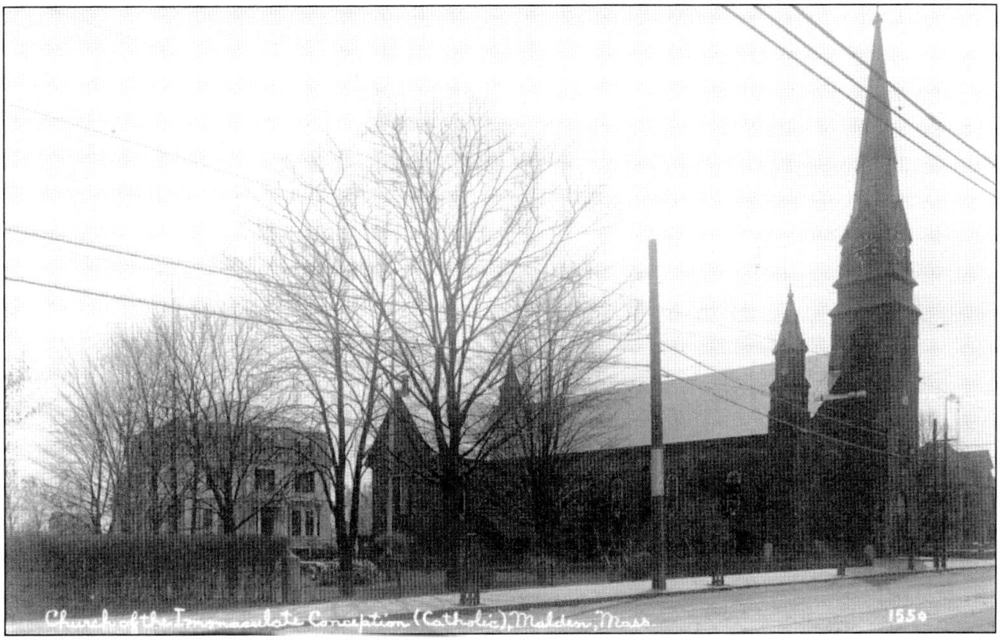

The Immaculate Conception Church was on Pleasant Street near the Medford line. Erected in 1855, Malden's first Catholic church was razed in 1963 and replaced by the present church.

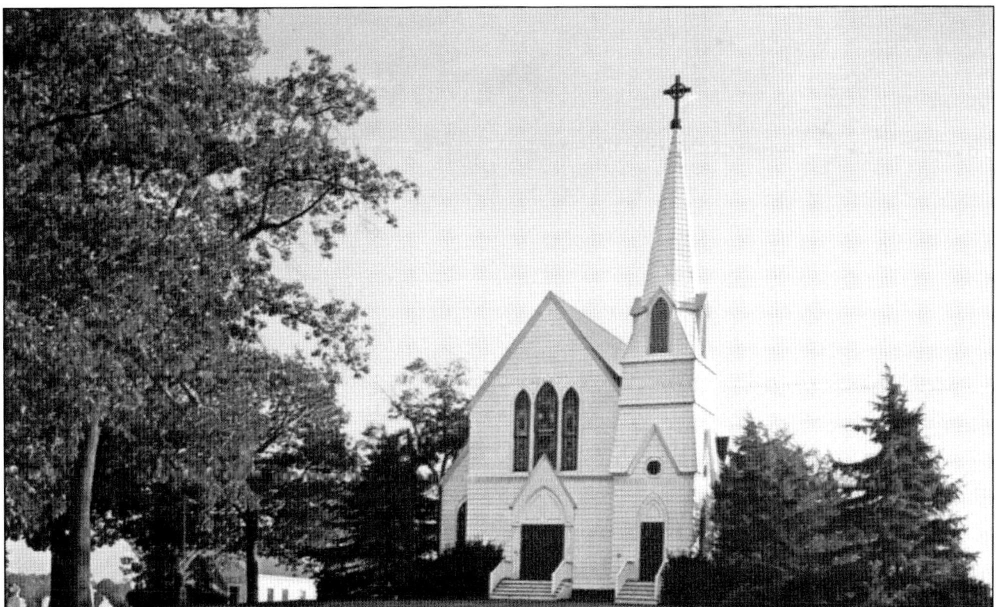
All Souls Chapel was located inside the Holy Cross Cemetery. It was removed in the 1980s.

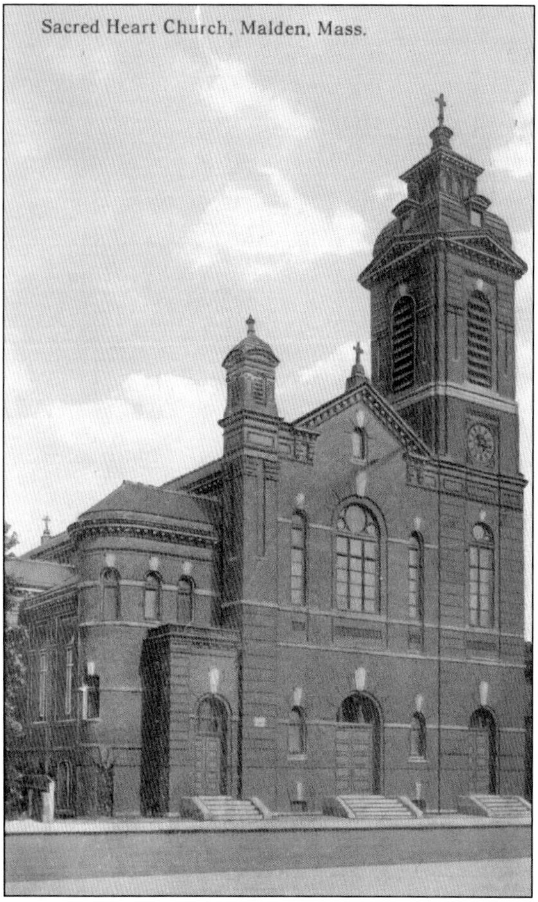

The second Catholic church in Malden, Sacred Hearts Church, is located on Main Street. It was built in 1892 by Fr. Thomas Shahan. Father Shahan was called the "church builder" because of the many churches he constructed in the diocese. This was said to be his last and greatest achievement.

The interior view of Sacred Hearts Church is seen here around 1912. The interior remains substantially the same today.

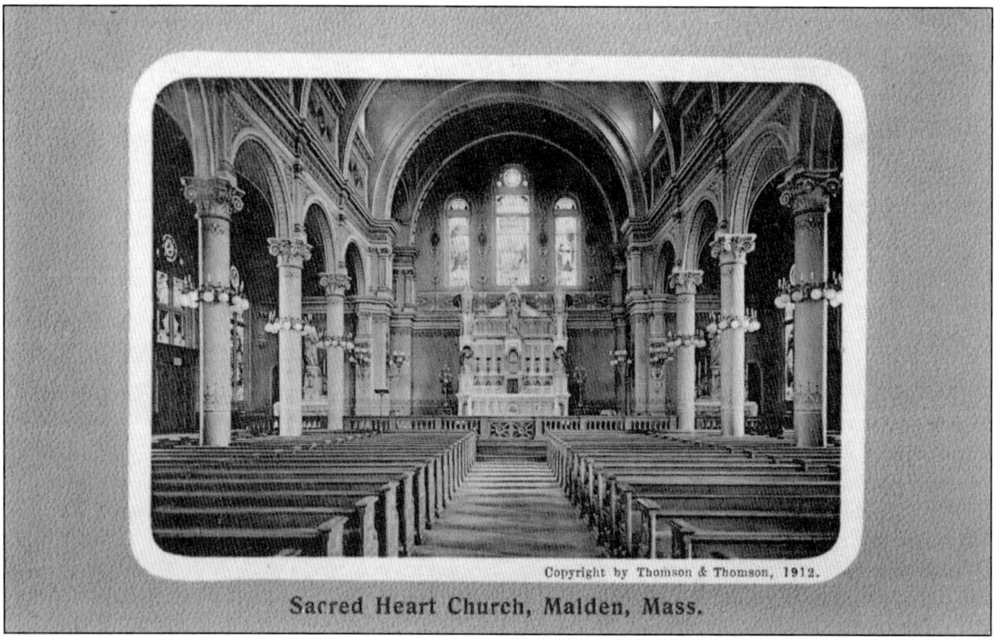

Two

SCHOOLS

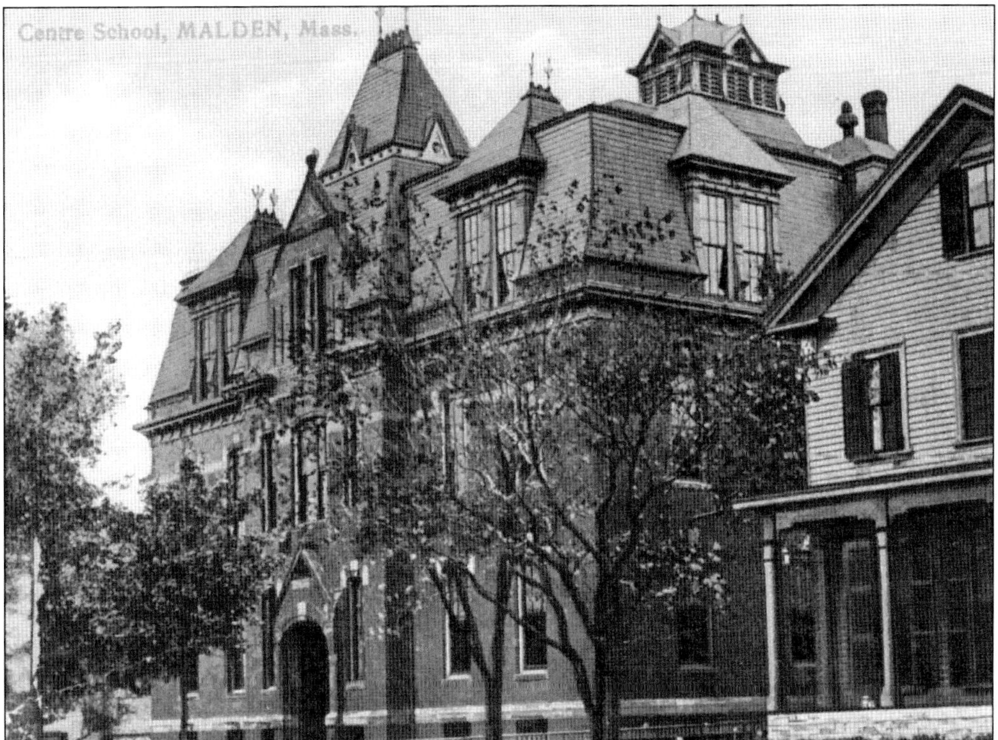

The first school in Malden was established in 1665. Beginning in the late 1800s, due to its large population and the importance of education to its residents, Malden built a number of schools for its children. At one time, there were over a dozen elementary or grammar schools and three junior high schools. One high school saw many alterations over the years to keep up with demand. The Centre Grammar School, seen above, was located on Ferry Street. It was built in 1875 and contained 16 classrooms. Razed in the 1960s, the site presently is Msgr. Foley Hall of the Cheverus School.

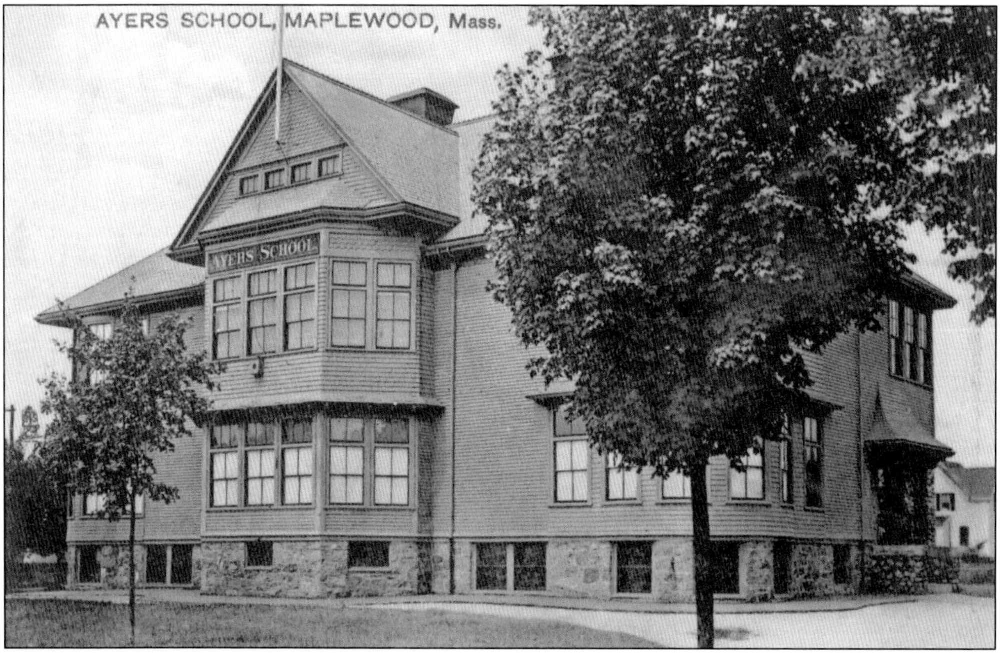

The Ayers School was built in 1891 and located on Cherry Street in the Maplewood section of Malden. It contained six classrooms.

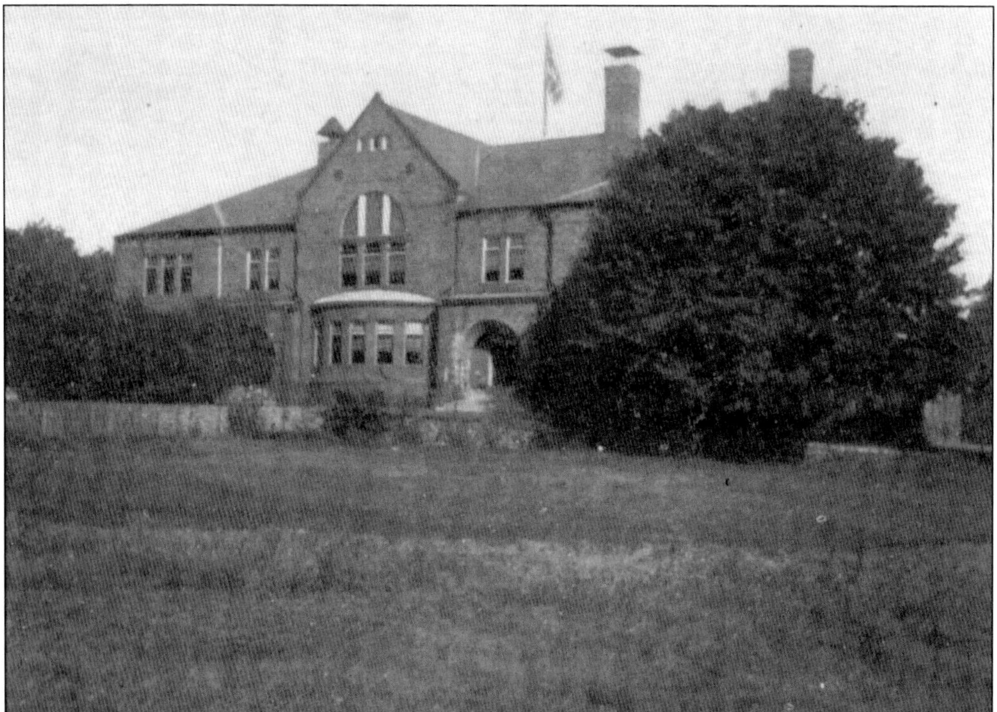

The West School was built in 1885 on Pleasant Street, opposite the Beebe School. It was later renamed the Laura A. Leonard School for its longtime principal. The building has been adapted for reuse as medical and professional offices.

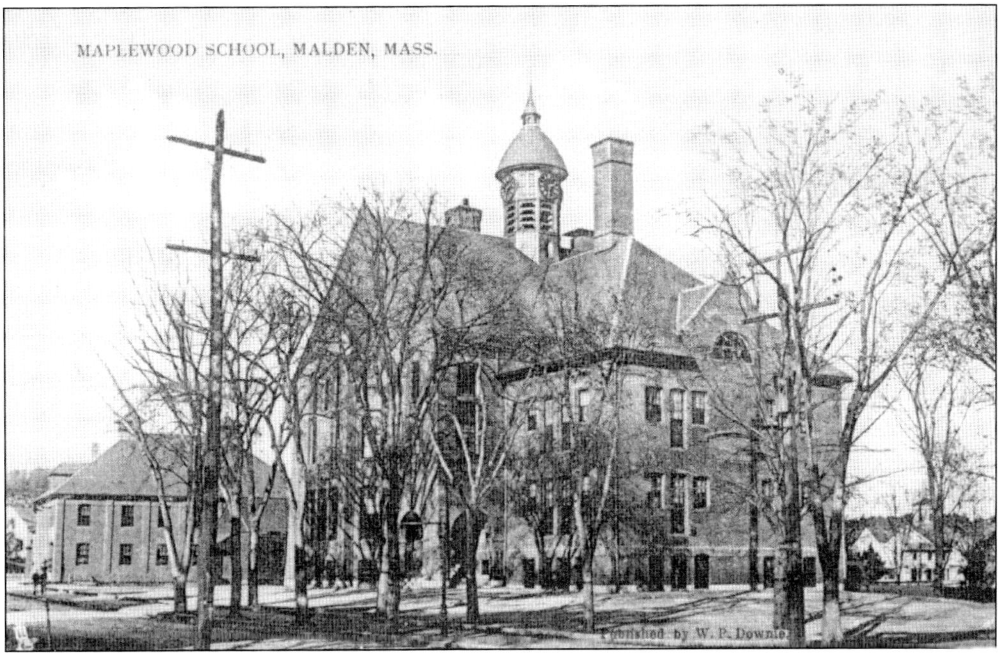

The Maplewood School was located at the corner of Salem and Laurel Streets. Erected in 1886, it contained 12 classrooms. Razed in the 1960s, it was replaced by a new Maplewood School. The site is presently the Mystic Valley Regional Charter School. Note the Maplewood Fire Station to the left.

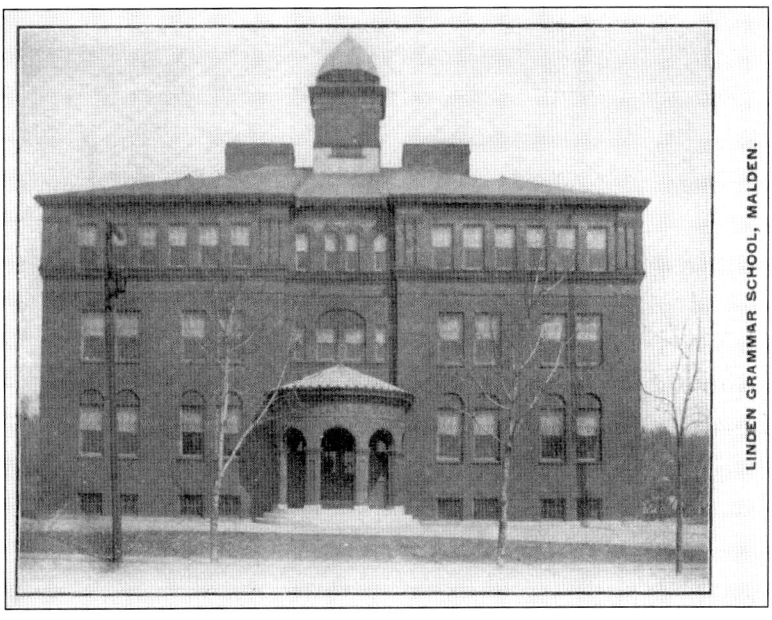

The Linden Grammar School was built in 1895 at the corner of Oliver and Springdale Streets. It contained 10 classrooms. It was demolished in the 1960s to accommodate the Linden senior housing project.

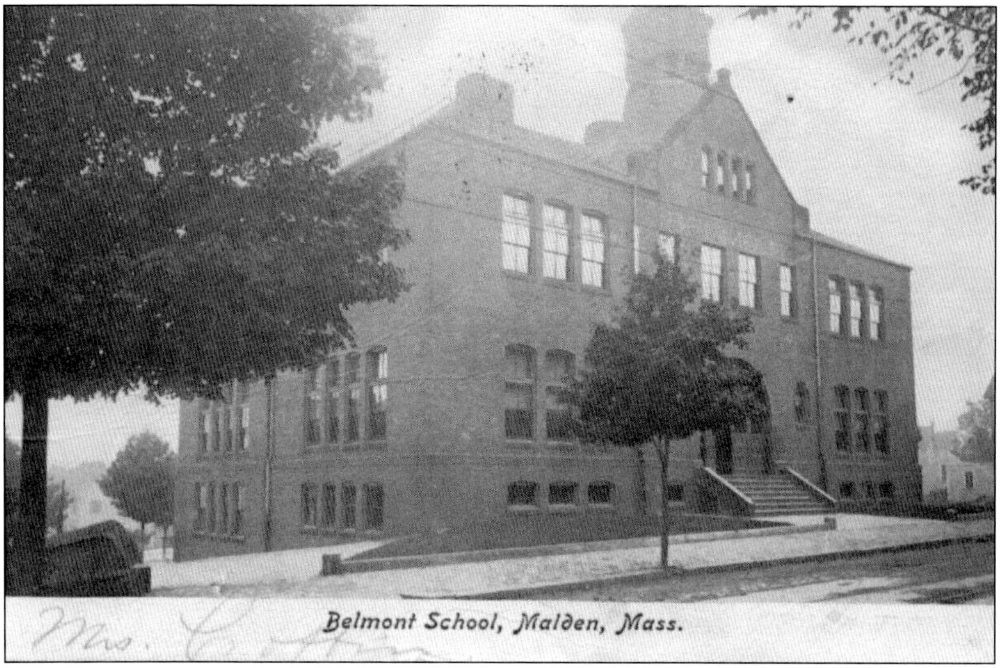

The Belmont School was built in 1889 on Cross Street at the corner of High Street. It contained eight classrooms originally. An addition was built in the 1930s. The school's last year of service was the 1999–2000 school year. It has since been converted to condominiums.

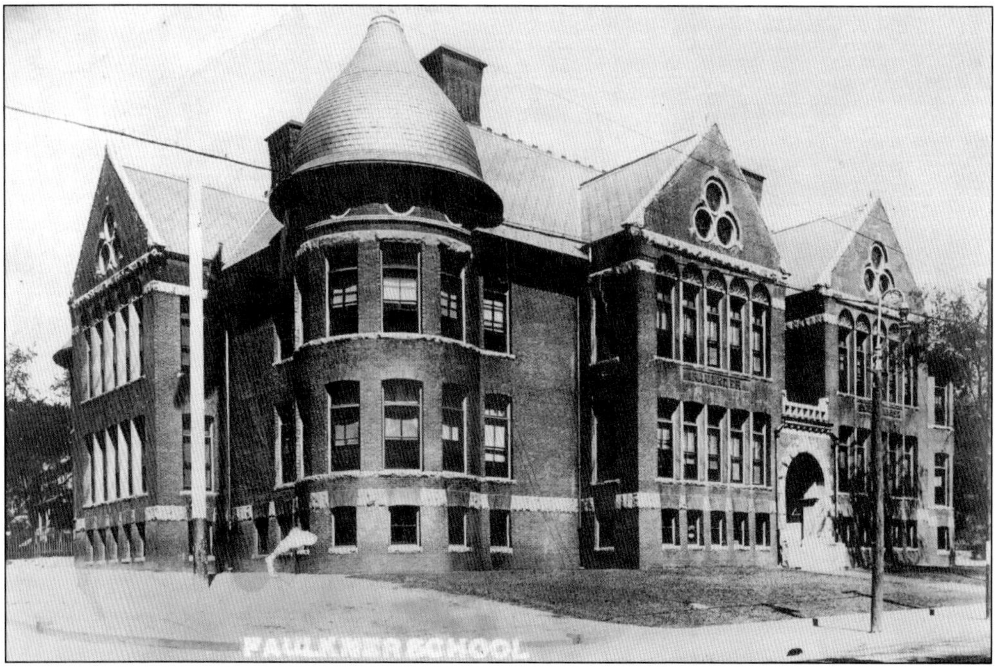

The Faulkner School was located at the corner of Salem and Pierce Streets. Built in 1893, it contained 12 classrooms. It was destroyed by fire in the 1960s. It is the present site of the Salem Towers apartment complex.

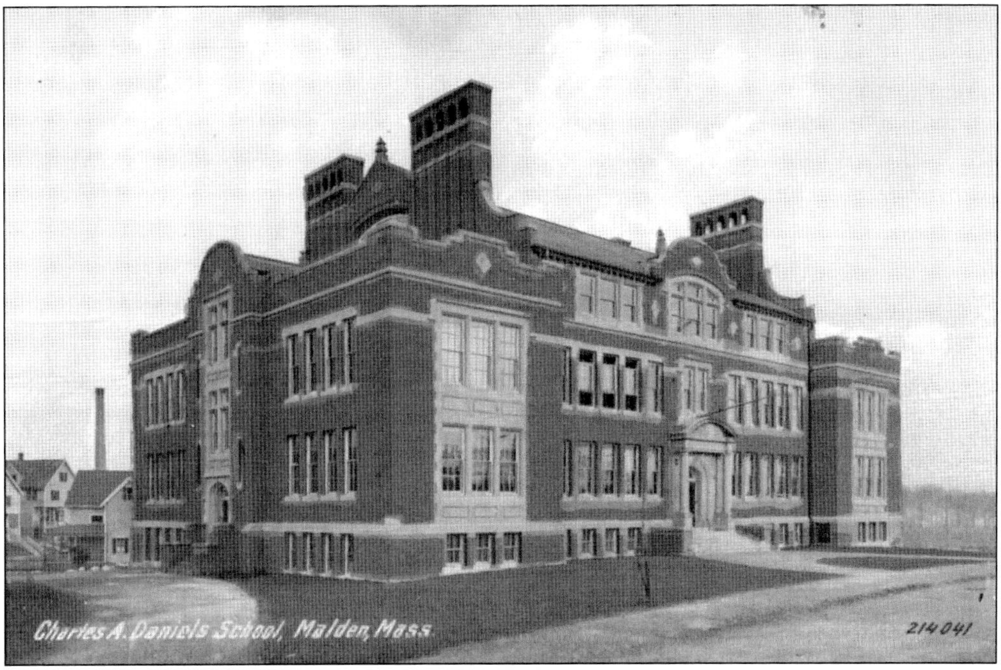

The Daniels School was named for Charles A. Daniels, an innovative, longtime administrator in the Malden Public Schools. Daniels was high school principal and superintendent of schools. Built in 1907 and located at Eastern Avenue and Daniels Street, the Daniels School has been converted to residential use. It is listed in the National Register of Historic Places.

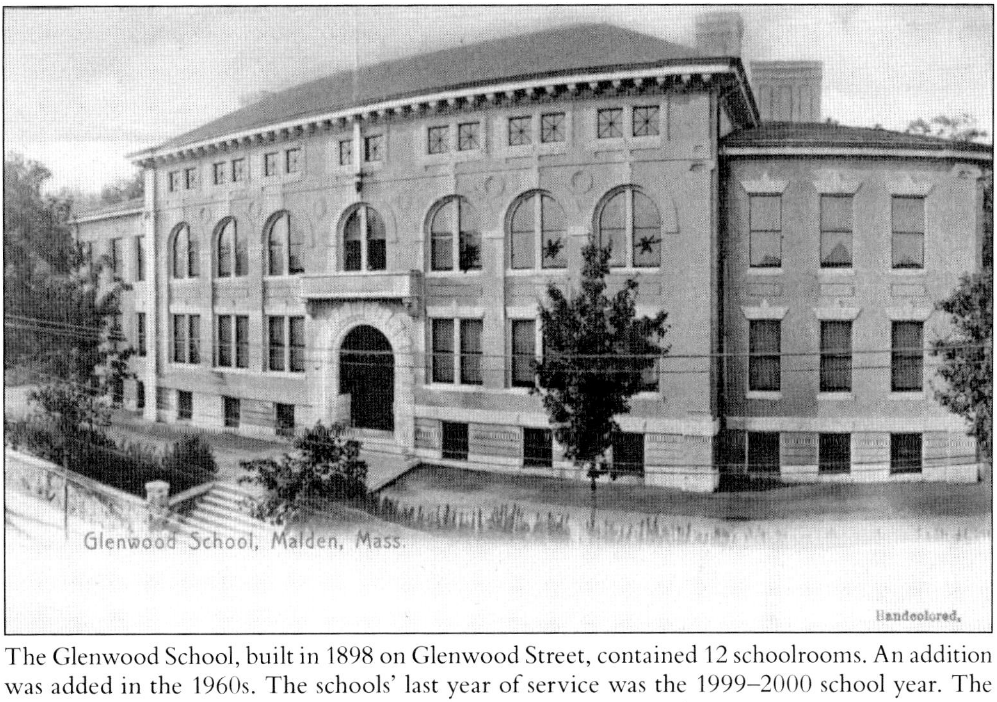

The Glenwood School, built in 1898 on Glenwood Street, contained 12 schoolrooms. An addition was added in the 1960s. The schools' last year of service was the 1999–2000 school year. The addition was removed, and the original school converted to condominiums.

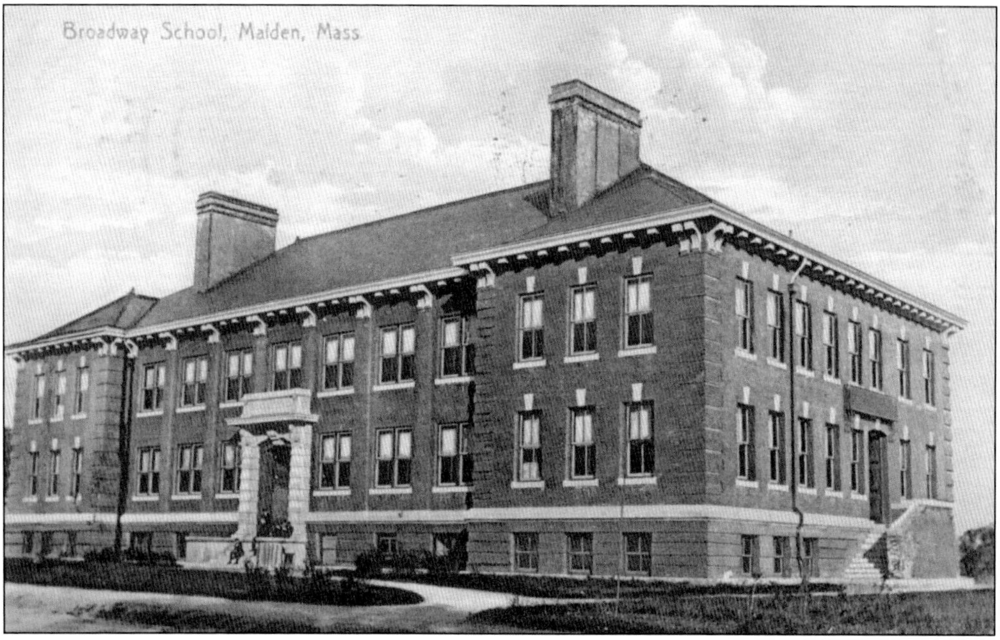

The Broadway School on Broadway is seen in this view. It was one of three junior high schools in Malden. Later renamed the Marcia P. Browne Junior High School, it is now used as Maplewood Place, an assisted living facility.

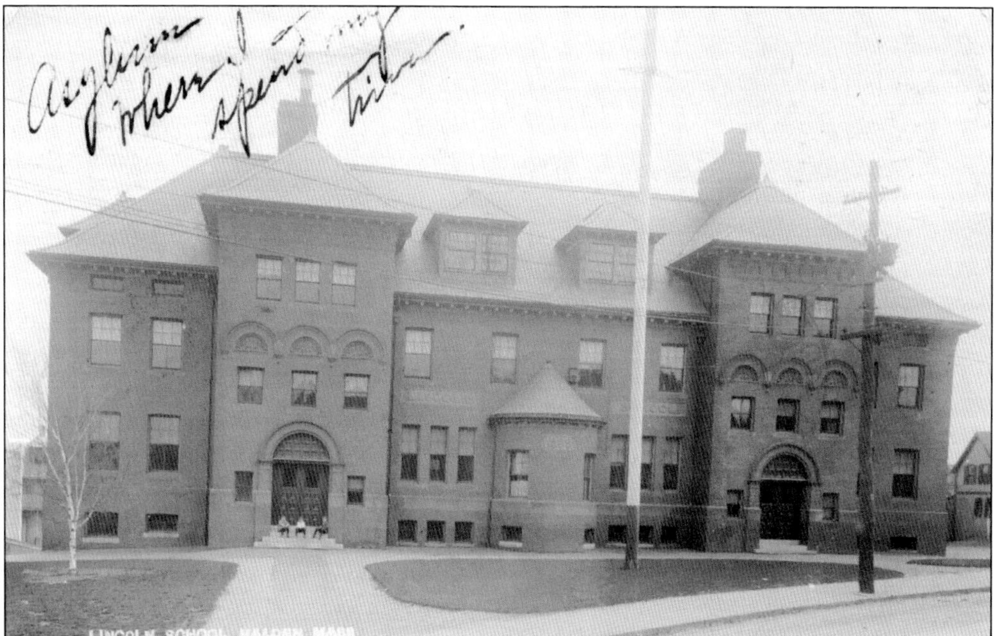

The Lincoln School was located on Cross Street on the site of the present Lincoln Commons. Built in 1895, it contained 12 classrooms. It was expanded before becoming Lincoln Junior High School in the 1930s.

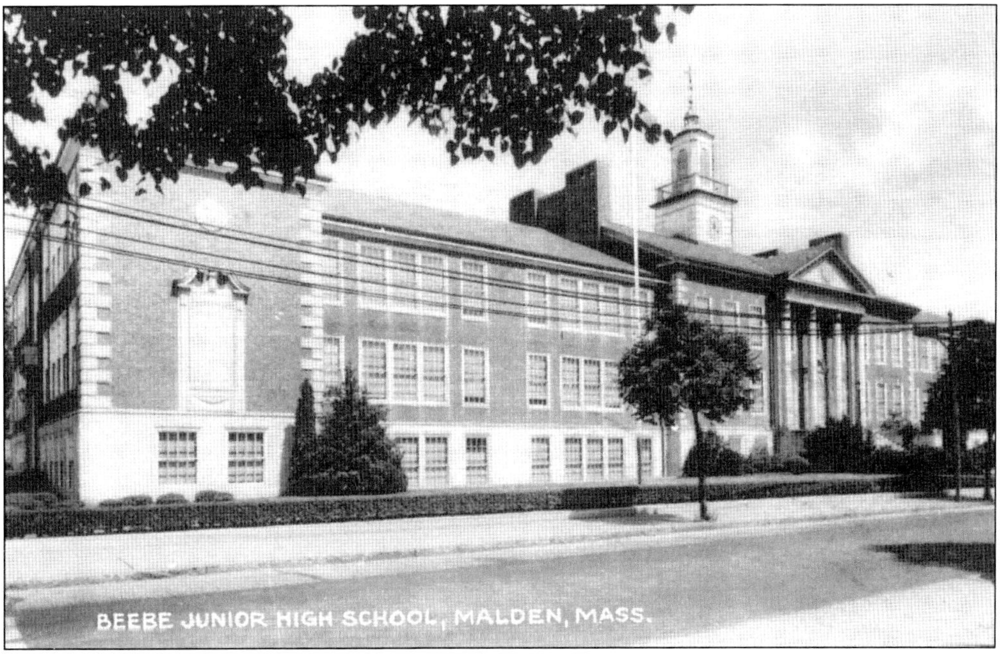

The Beebe Junior High School was built in 1929 on Pleasant Street on the site of the former Marcus Beebe estate. It was demolished in 1998 and replaced by the present Beebe School.

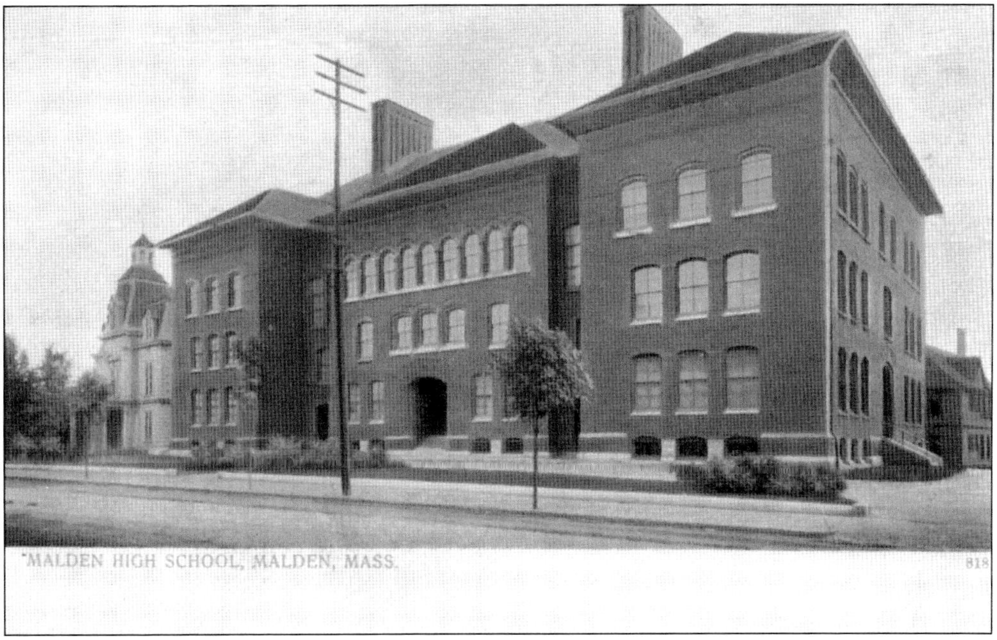

Malden High School on Salem Street is seen in this view. Visible are the original 1872 wooden high school (left) and the 1895 new high school. Prior to 1872, the high school was located in rooms in the original Centre Grammar School on Pleasant Street and later in rooms in the town house.

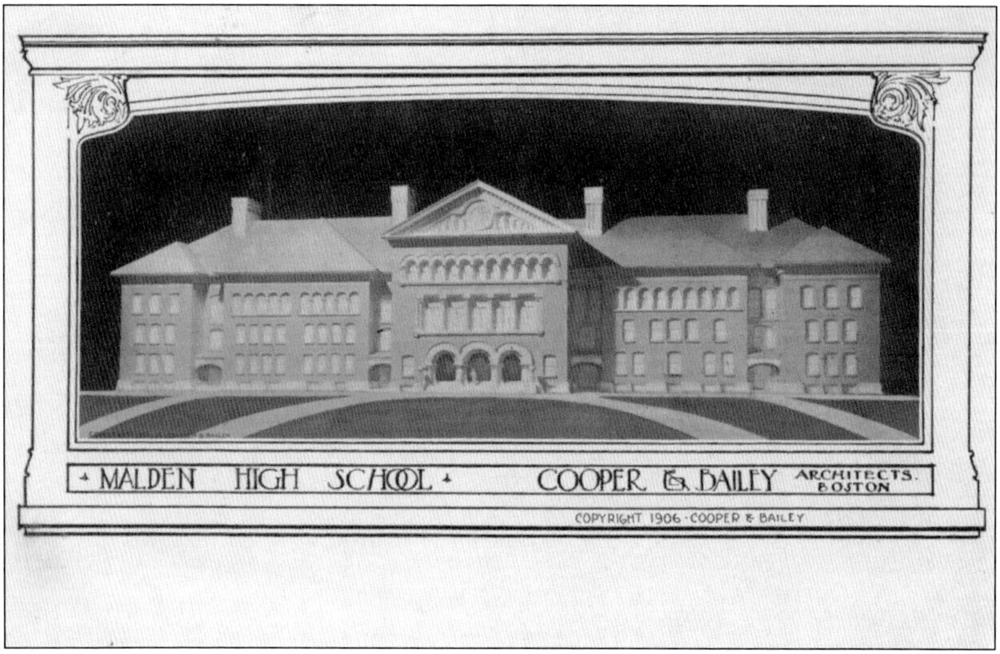

Seen here is an architectural rendering of the enlarged 1906 redbrick Malden High School. Malden's rapid growth necessitated the addition to the 1895 redbrick building seen in the previous view.

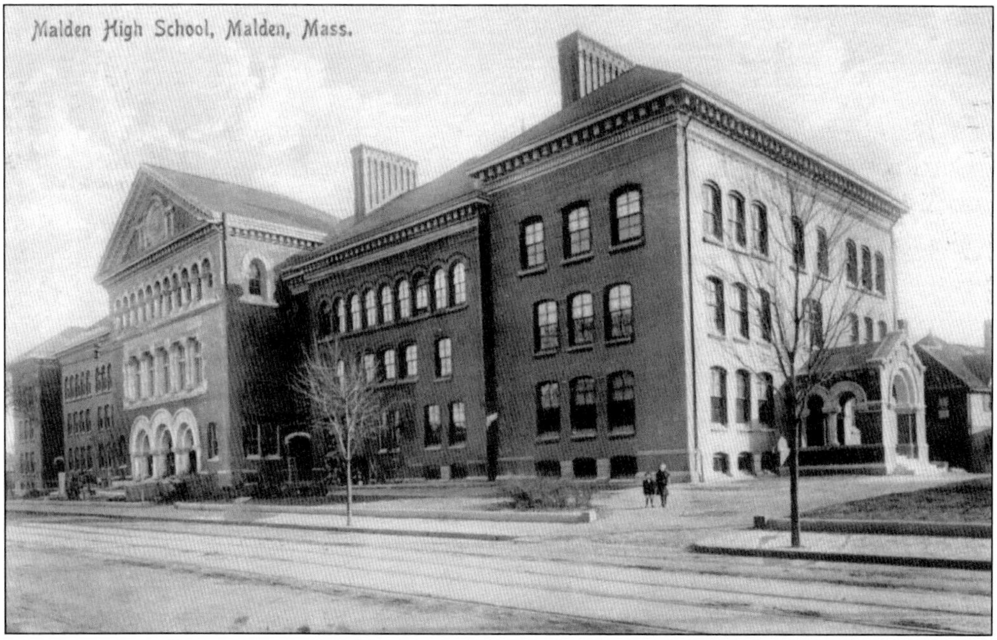

Malden High School is seen in this c. 1907 view following an addition and expansion of the original redbrick school. Note the city seal atop the peak of the building, which has been preserved at the corner of Ferry and Salem Streets on the present high school grounds. This building was razed in 1978.

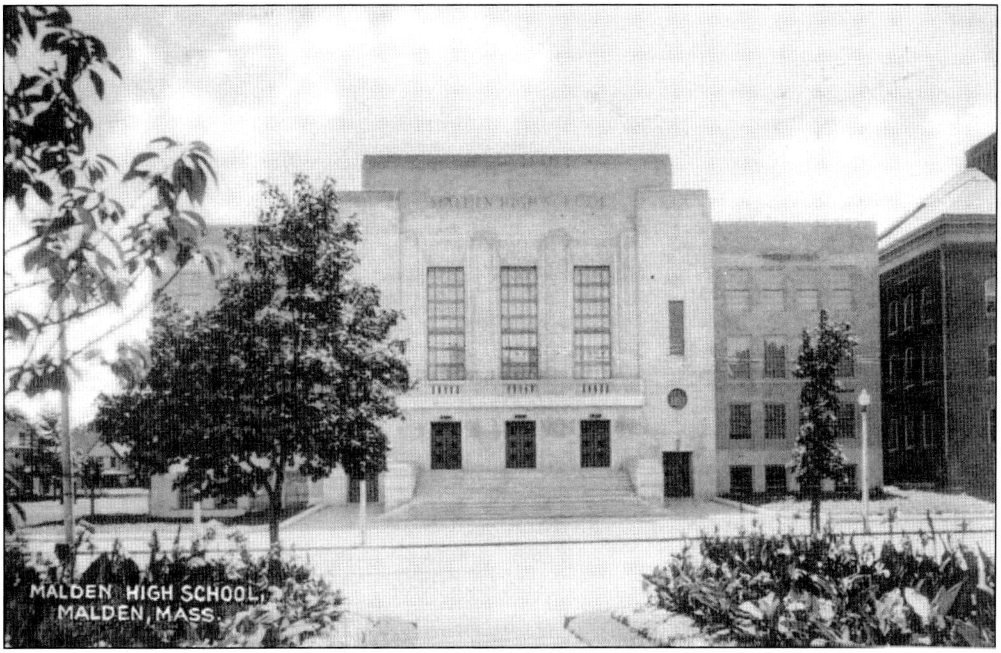

The 1939 Art Deco addition to Malden High School is seen in this view. Built by the Works Progress Administration, this building replaced the 1872 wooden high school. The first class to graduate from this facility was the class of 1940. The structure is still used as part of the high school today.

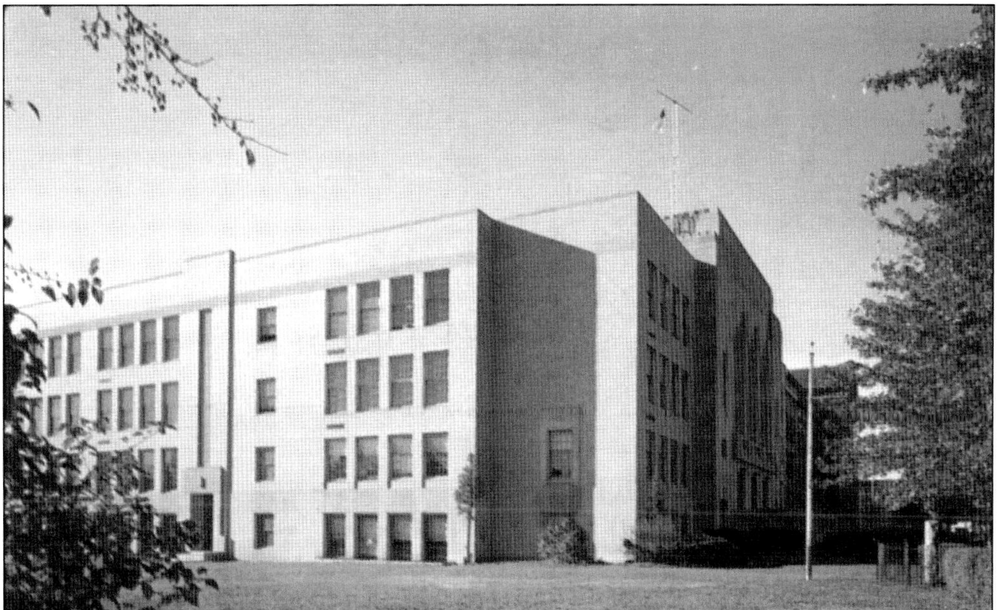

The Art Deco features of the 1939 Malden High School are apparent in this view taken from the corner of Salem and Holden Streets.

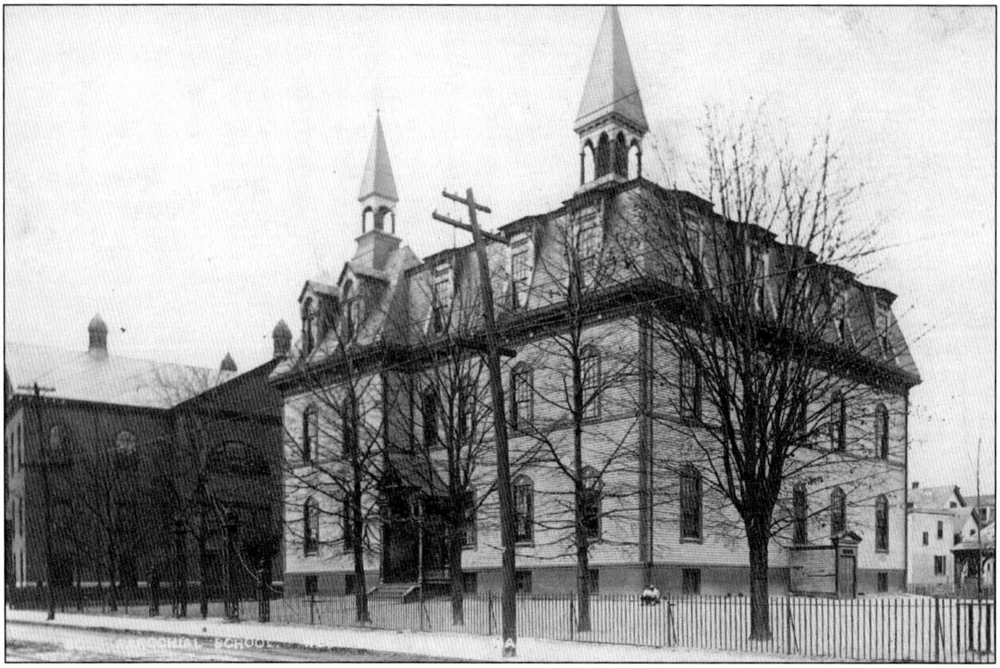

The Boys Parochial Grammar School was located at the corner of Charles Street and Highland Avenue and was part of the Immaculate Conception Parish. Built in the late 19th century, it was destroyed by fire in 1946. It was staffed by the School Sisters of Notre Dame.

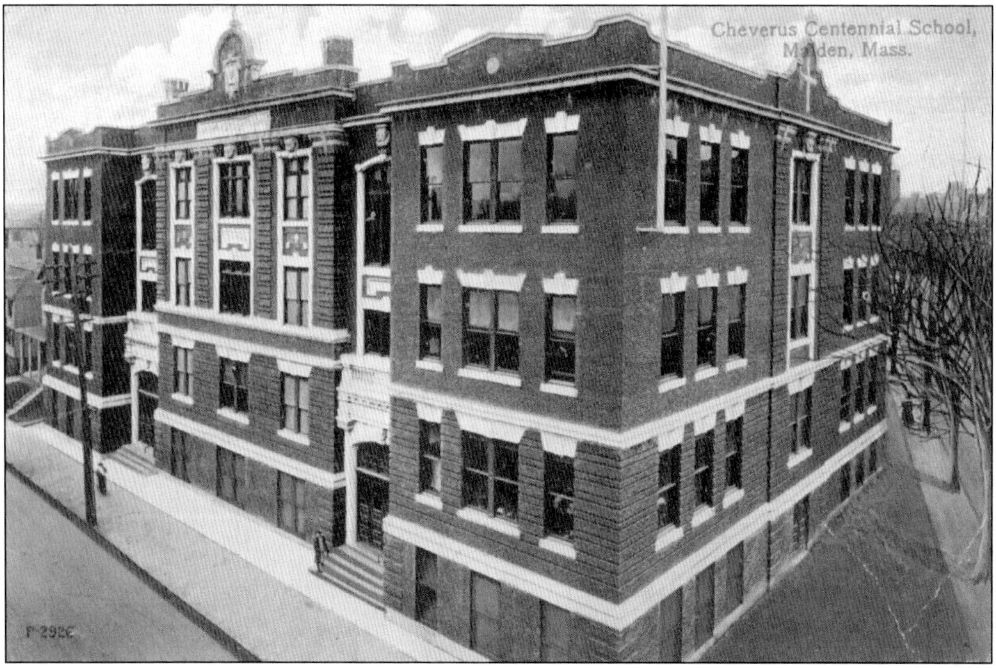

The Cheverus Centennial School, located at the corner of Ferry and Irving Streets, is seen in this view. It is part of Sacred Hearts Parish and remains in use today.

Three

BUSINESSES

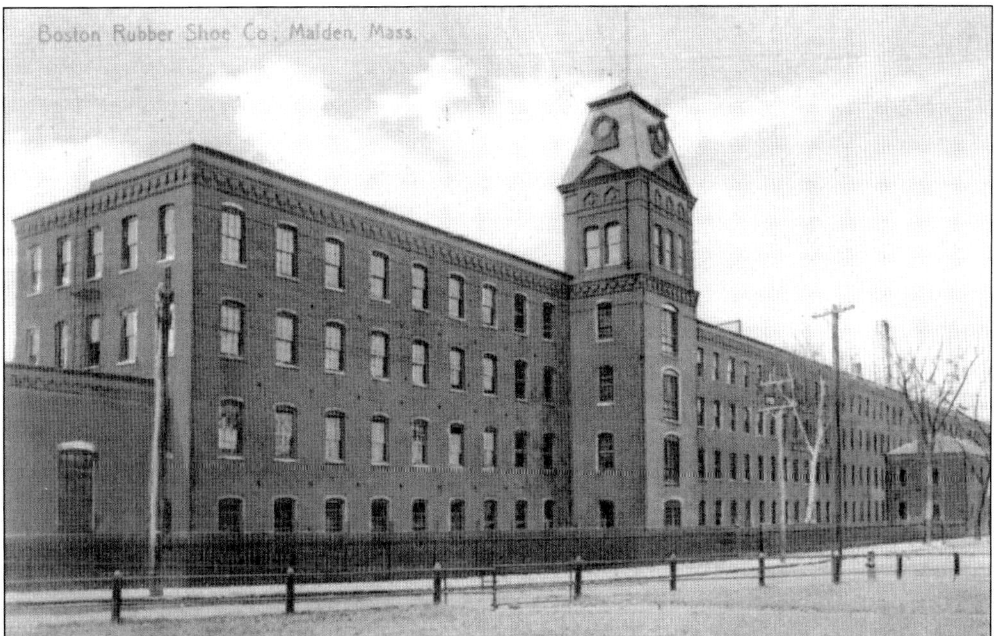

The Boston Rubber Shoe Company was located on Commercial Street. Founded in 1853 by Elisha Converse, this mill replaced the first one, which was destroyed by fire in 1875. The building was razed in the 1960s as part of urban renewal.

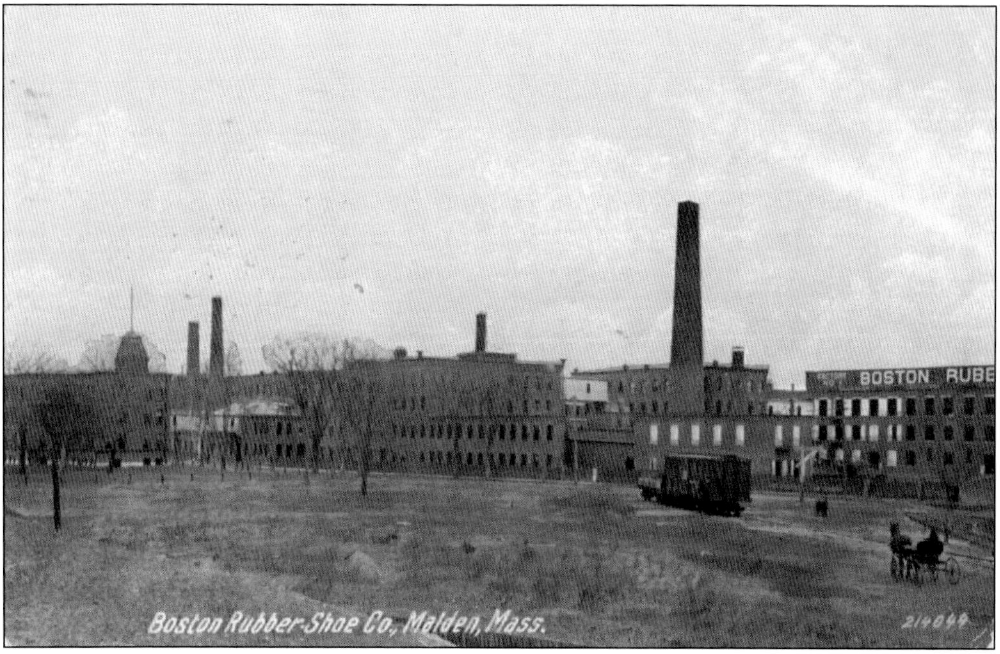

The Boston Rubber Shoe Company, as seen from Commercial Street, gives a sense of the enormity of the rubber works.

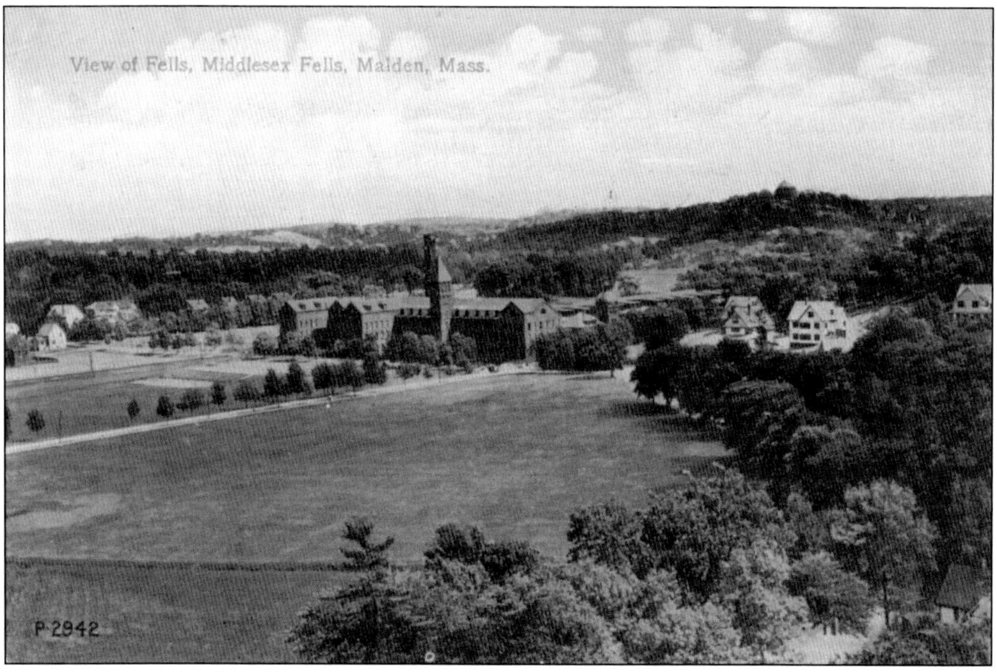

Seen in this view is the second factory of the Boston Rubber Shoe Company, just over the line in Melrose from Oak Grove, which was built in 1882. Note Waitt's Mount in the distance to the right, with the water standpipe on its summit.

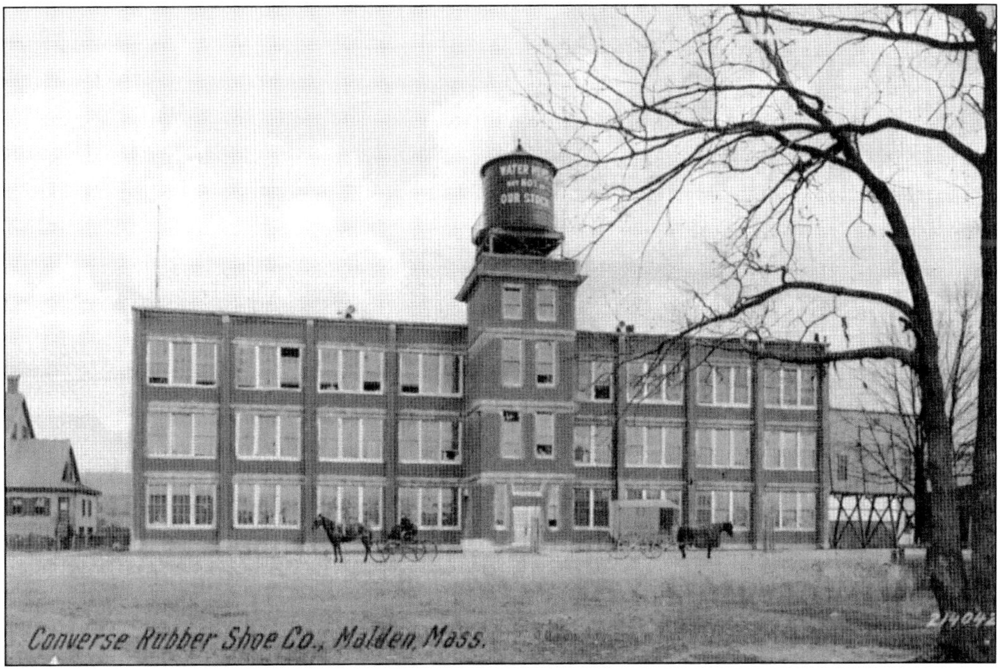

The Converse Rubber Shoe Company was founded in 1908 by Marquis M. Converse. For many years, it was one of Malden's largest employers.

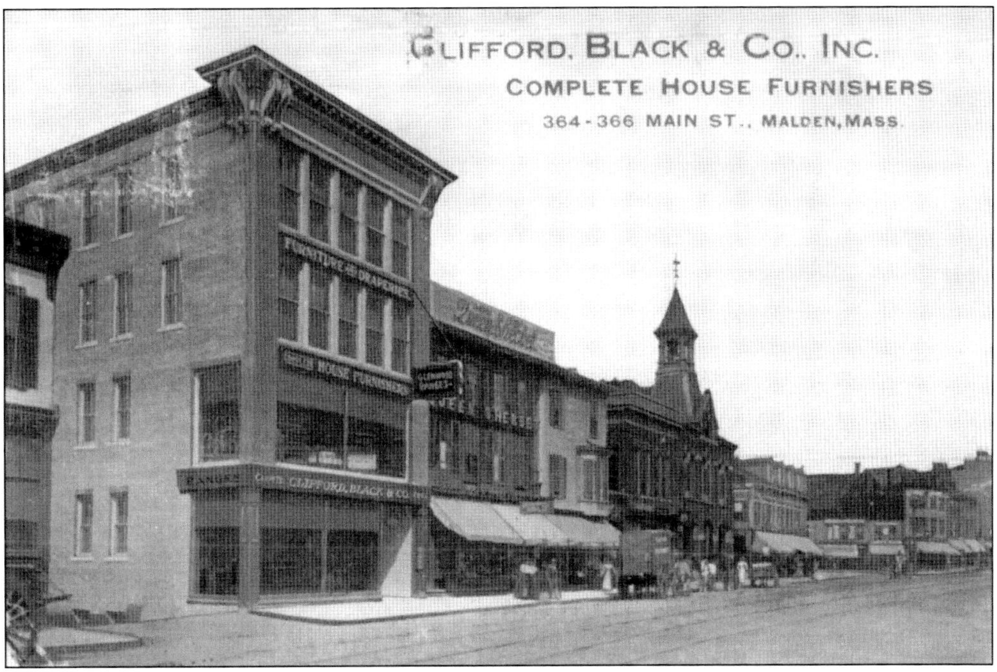

Many a Malden resident bought furniture from the Clifford-Black Company, located on Main Street in Malden Square. Also visible is the central fire station with the spire, located where Exchange Street now meets Main Street.

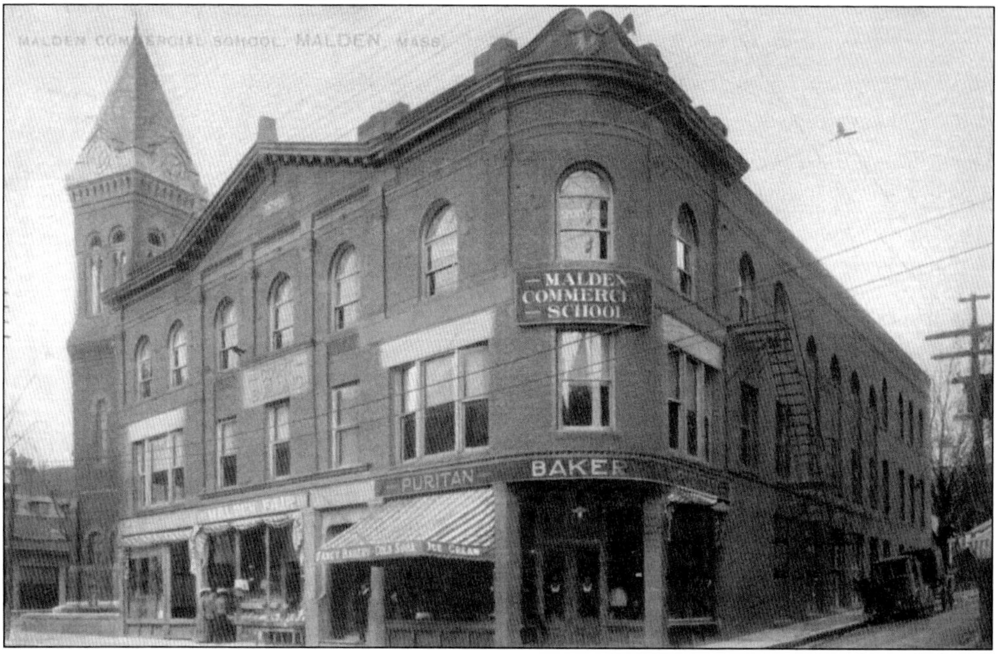

The Malden Commercial School was located in the Court Building, which was situated on Pleasant Street at the corner of Linden Avenue. The upper floors housed the Malden District Court.

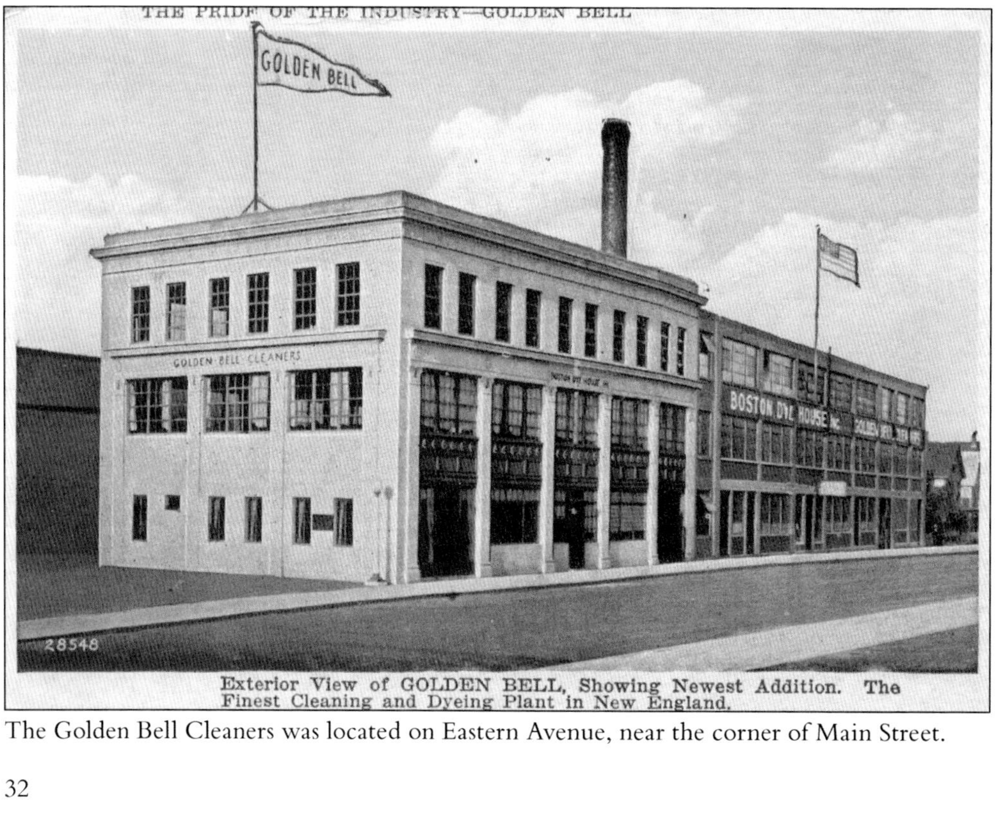

The Golden Bell Cleaners was located on Eastern Avenue, near the corner of Main Street.

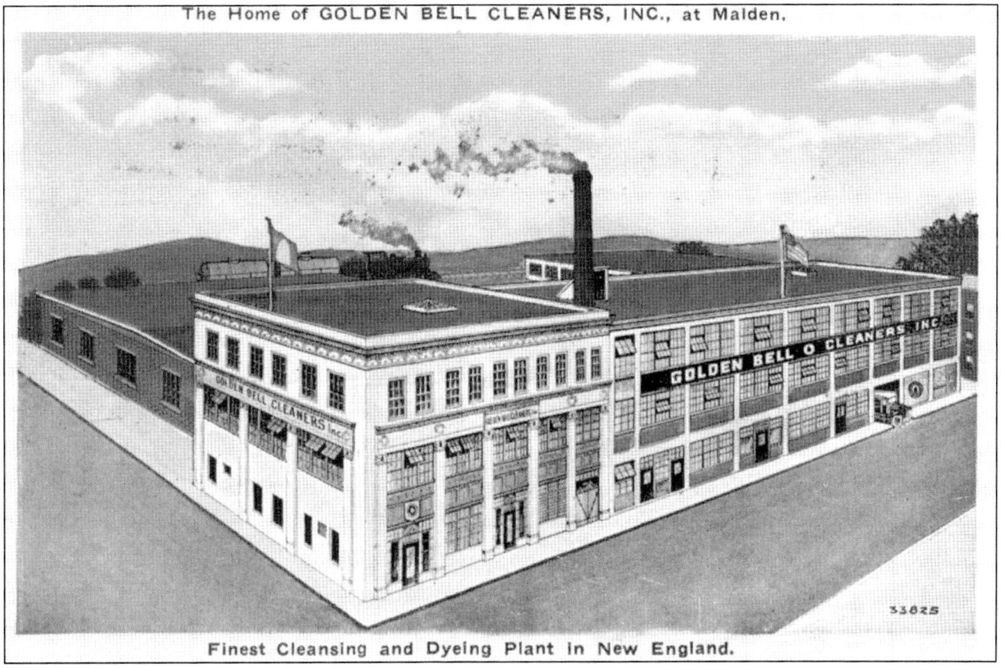

The Golden Bell Cleaners building still stands and has been adapted for commercial, retail, and office use.

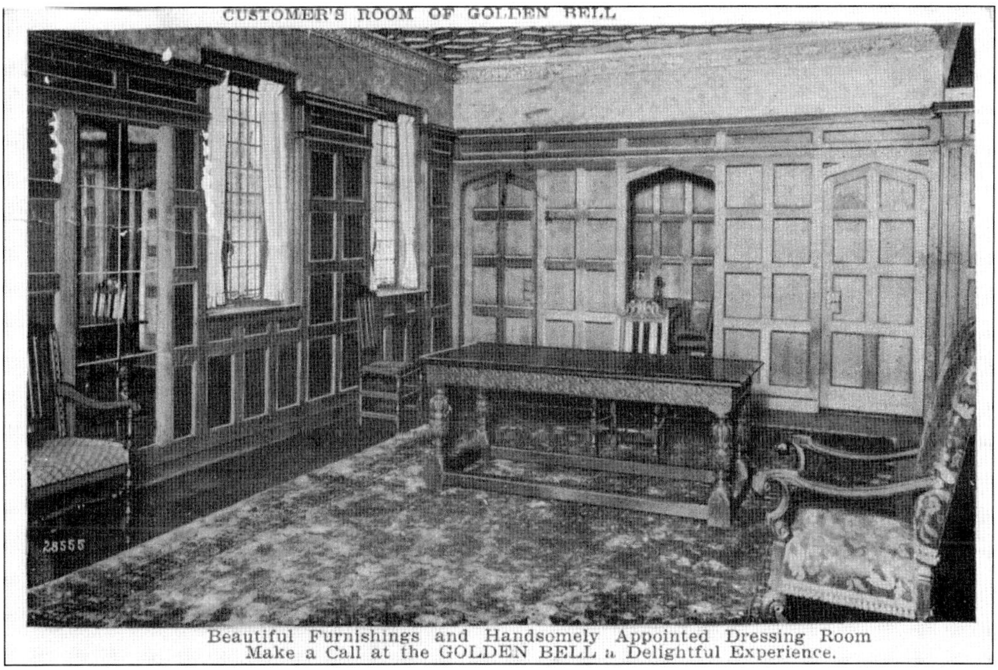

Pictured is the customers' room in the interior of the Golden Bell Cleaners. The opulent interior reflected the taste of the clientele of this establishment in the early 20th century.

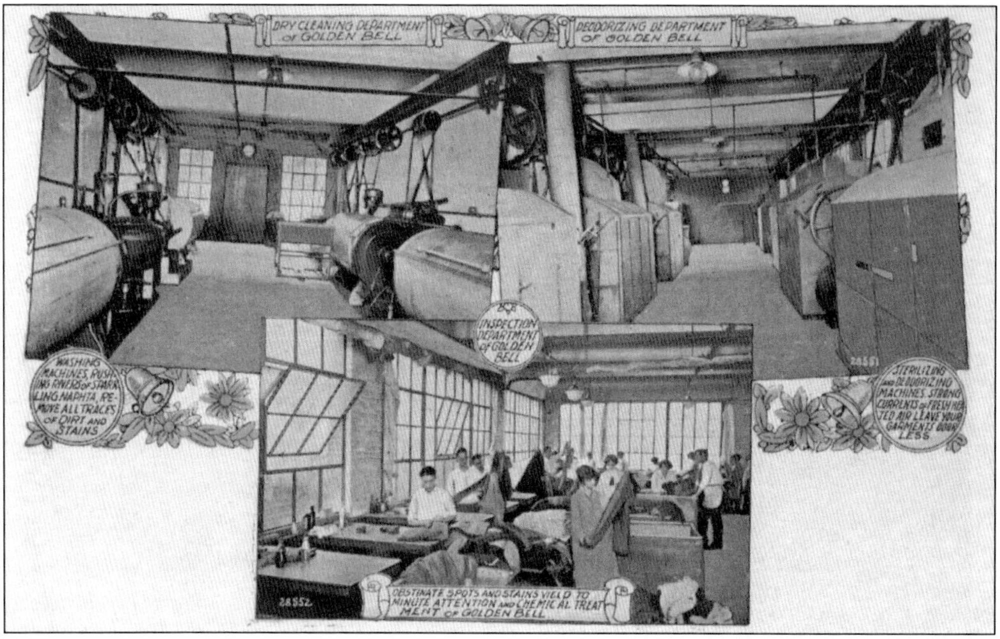

This multi-view card shows the various departments of Golden Bell Cleaners: the dry cleaning department, deodorizing department, and inspection department.

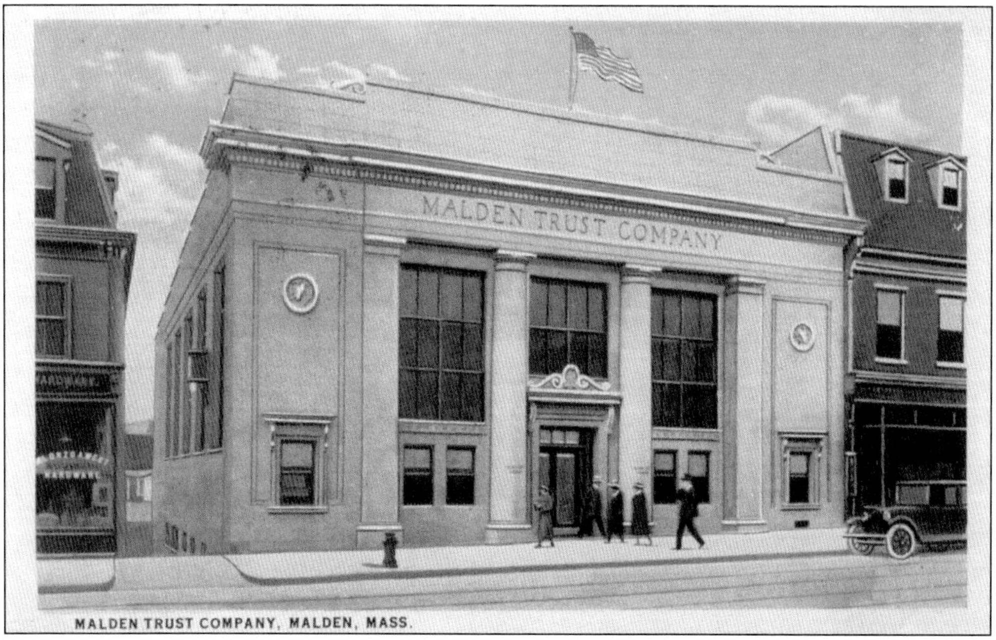

The Malden Trust Company was located on Pleasant Street in Malden Square in this building, erected in 1923. The building still stands, but the trust company was absorbed into Eastern Bank in the 1990s.

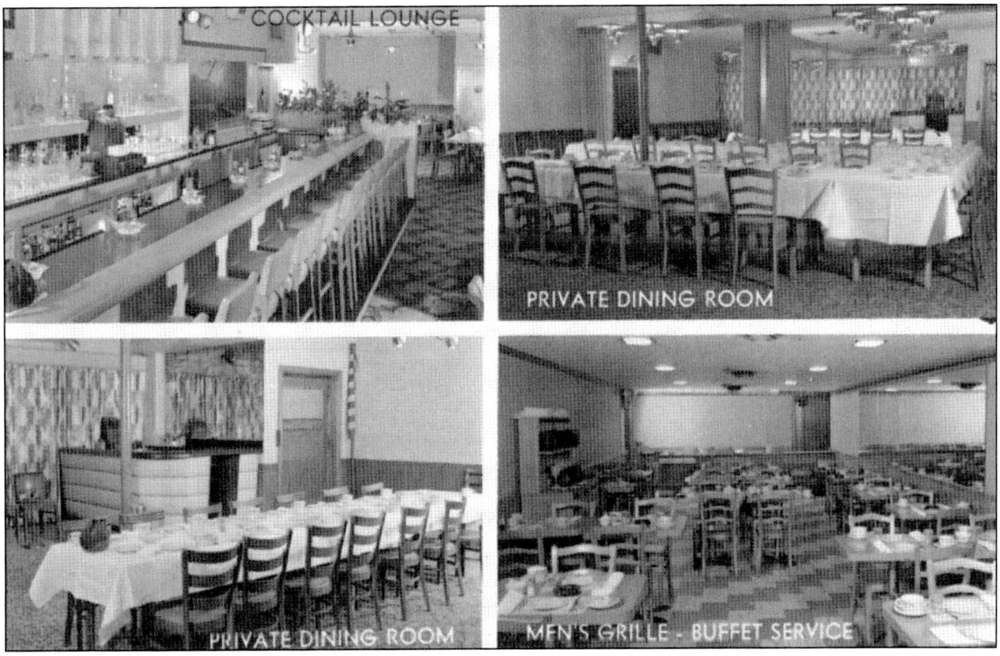

The Kernwood Restaurant on Dartmouth Street was a favorite of Malden area residents for many years. It closed in the 1970s.

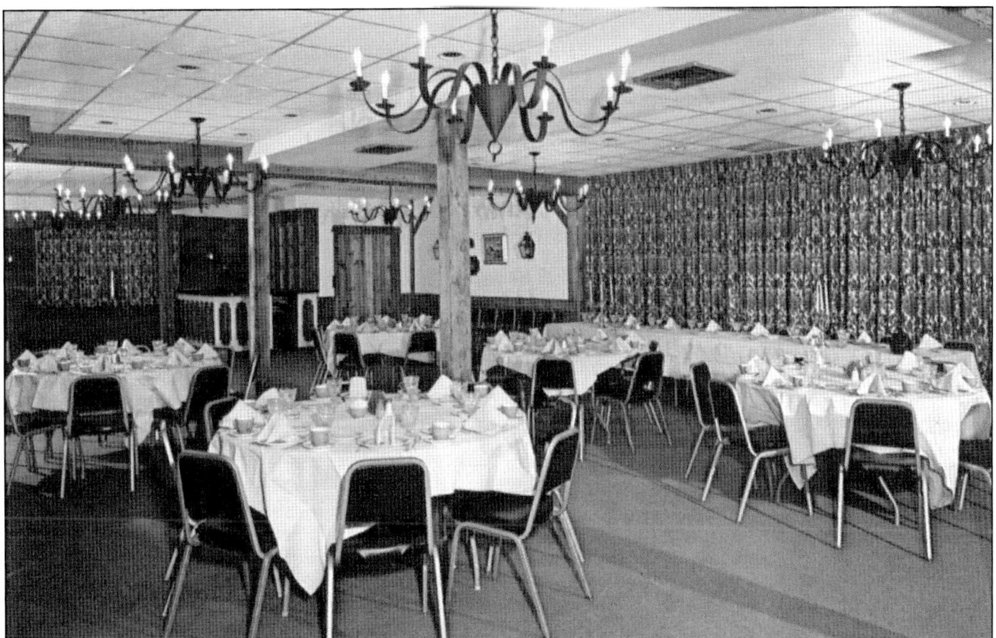

The third-floor banquet rooms of the Kernwood Restaurant hosted Malden functions and banquets for many years.

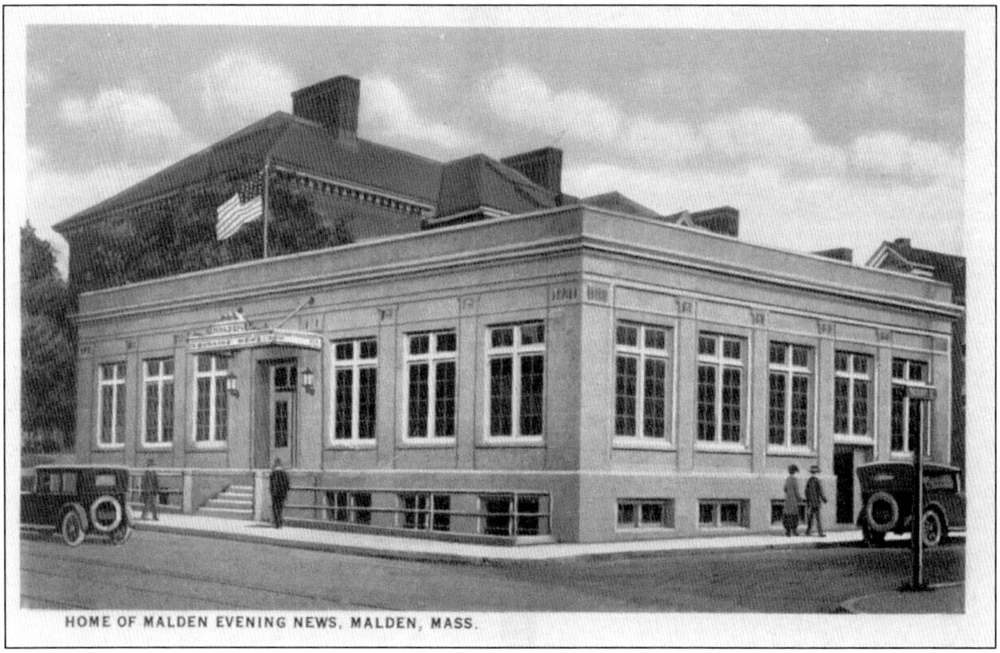

The *Malden Evening News* was founded in 1882 and still publishes today. This view shows its plant when it was located on Ferry Street adjacent to Malden High School. The structure was removed around 1977 as part of the high school building project. The paper relocated to offices on Commercial Street.

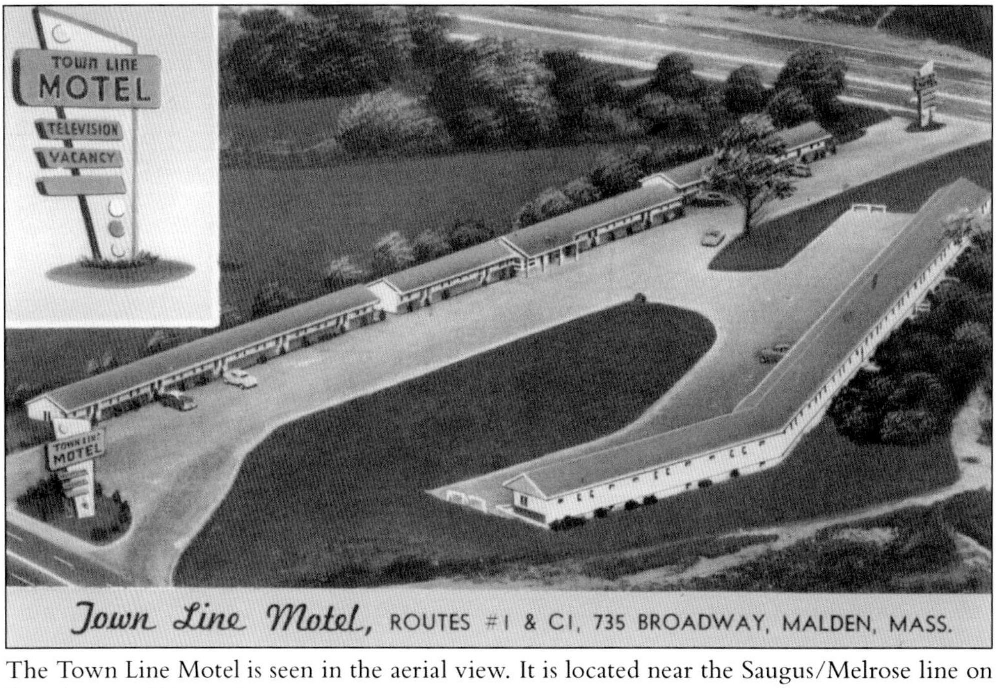

The Town Line Motel is seen in the aerial view. It is located near the Saugus/Melrose line on Broadway and Route 1.

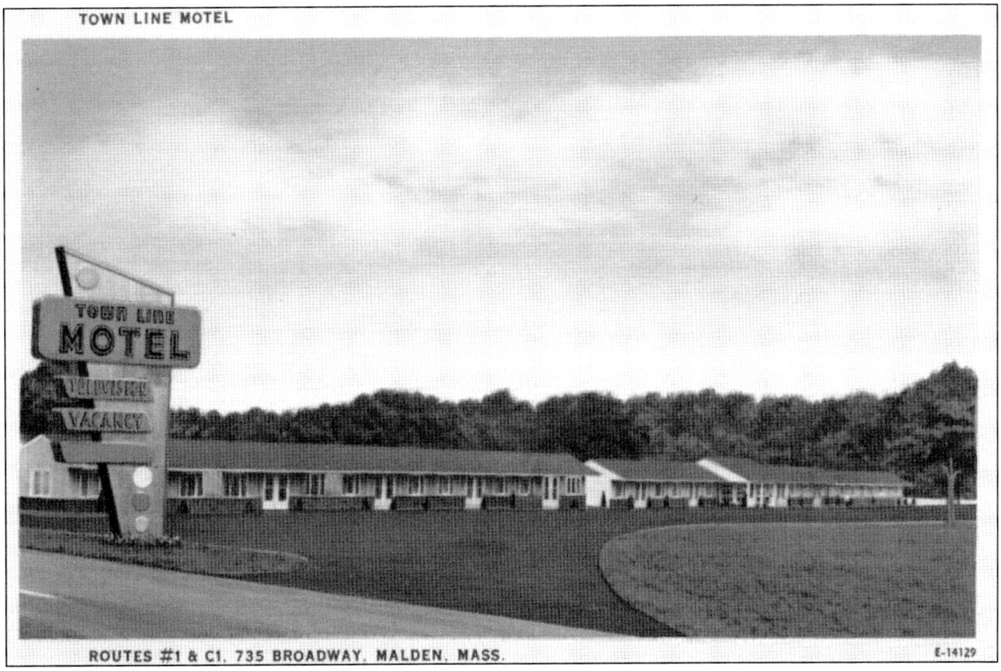

This view of the Town Line Motel shows how the business looked shortly after its construction in the 1950s.

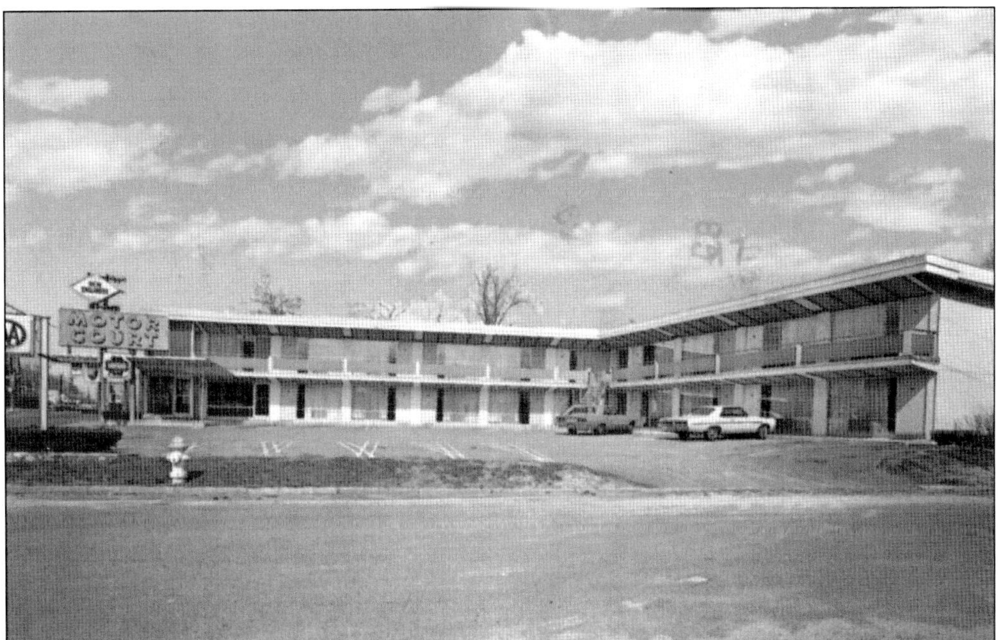

Broadway was the home to many small motels, as is evidenced by this view of the New Englander Motor Court on Broadway, Route 99.

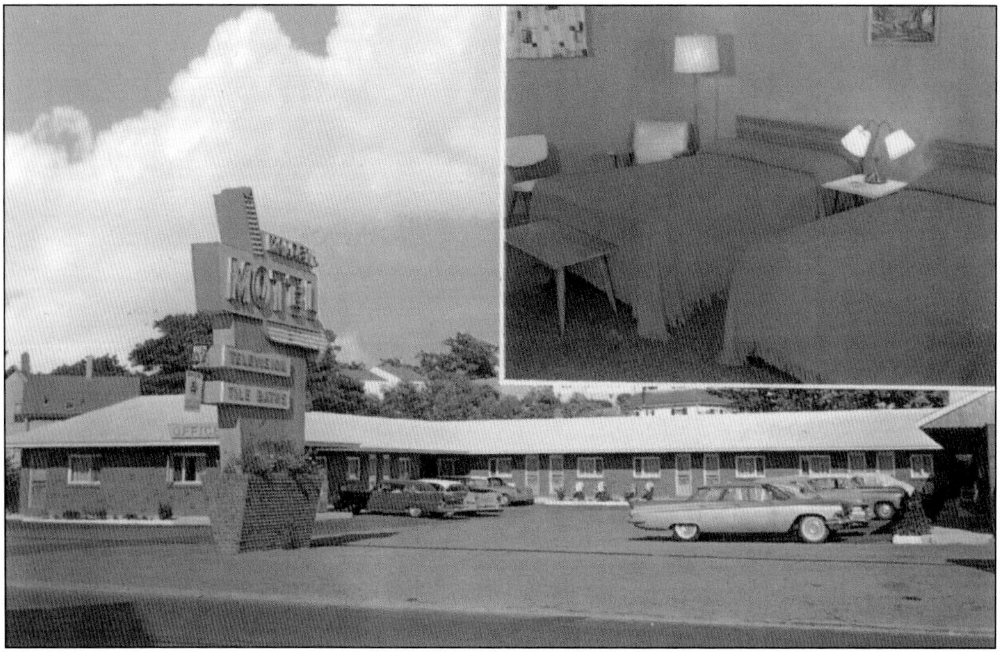

The Malden Motel was located at 573 Broadway and boasted television and tile baths, the latest in amenities for travelers.

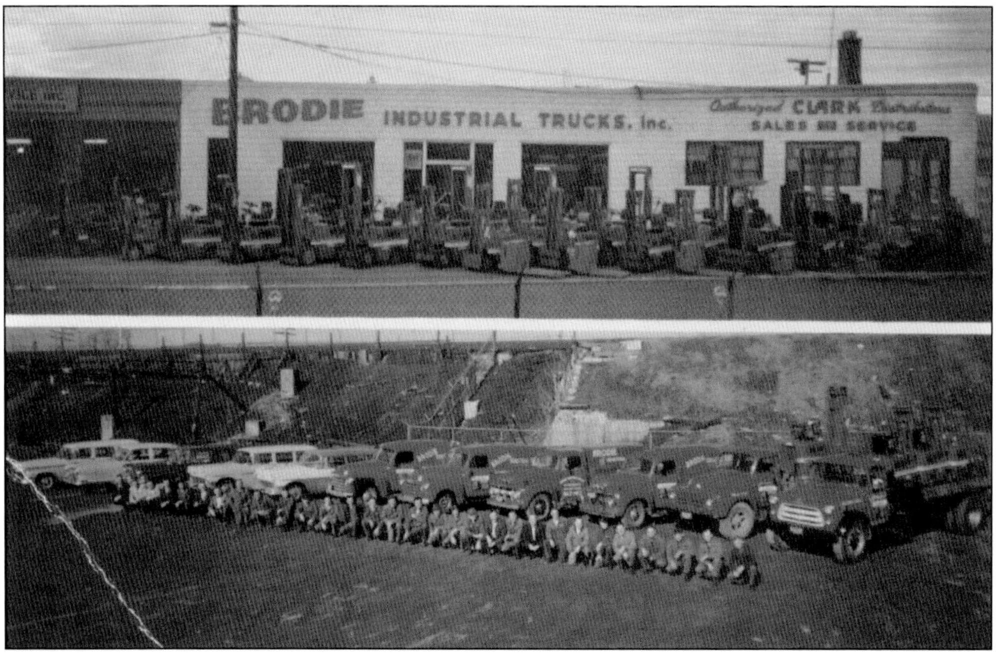

For many years, Brodie Industrial Trucks sold forklifts and material handling equipment from its location at 50 Commercial Street. The business was relocated as part of the area's urban renewal.

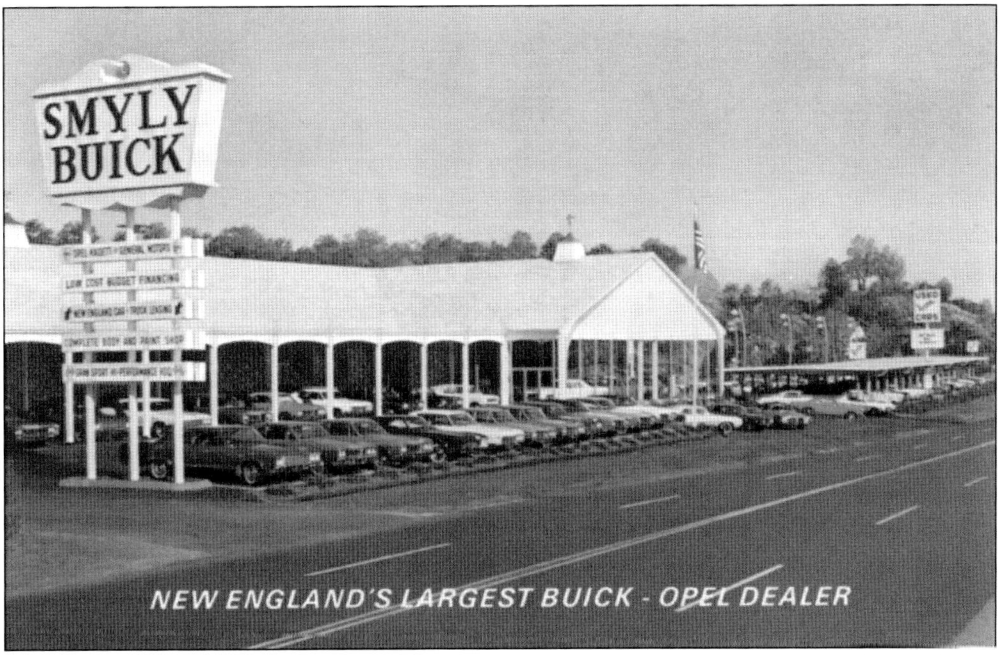

Many Malden residents bought a Buick from Smyly Buick on Broadway, near the Melrose/Saugus line.

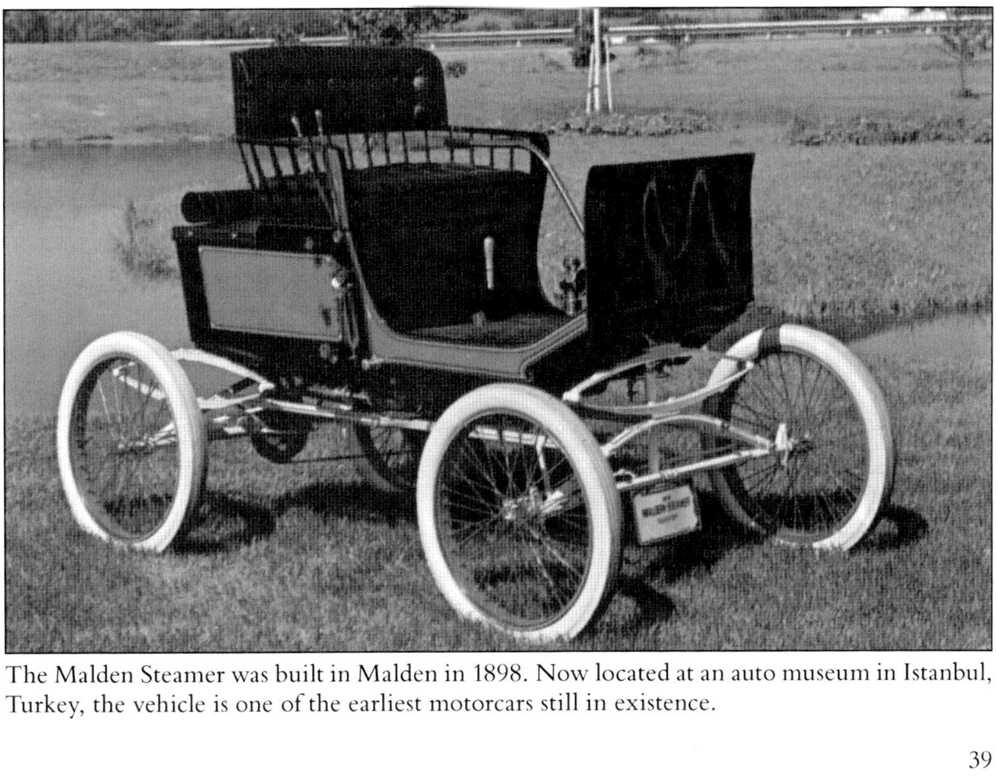

The Malden Steamer was built in Malden in 1898. Now located at an auto museum in Istanbul, Turkey, the vehicle is one of the earliest motorcars still in existence.

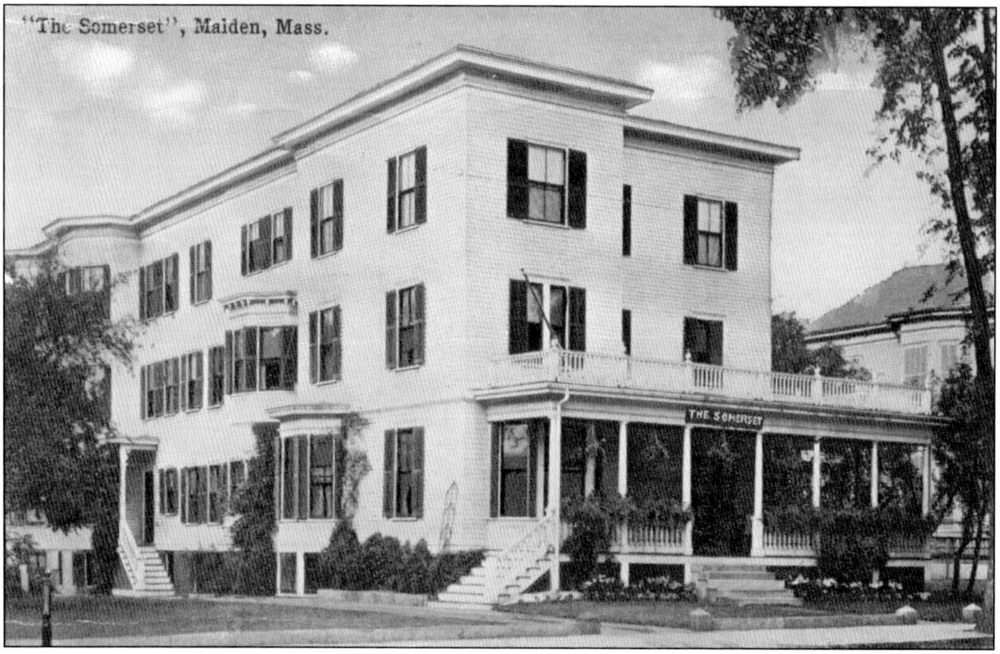

The Somerset Hotel was located on Summer Street in Malden. This area was home to many larger private homes and lodging houses.

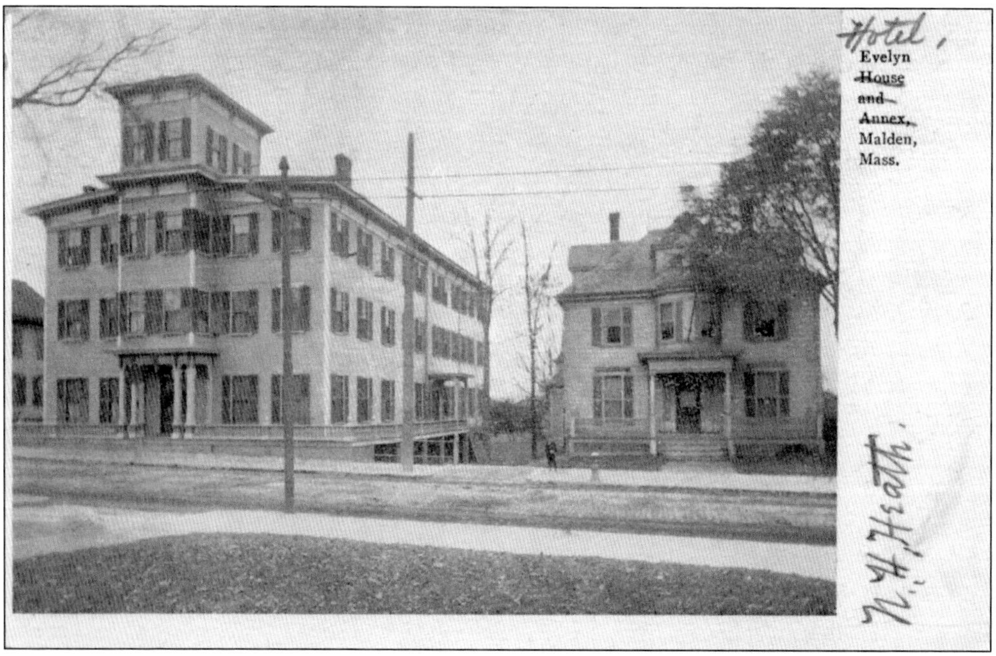

The Evelyn Hotel was located on Pleasant Street at the corner of Summer Street. It is the site of today's Gateway Apartments.

Four

MALDEN SQUARE

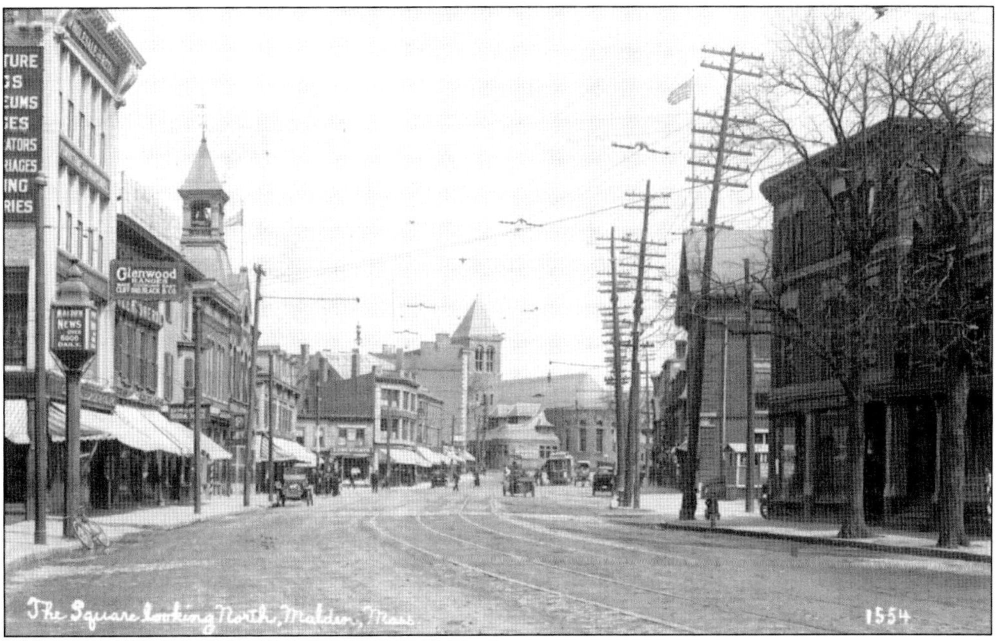

The business center of Malden, the Malden Square, is basically located at the junction of older roads that ran north-south and east-west (the Salem-Medford Road and the Reading-Charlestown Road). Because of this development, the Malden Square does not have one main thoroughfare, it has two main streets—Pleasant and Main Streets. There is no common in Malden; there is a square. This view of Malden Square is looking north along Main Street. The tower to the left is the Central Fire Station. Also, note the *Malden News* sign, which stood in front of the building housing the *Malden Evening News*.

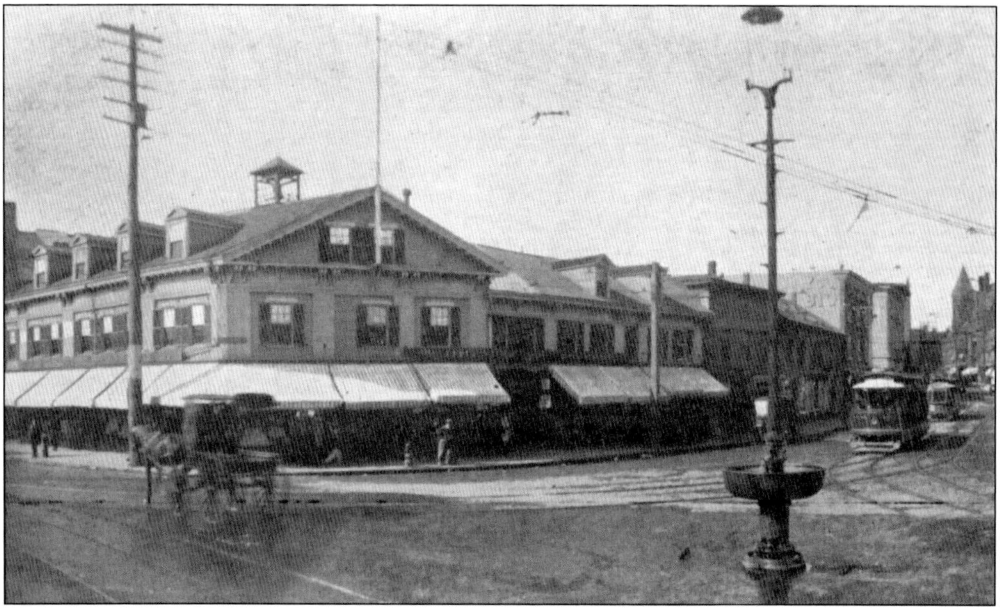

This is a c. 1910 view of the intersection of Main and Pleasant Streets in Malden Square. The large building to the left was F.N. Joslin's, also called "The Big Store."

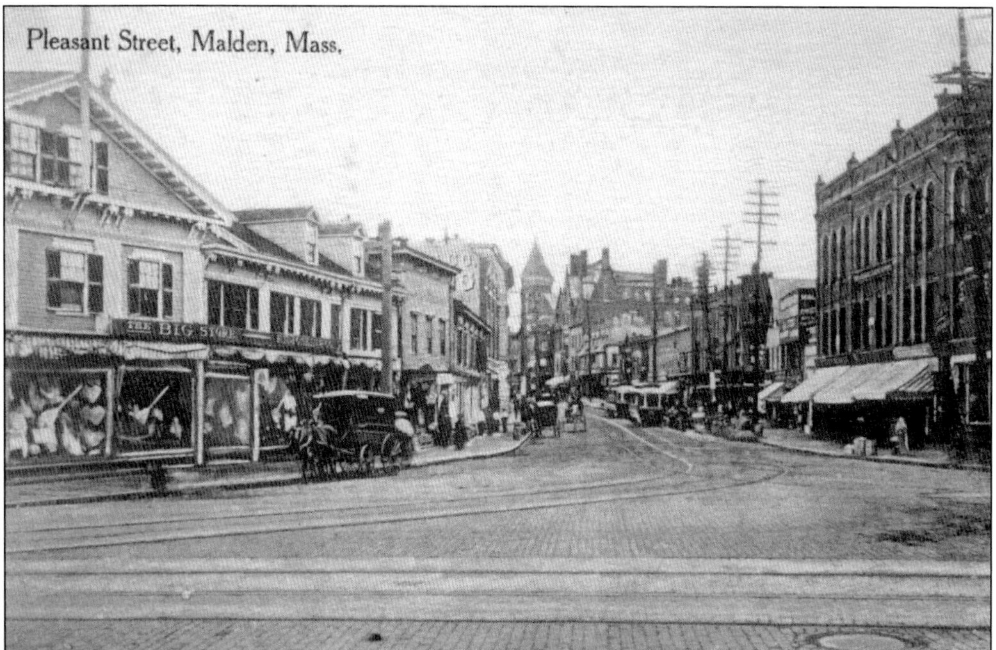

Pictured here is an early real-photo postcard of Pleasant Street running west. The bell tower in the center background is that of Centre Methodist Church, located at Washington and Pleasant Streets.

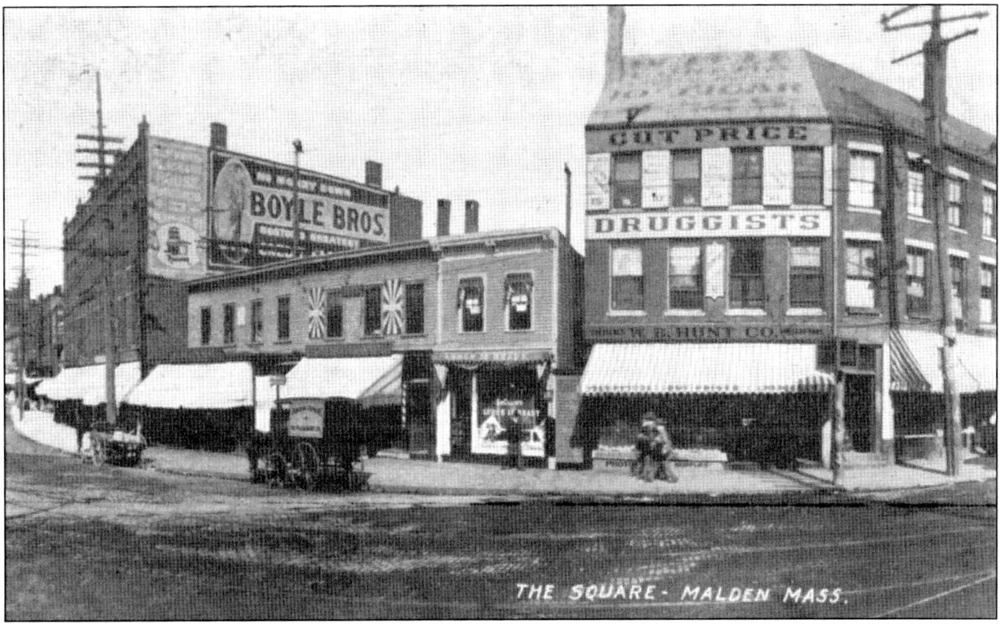

This view of Pleasant Street, taken from Main Street, is looking toward the west. The W.B. Hunt Company druggists, featured at right, later moved to the Melrose line and became a large store devoted to photography.

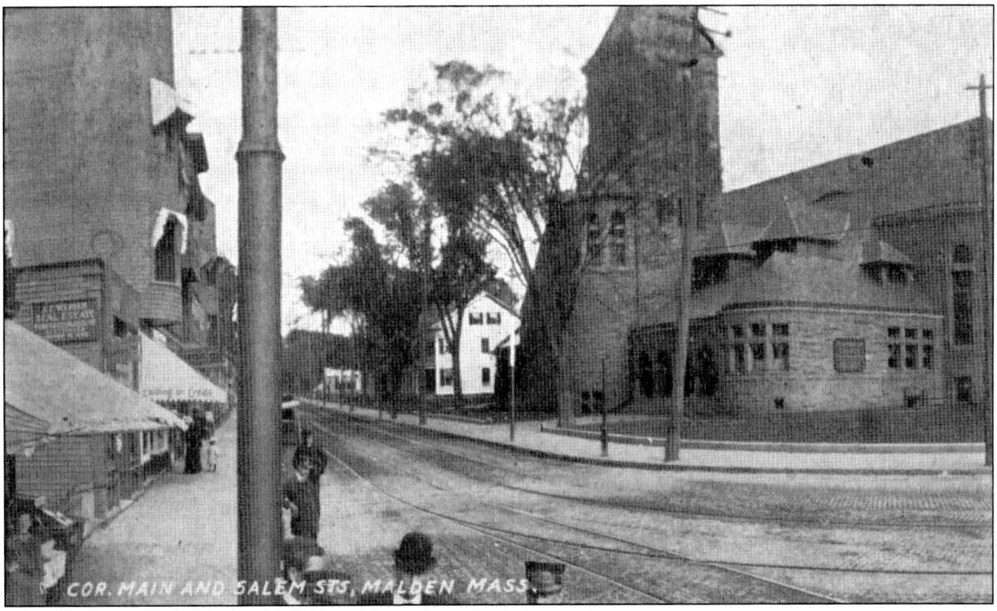

The corner of Main and Salem Streets is depicted in this c. 1910 photograph card. The First Baptist Church is at right.

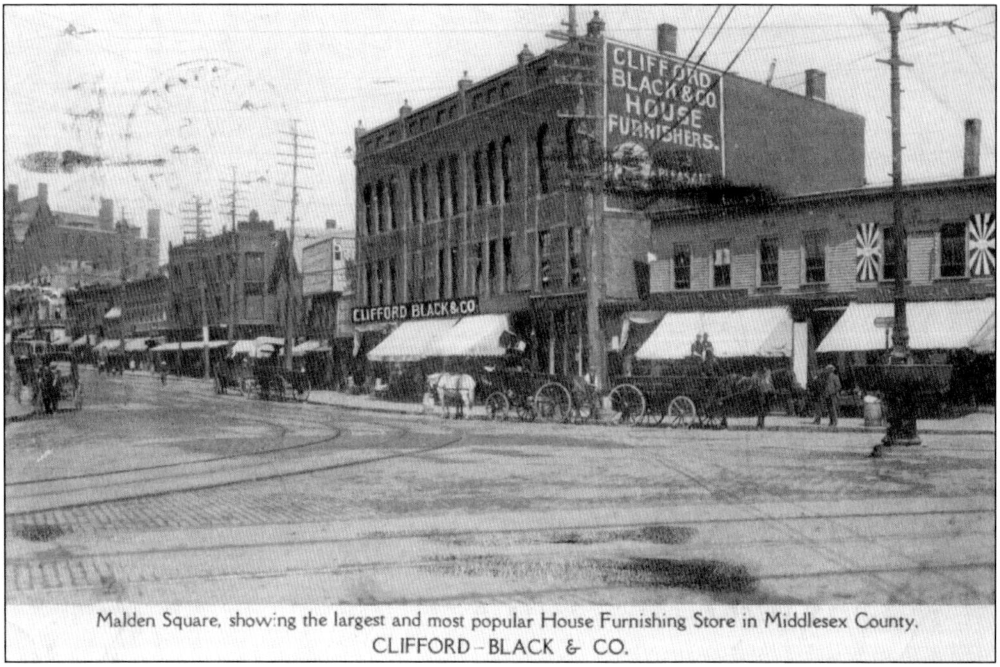

This advertising postcard shows the Clifford Black and Company store on Pleasant Street as it appeared around 1909.

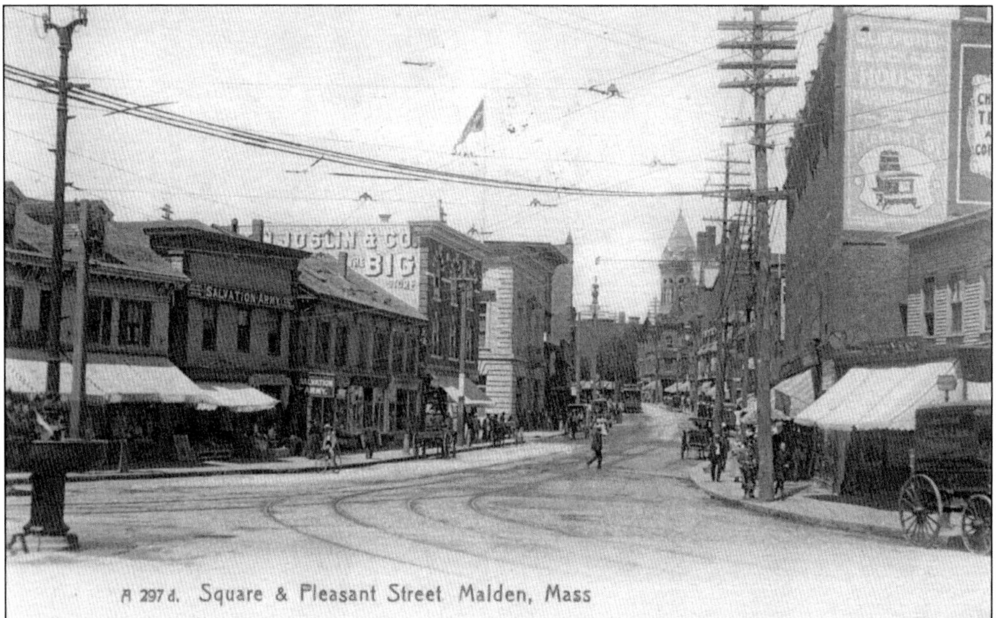

This image of Pleasant Street looking west shows the F.N. Joslin store, an early department store, at left center, at the corner of Pleasant and Middlesex Streets. Joslin's was later replaced by a Jordan Marsh store.

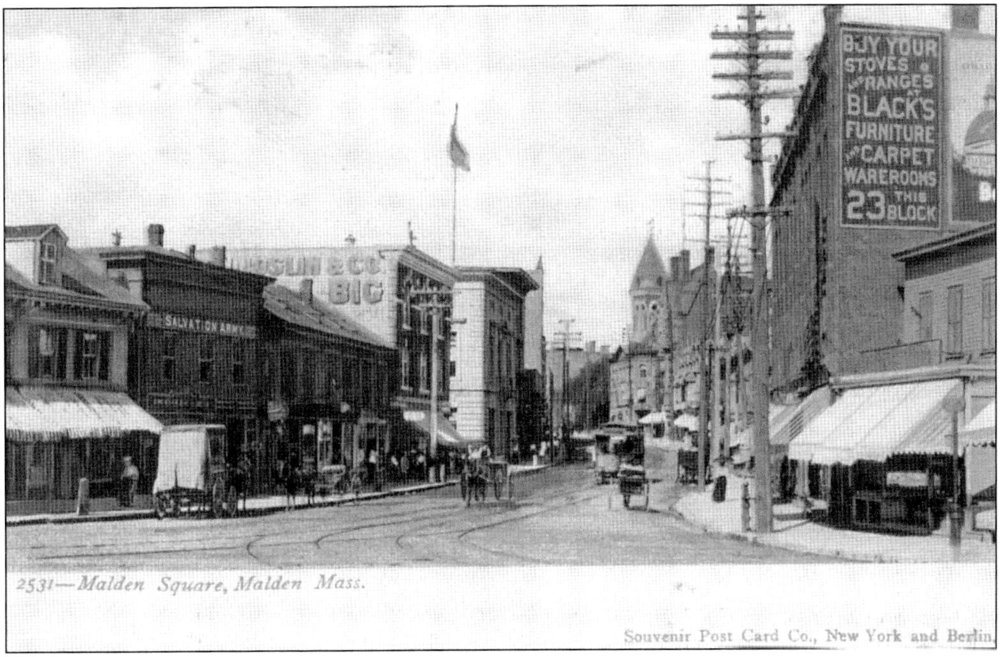

This is another view of Pleasant Street looking west. Note the Salvation Army building to the left and the horse carts on this busy street.

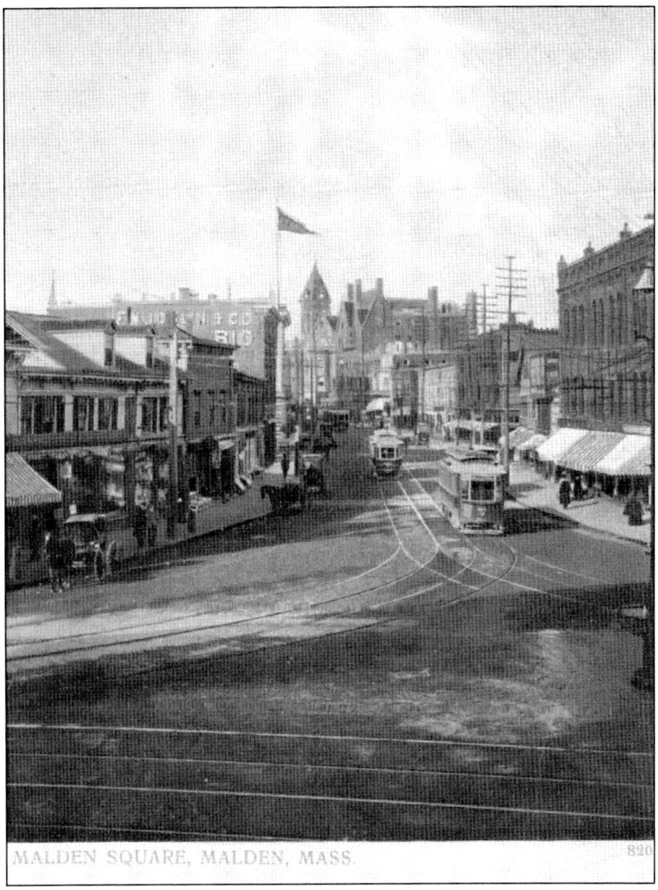

This view of Pleasant Street was taken from an elevated position looking west. The large structure to the right of the Methodist church tower is the old YMCA building.

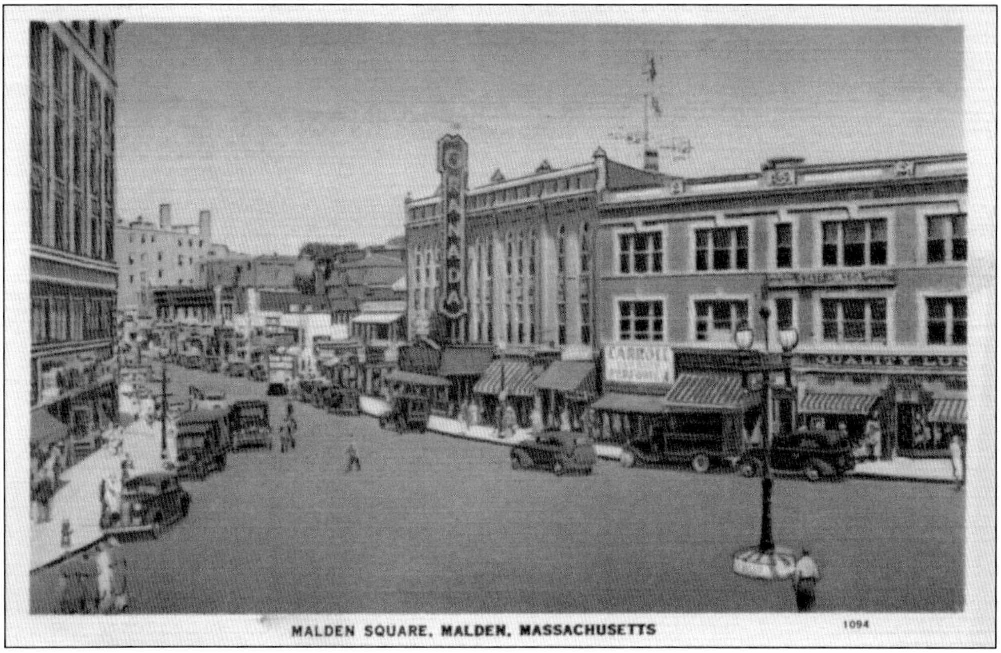

This linen postcard features a view of Pleasant Street from Main Street. The Granada Theater, at center in this postcard, was one of five cinemas in Malden Square at one time.

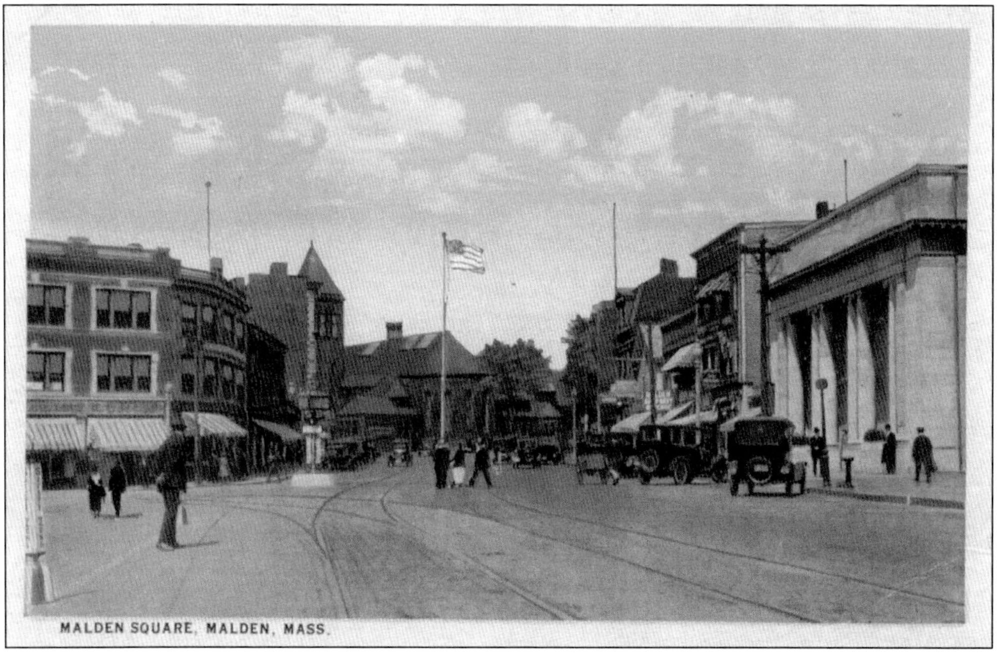

This view looks east on Pleasant Street. The columned building to the right was the Malden Savings Bank.

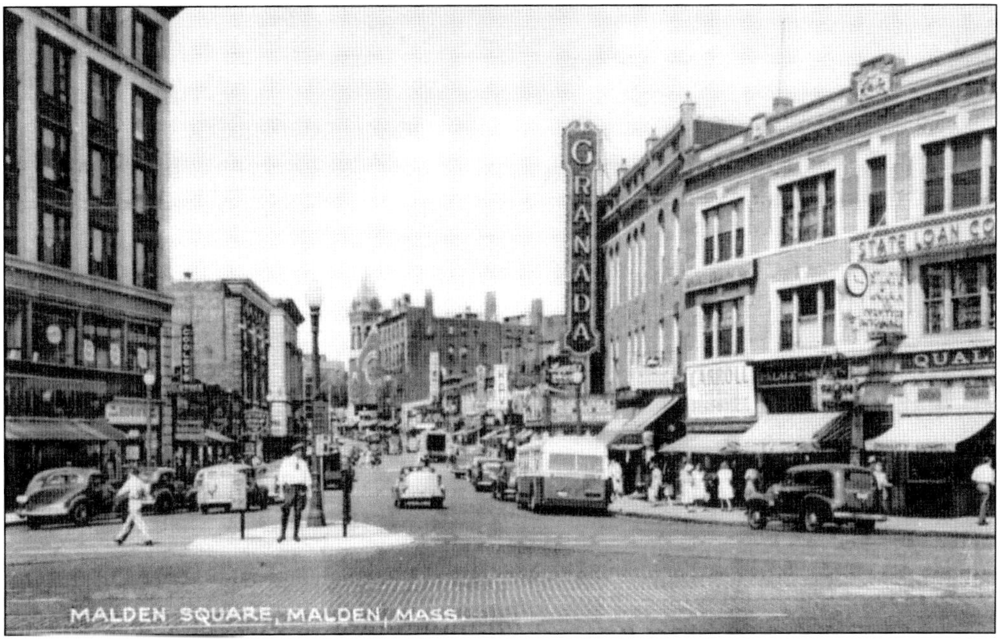

Pleasant Street is shown in this c. 1940 real-photo postcard. By the 1940s, Malden Square had become a popular shopping destination. The Granada Theater, at right, was a popular attraction.

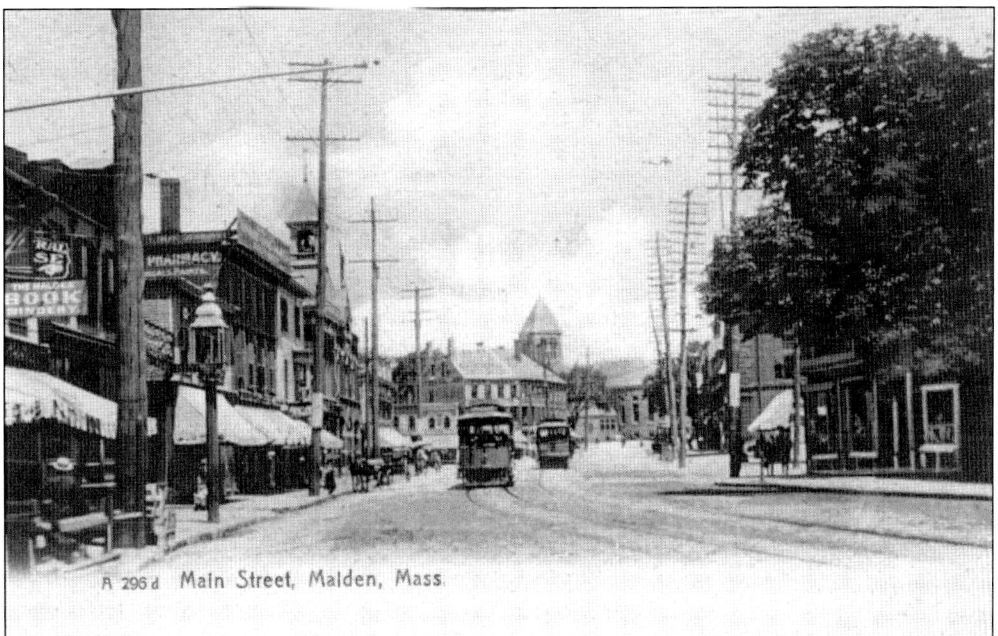

This early real-photo postcard of Main Street looks north. The Malden Book Bindery can be seen at left.

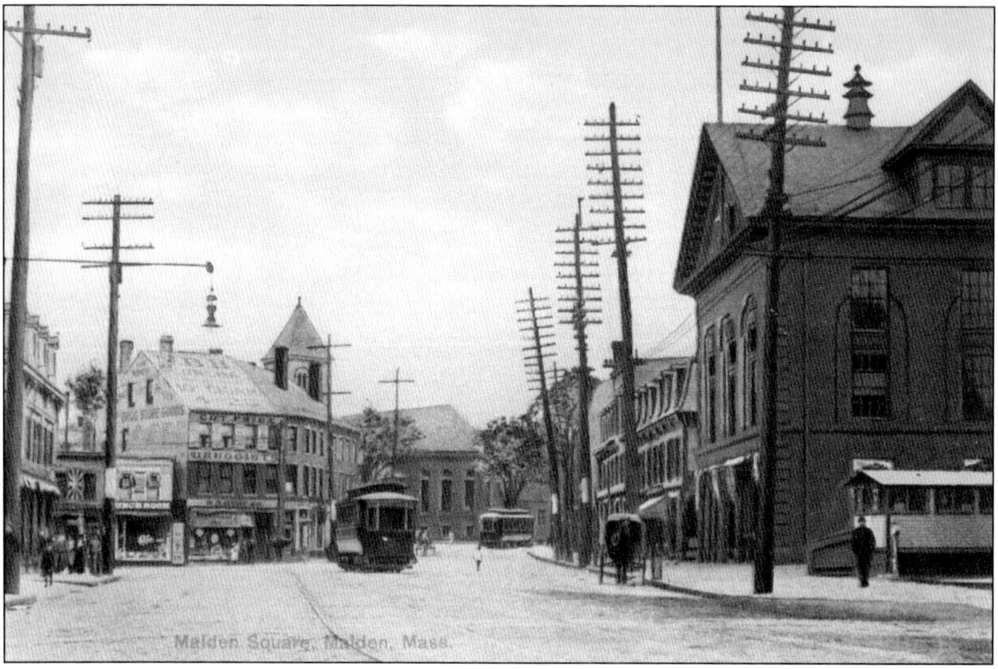

This view of Main Street shows the Malden City Hall at right. To the right of city hall is a small restaurant.

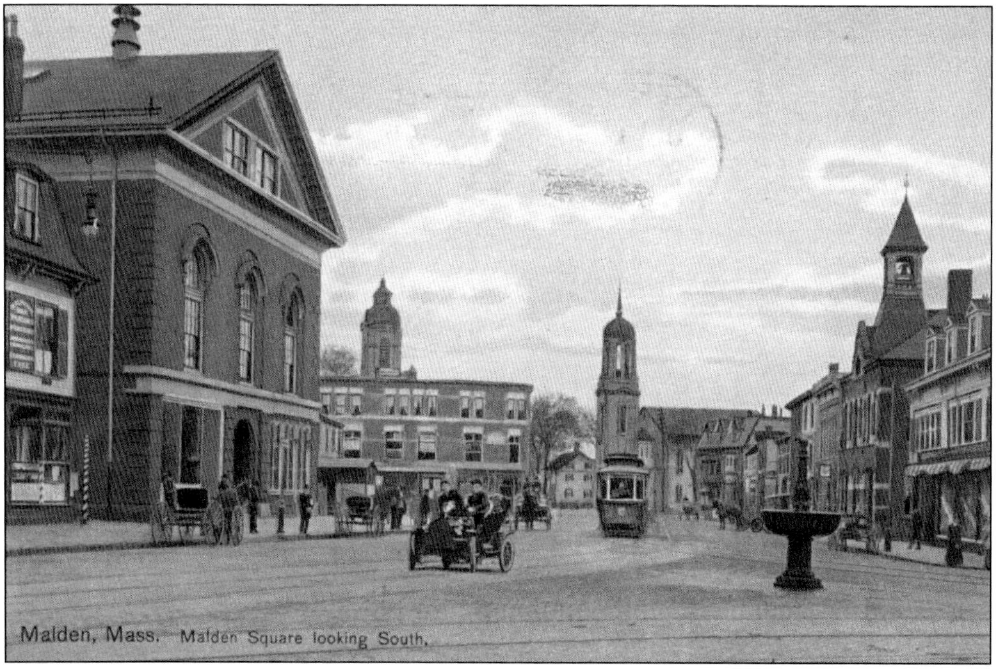

This view of Main Street is looking south, with the city hall to the left, the First Parish Church (Universalist) in the center, and the Sacred Hearts Church tower in the middle.

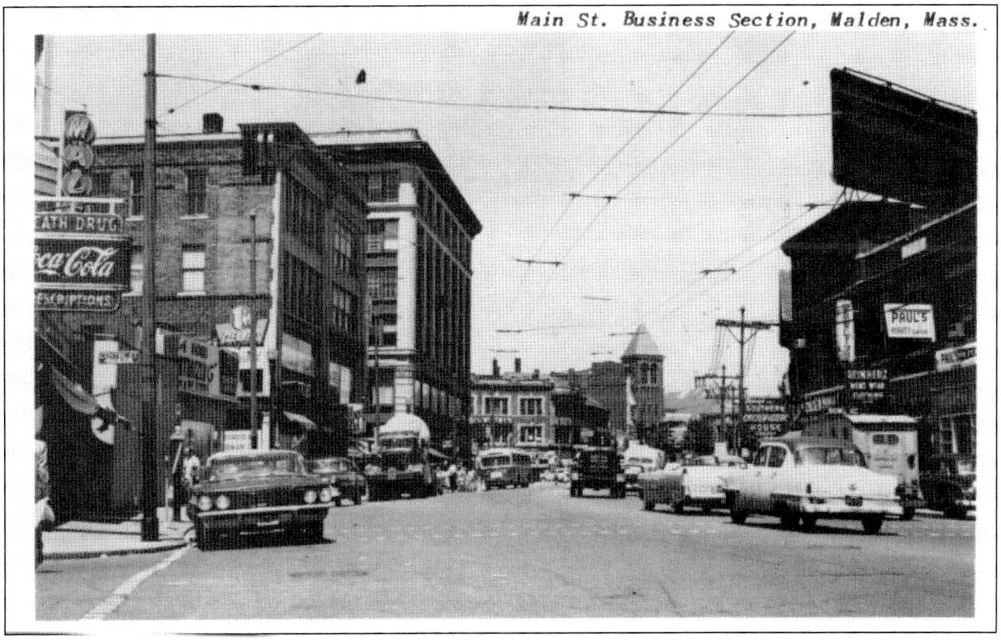

This photograph is of Main Street as it appeared in the 1950s. The Clifford-Black Furniture Company is on the left just before the Dowling Building. This view is looking toward the intersection of Main and Pleasant Streets.

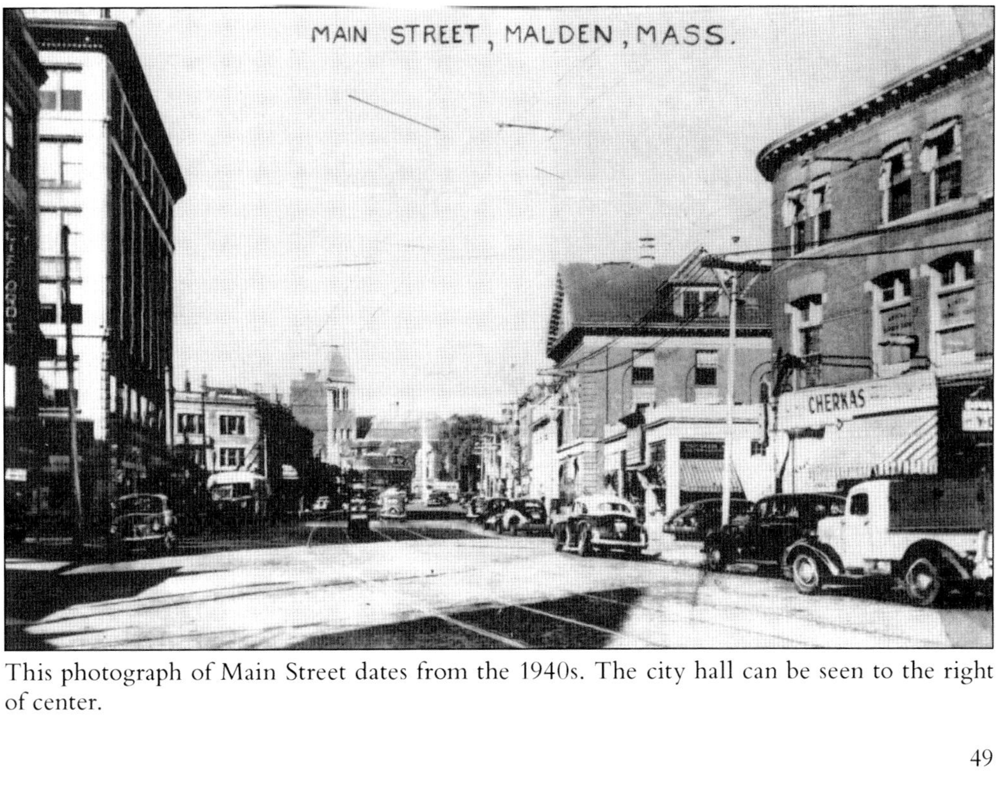

This photograph of Main Street dates from the 1940s. The city hall can be seen to the right of center.

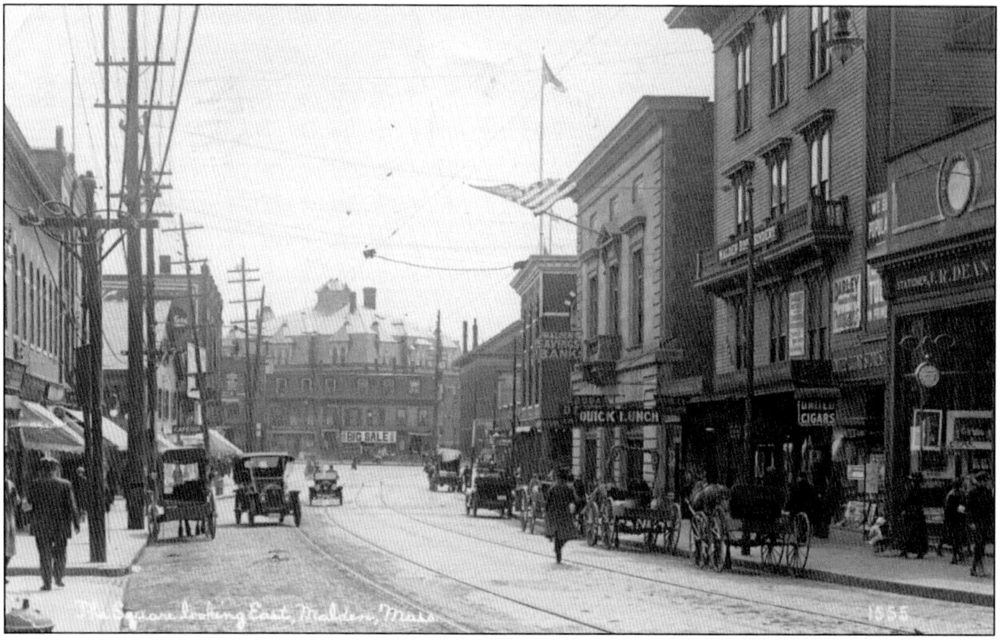

This c. 1915 view of Pleasant Street is looking to the east toward Main Street. The Centre Grammar School is visible in the center of this card. The First National Bank of Malden is at right center.

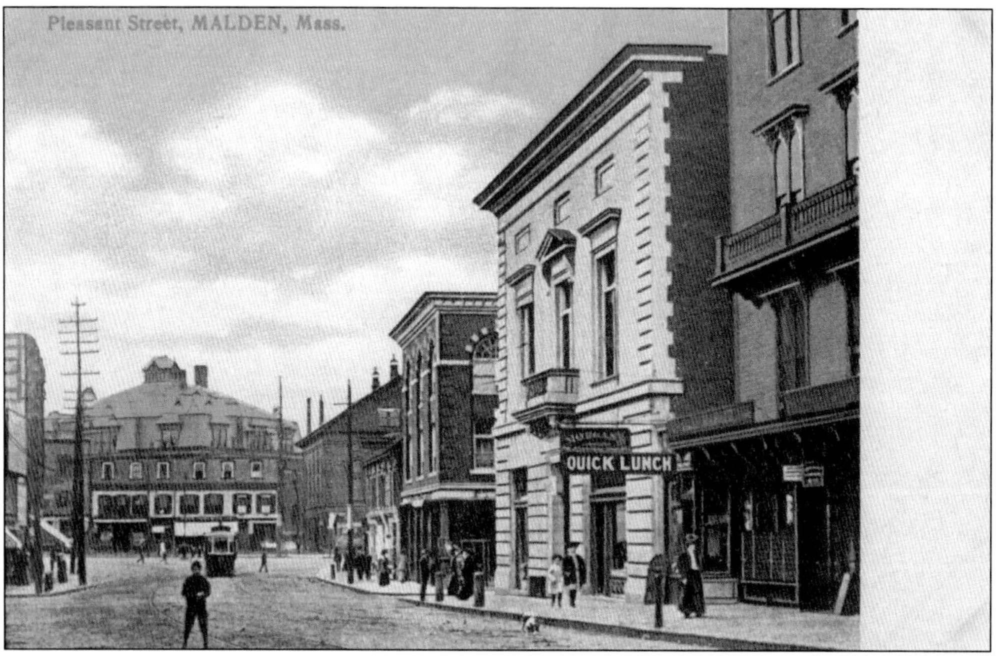

This view of Pleasant Street is facing east. The building to the left of the Quick Lunch is the First National Bank of Malden, which is at the corner of Middlesex and Pleasant Streets.

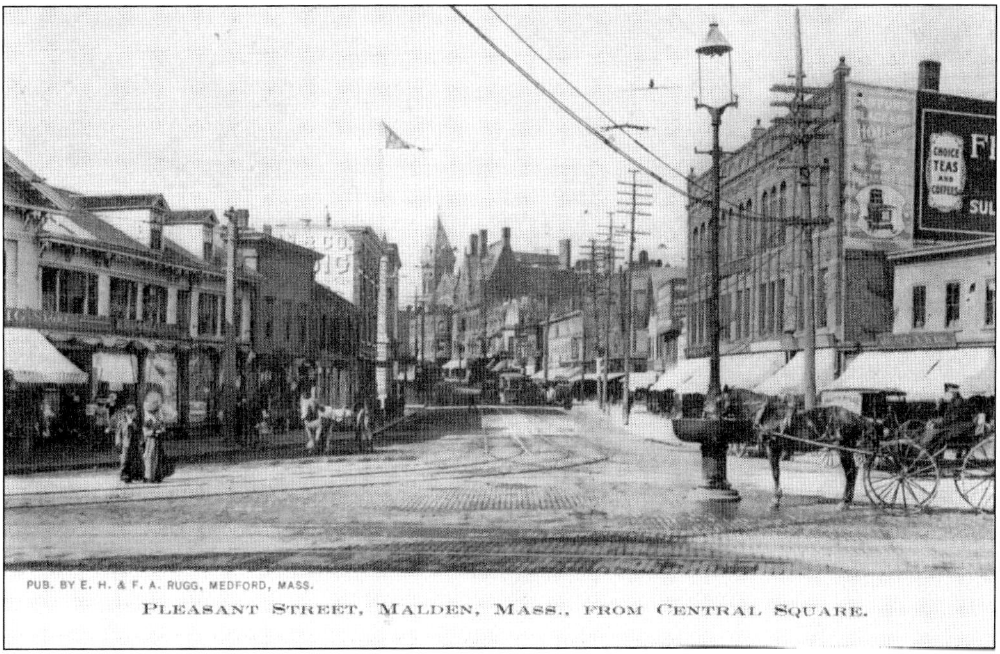

Pictured is Pleasant Street as seen from Central Square (the intersection of Pleasant and Main Street was known as Central Square in the 1900s). Note the horse at the water trough to the right.

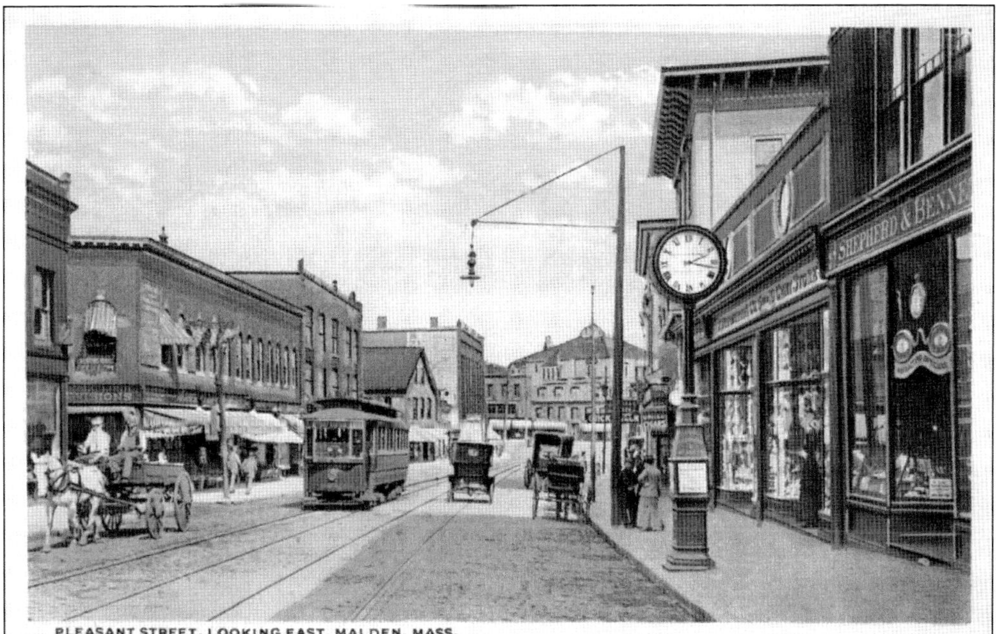

This c. 1907 photograph of Pleasant Street looks east. Note the trolley, horse carts, and the eyeglass trade sign near the clock.

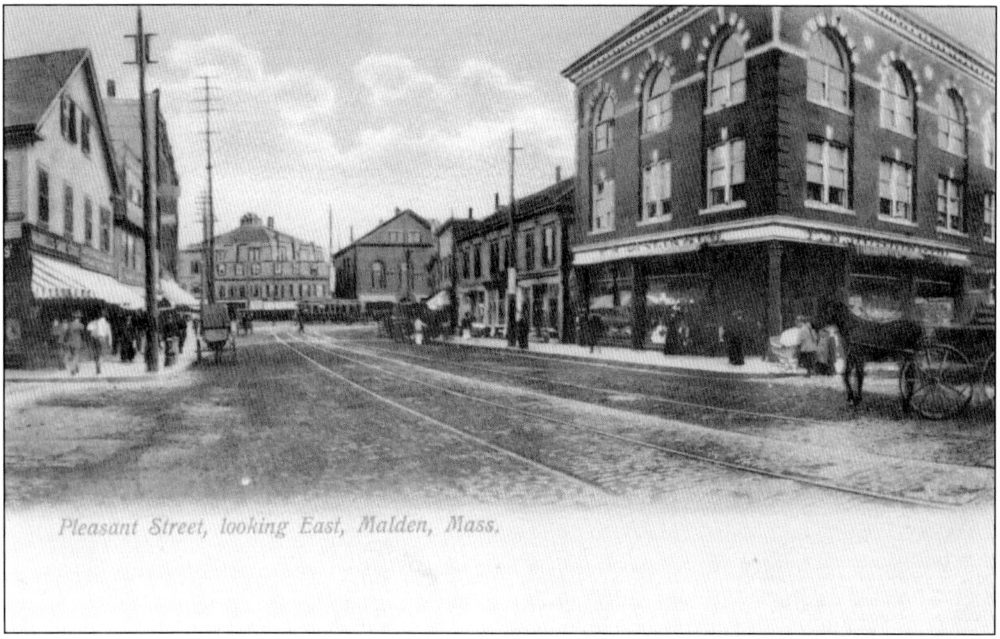

This view of Pleasant Street looking east toward Main Street shows F.N. Joslin's store to the right, at the corner of Middlesex Street, which is partially obscured by the horse and cart.

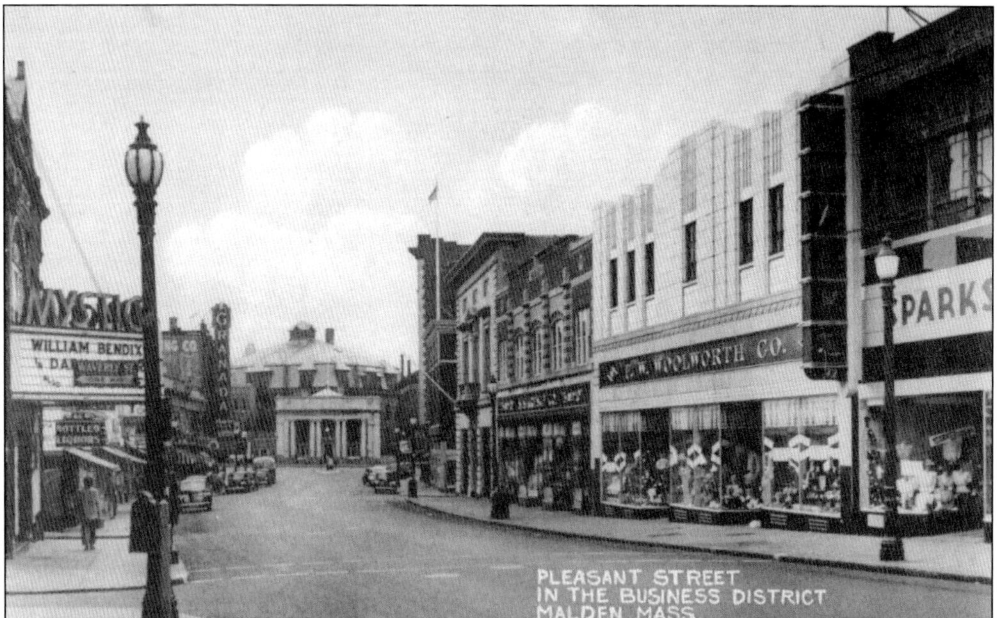

The Mystic Theater, at left, was on Pleasant Street, opposite F.W. Woolworth Company. The marquee presents enough information to date this photograph to exactly 1946, when *The Dark Corner* starring William Bendix was the feature film.

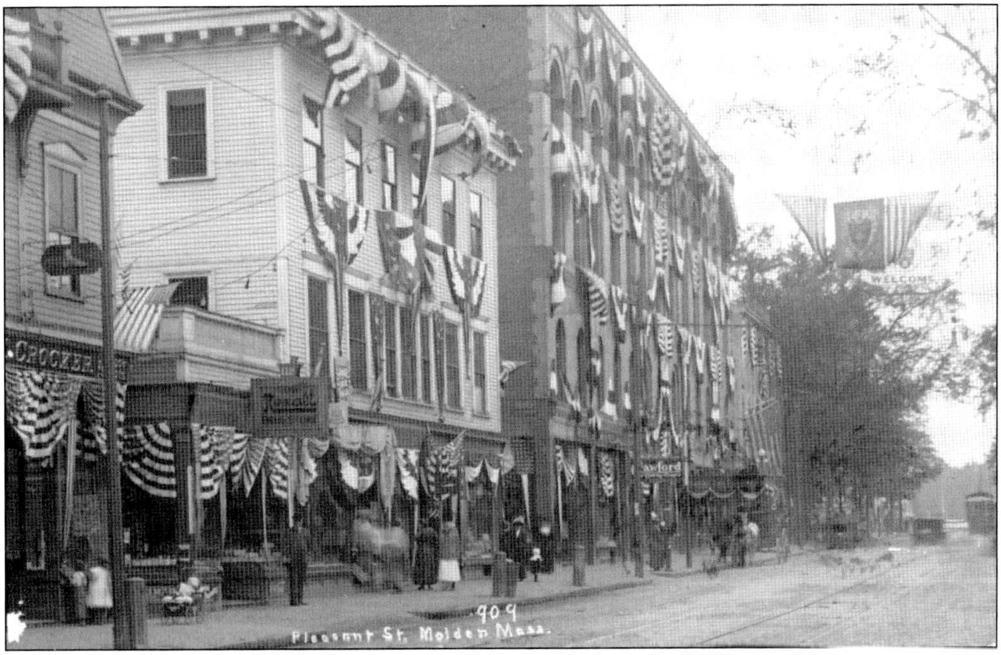

This photograph of Pleasant Street shows the Malden Square area decked out for a patriotic celebration, probably President Taft's visit in September 1912.

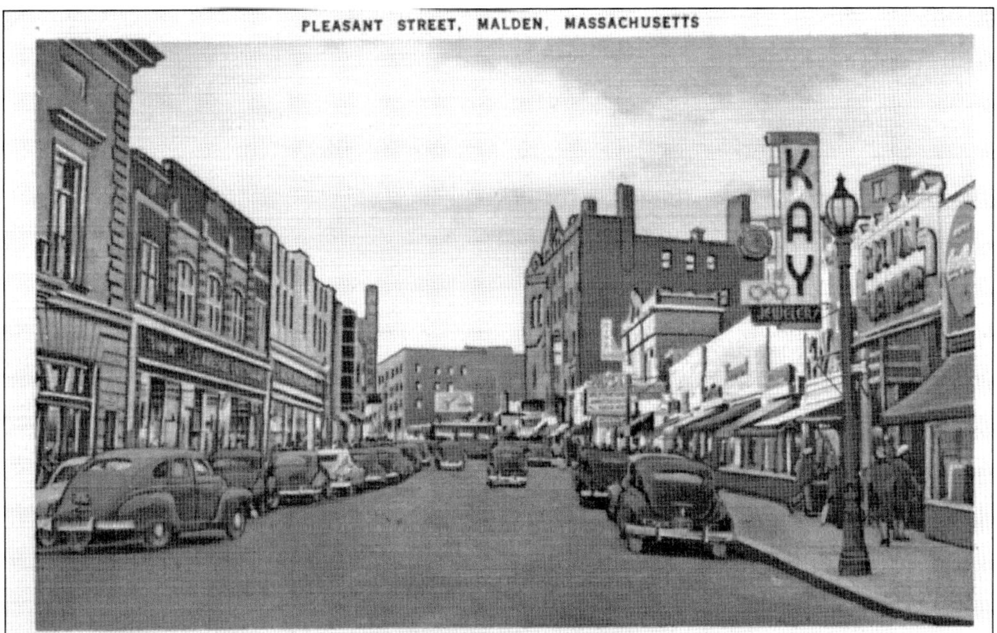

A linen postcard of Pleasant Street in the 1940s shows the S.S. Kresge and F.W. Woolworth stores, which can be identified by their signs at left.

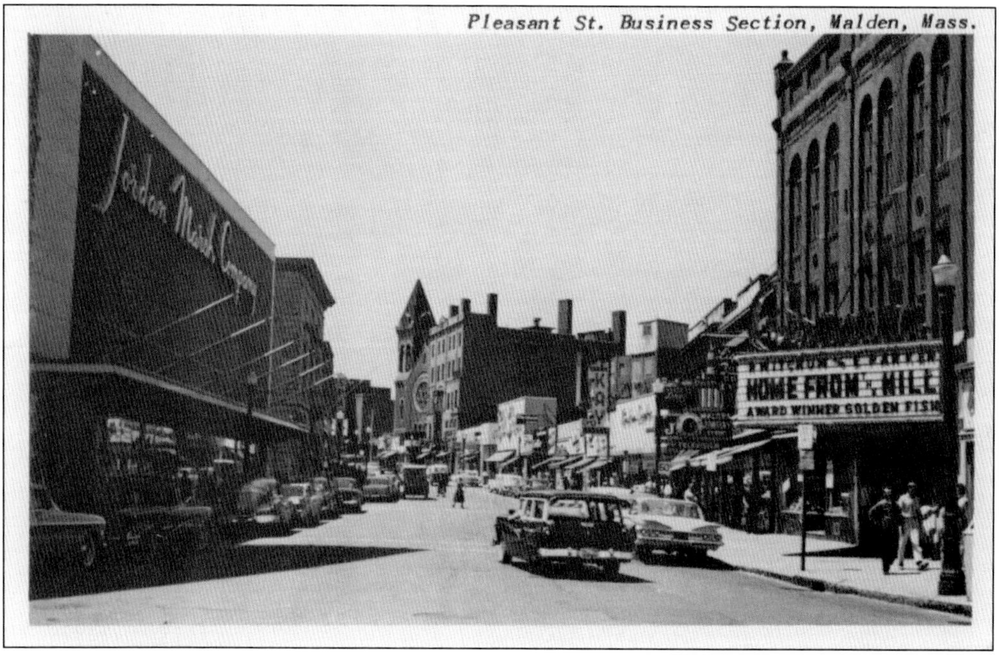

This view of Pleasant Street includes the marquee of the Granada Theater, which features *Home From the Hill*, a 1960 film starring Robert Mitchum. The Jordan Marsh department store, successor to Joslin's, is on the left.

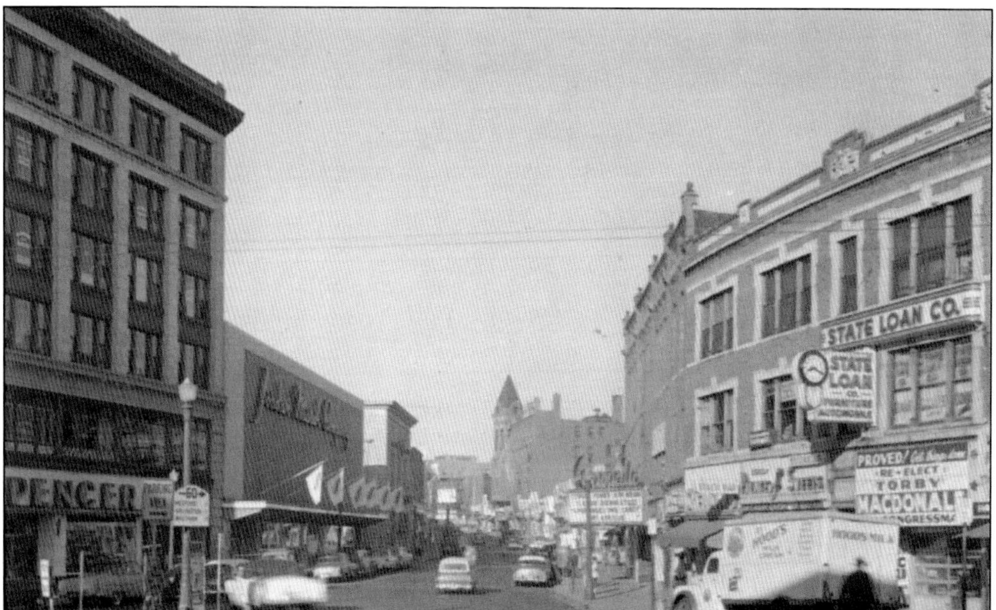

As seen in this Kodachrome postcard, the Granada Theater now features *The Eddie Duchin Story*, a 1956 film starring Tyrone Power and Kim Novak. To the right, a sign declares that Torbet Macdonald is running for reelection to Congress. Also seen is the popular Palace of Sweets.

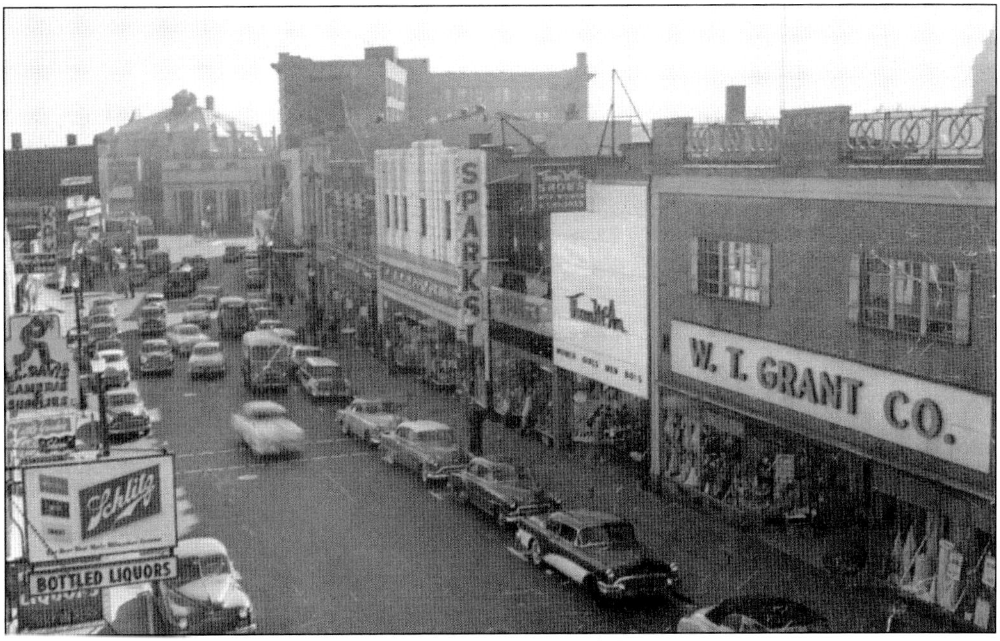

This elevated view of Pleasant Street is looking east and features a view of a number of local stores in the early 1960s. W.T. Grant, Thom McAn, Sparks, F.W. Woolworth, and S.S. Kresge have all departed now; the last store, Sparks, closed in 2014.

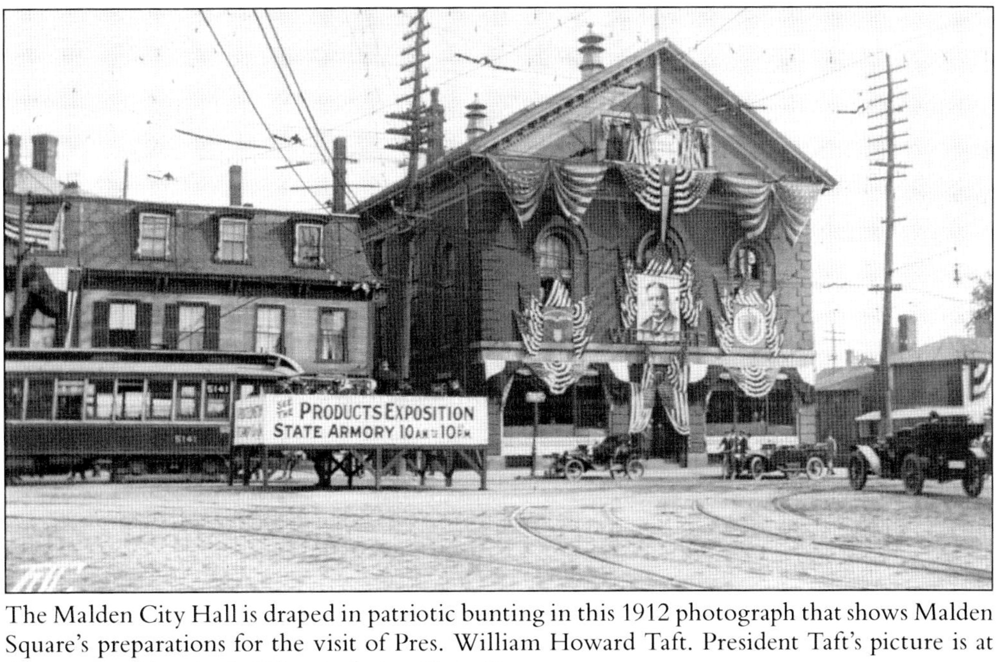

The Malden City Hall is draped in patriotic bunting in this 1912 photograph that shows Malden Square's preparations for the visit of Pres. William Howard Taft. President Taft's picture is at the center of the city hall facade facing Main Street.

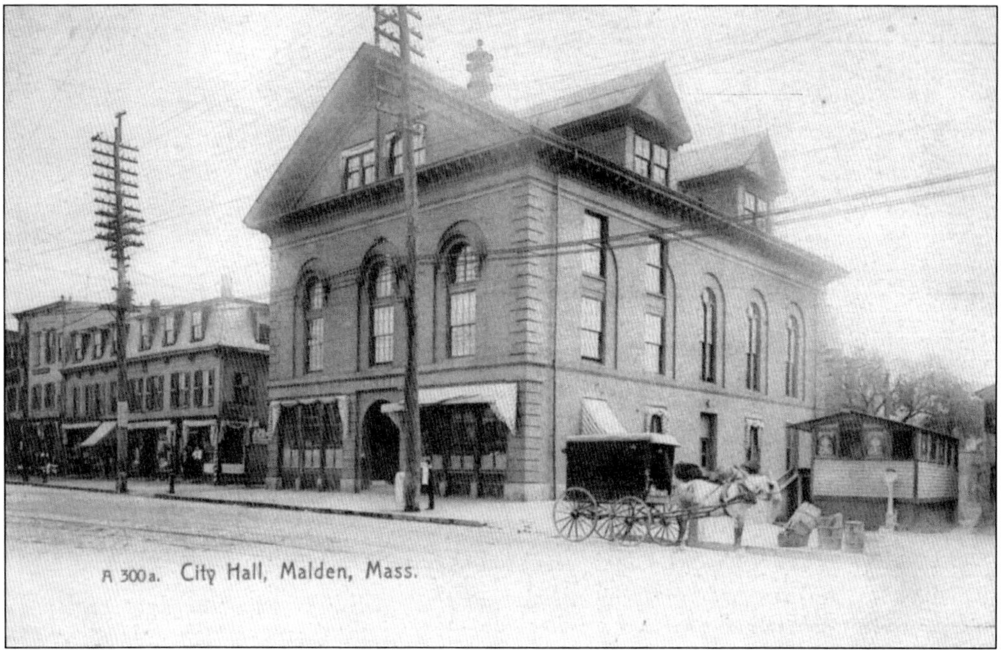

This view of the old Malden City Hall shows the structural and cosmetic changes made to the 1857 building in the 1890s. The small building near the horse cart is a diner.

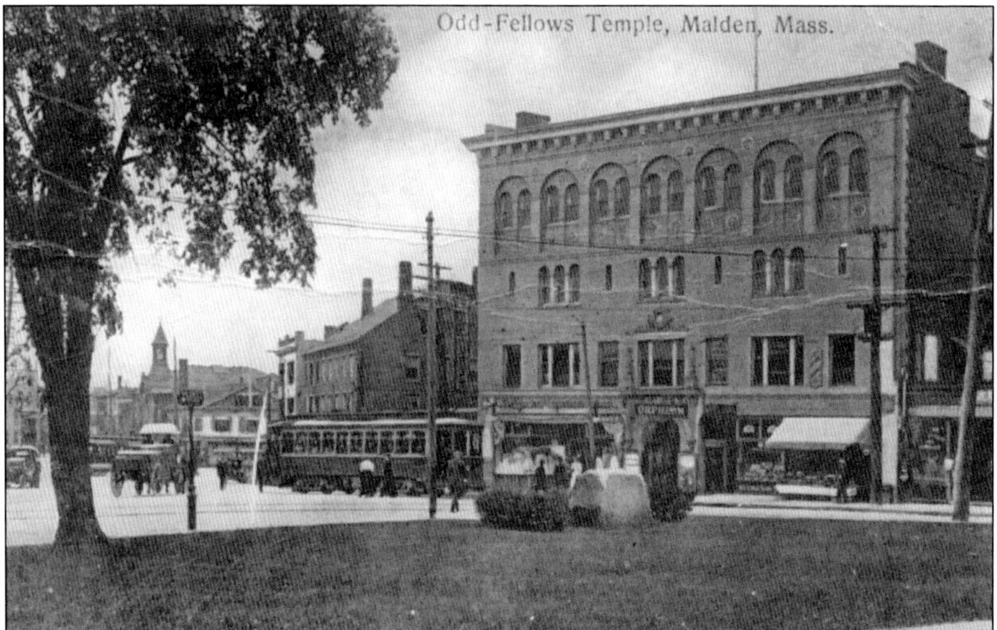

The Odd Fellows Temple on Main Street, built in 1907, is pictured here from the First Baptist Church front lawn. At the center of the Odd Fellows Temple is the entrance to the Orpheum Theater, a movie house.

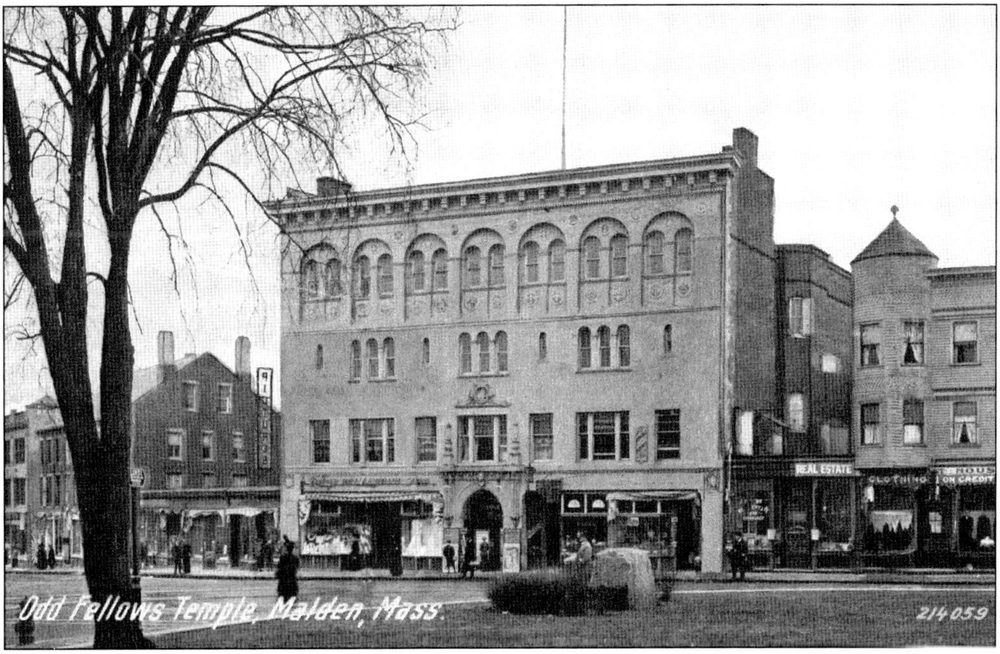

Here is another view of the Odd Fellows Temple in Converse Square as seen from the First Baptist Church. The Odd Fellows Temple is listed in the National Register of Historic Places.

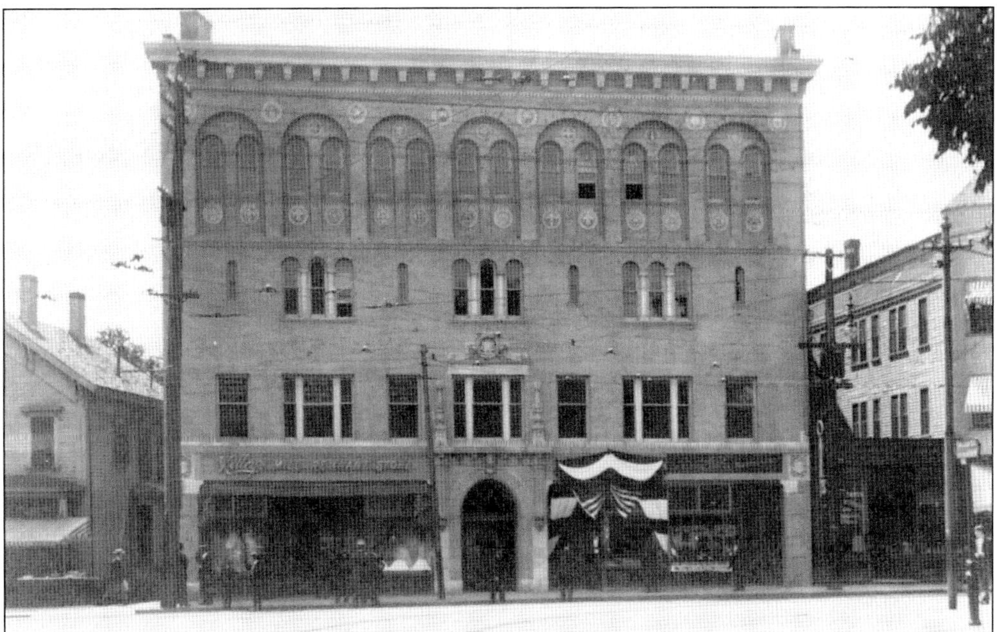

This is a direct view of the Odd Fellows Temple on Main Street around 1911. Kelly's Mill Remnant Store occupies the lower left side of the building.

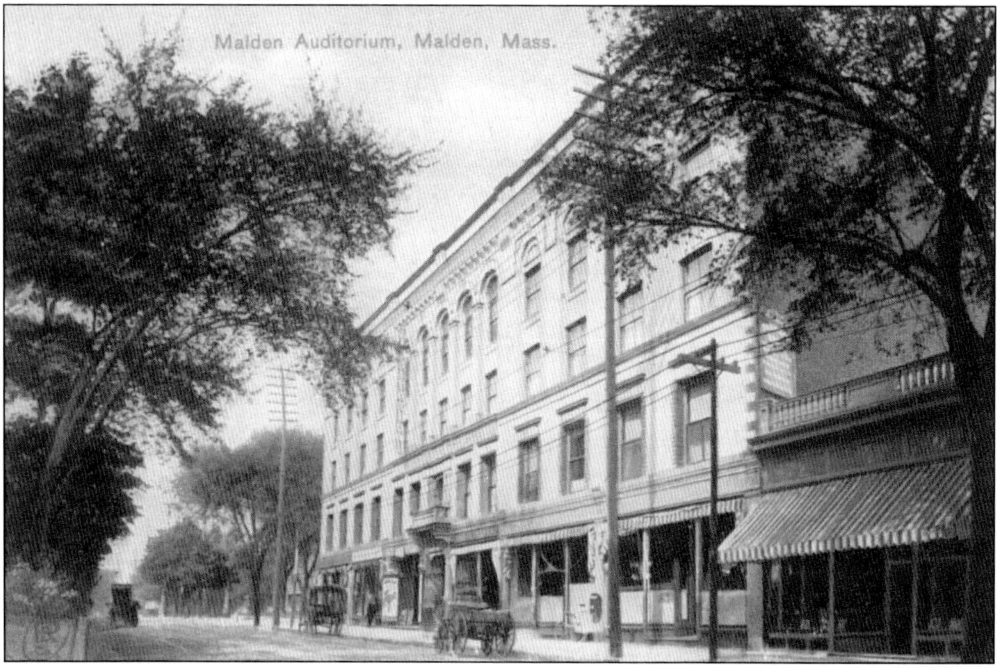

Pictured here is the Malden Auditorium Theater, Malden's finest theater when it opened. Located on Pleasant Street, it originally hosted plays and vaudeville acts and was later converted to a movie theater.

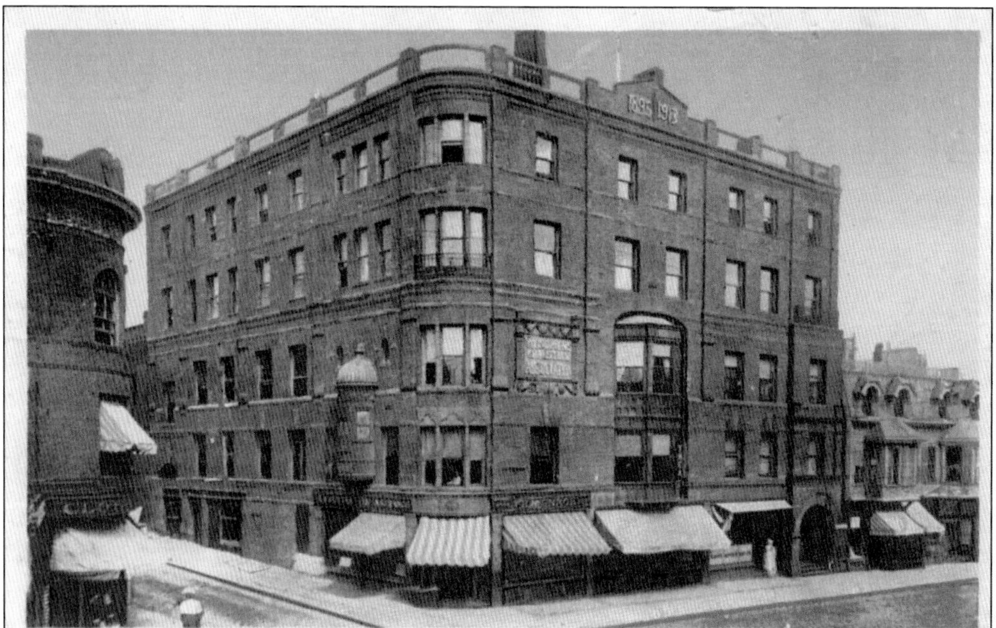

The YMCA building on Pleasant Street is shown in this postcard. The building as pictured was refurbished in 1913.

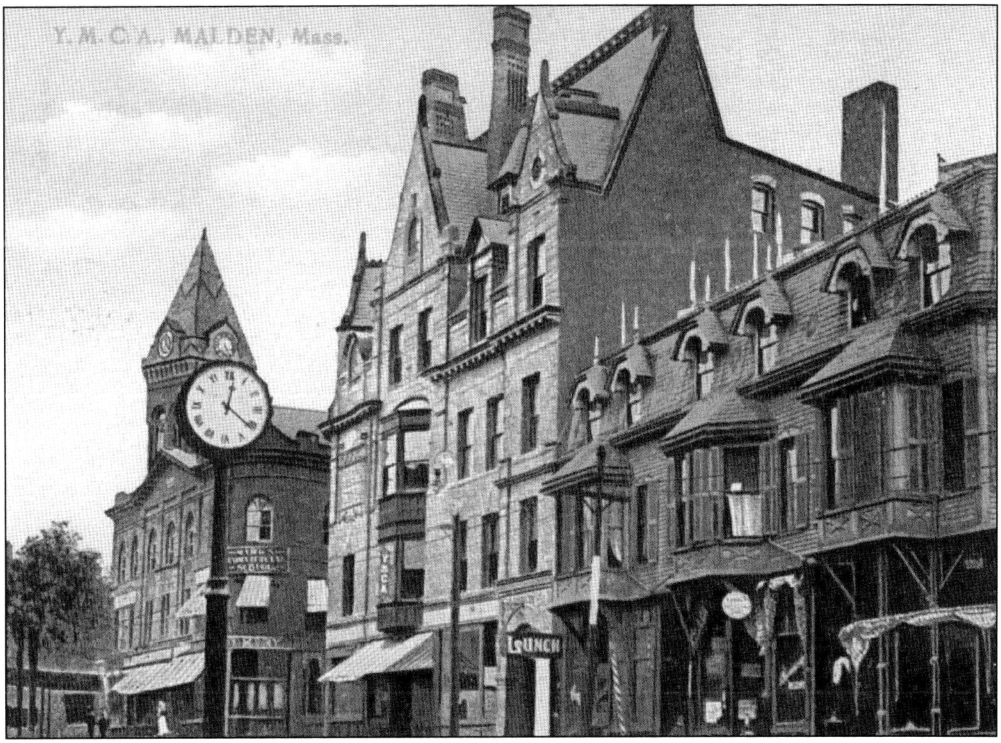

This view of the YMCA building shows the original structure on Pleasant Street, constructed in 1895.

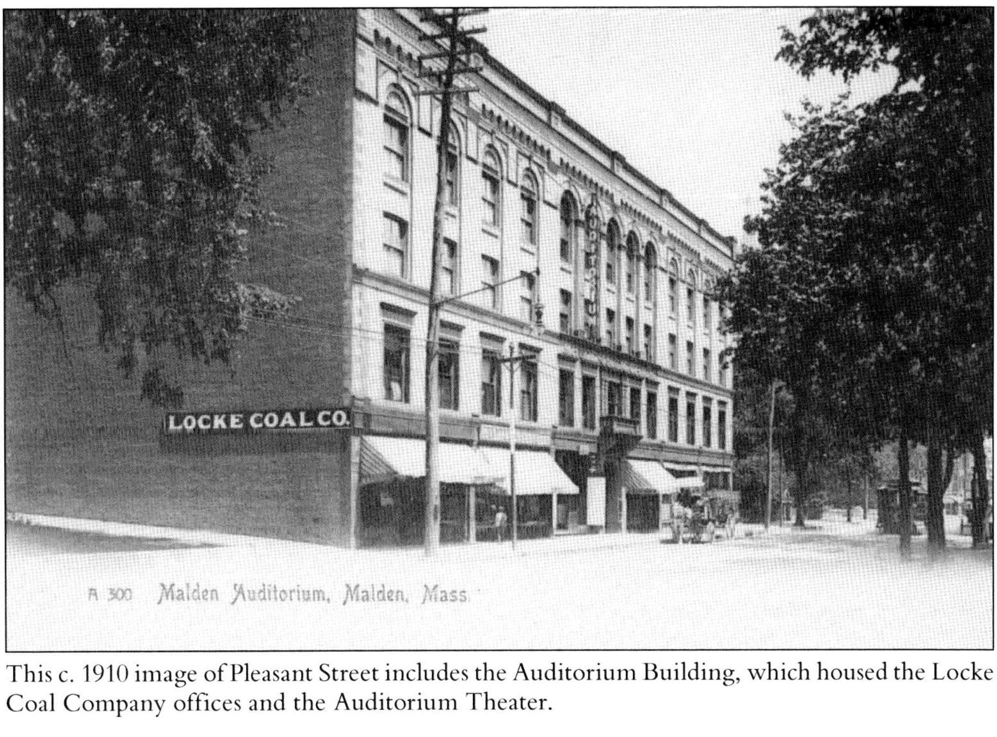

This c. 1910 image of Pleasant Street includes the Auditorium Building, which housed the Locke Coal Company offices and the Auditorium Theater.

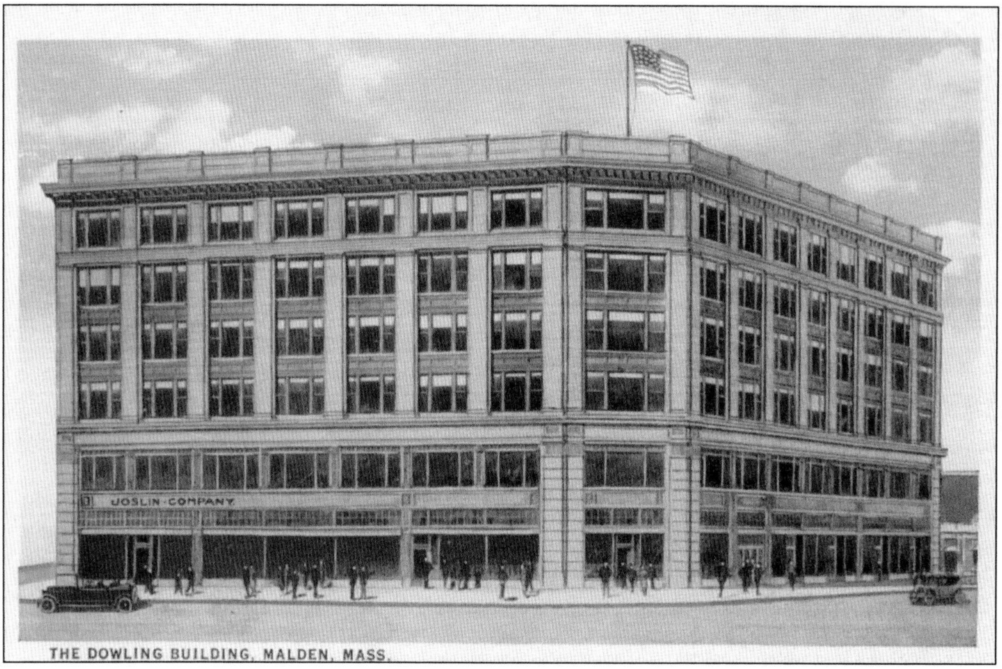

The Dowling Building, located on the corner of Pleasant and Main Streets, contained numerous professional offices. The ground floor was a large department store, occupied by F.N. Joslin's and later by Jordan Marsh.

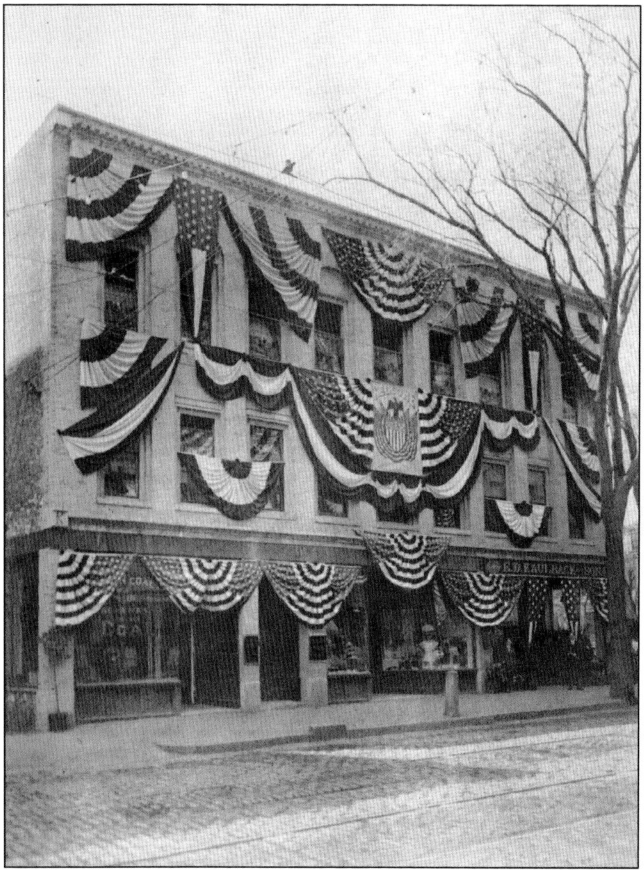

This early real-photo postcard shows the Kaulback Building decked out in patriotic bunting, perhaps in honor of President Taft's visit to Malden in 1912.

Five

Houses and Neighborhoods

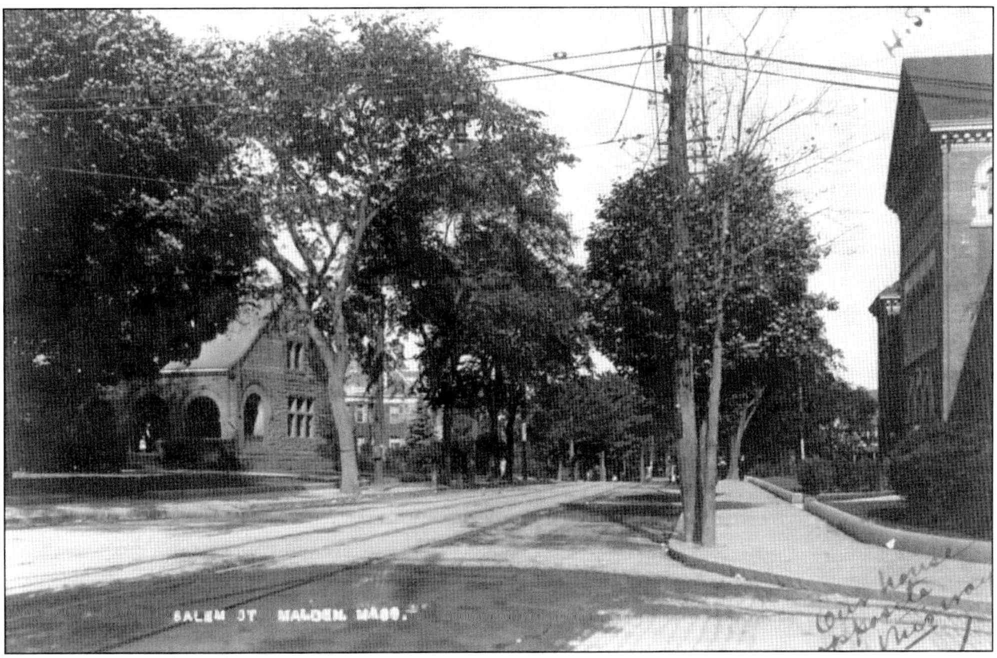

This summertime view of Salem Street looking east depicts the Malden Public Library on the left and Malden High School on the right. As Malden businessmen grew wealthier, they built residences that reflected this new wealth. However, because these were private dwellings, very few of the houses appear on postcards; only some residences are shown adapted to later uses. Views of many neighborhood streets showing residences of the middle class were also produced.

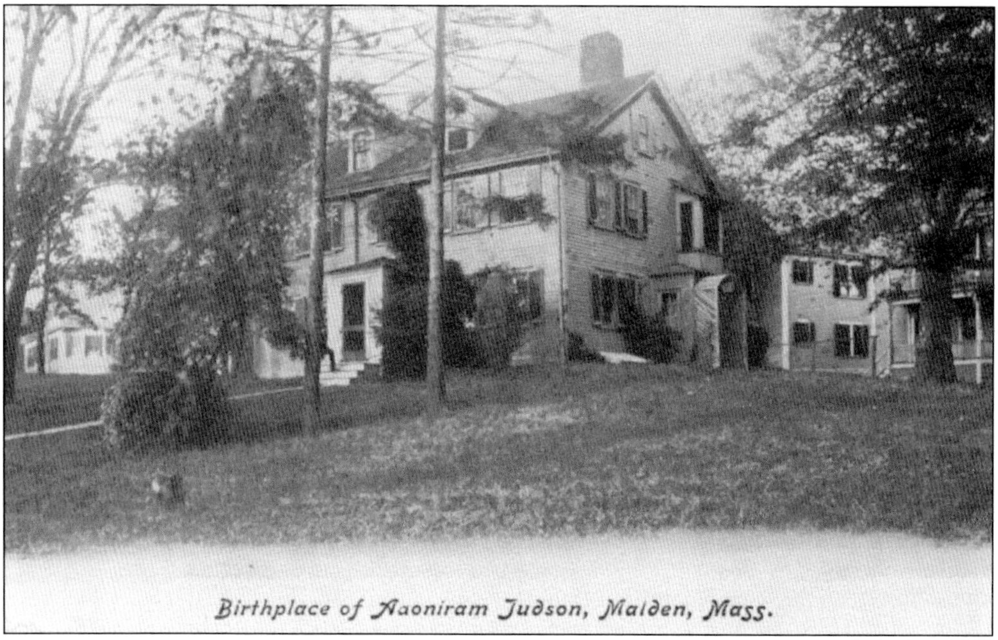

The birthplace of Adoniram Judson (1788–1850), missionary to Burma and the translator of the Bible into Burmese, is pictured as it looked in the 1900s. The house still stands today across from Bell Rock Park, although it has been greatly altered.

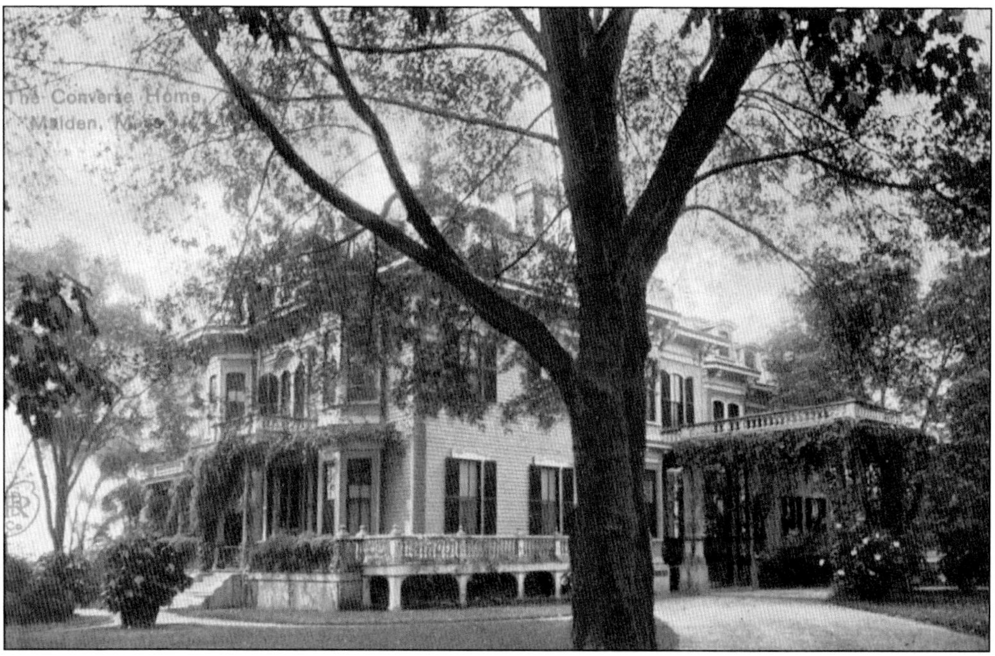

The stately Victorian home of Elisha Converse on Main Street was located between Perkins Avenue and Wyllis Avenue. It was razed in the 1940s. Converse was the first mayor of Malden, the owner and president of the Boston Rubber Shoe Company, an officer of many business organizations, and a noted and generous philanthropist.

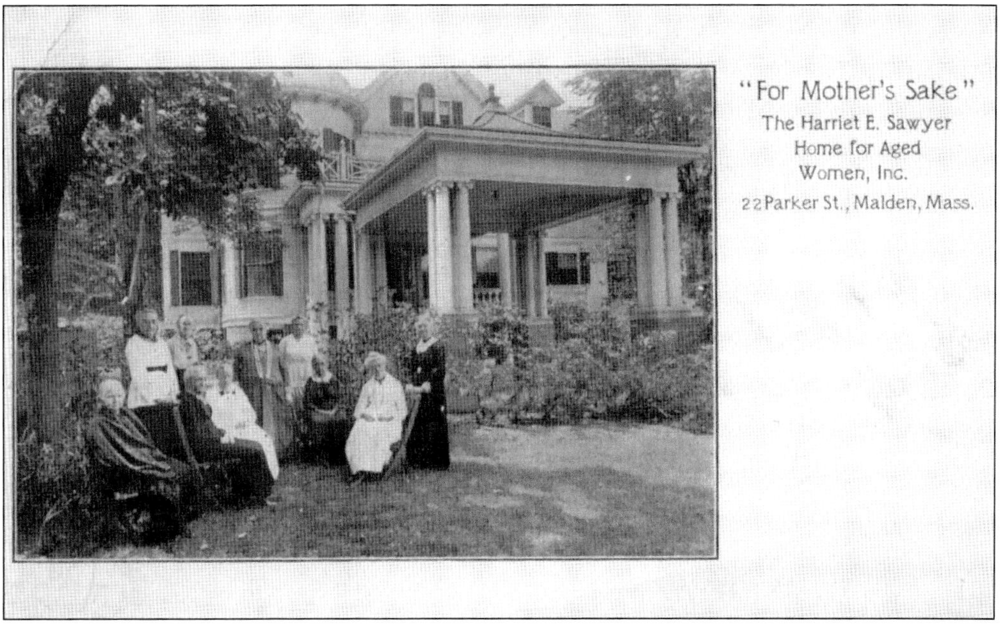

The exterior entrance to the Harriet E. Sawyer Home for Aged Women, formerly the Millet mansion, located at 22 Parker Street, is shown in this early photograph of the residents gathered in the front yard.

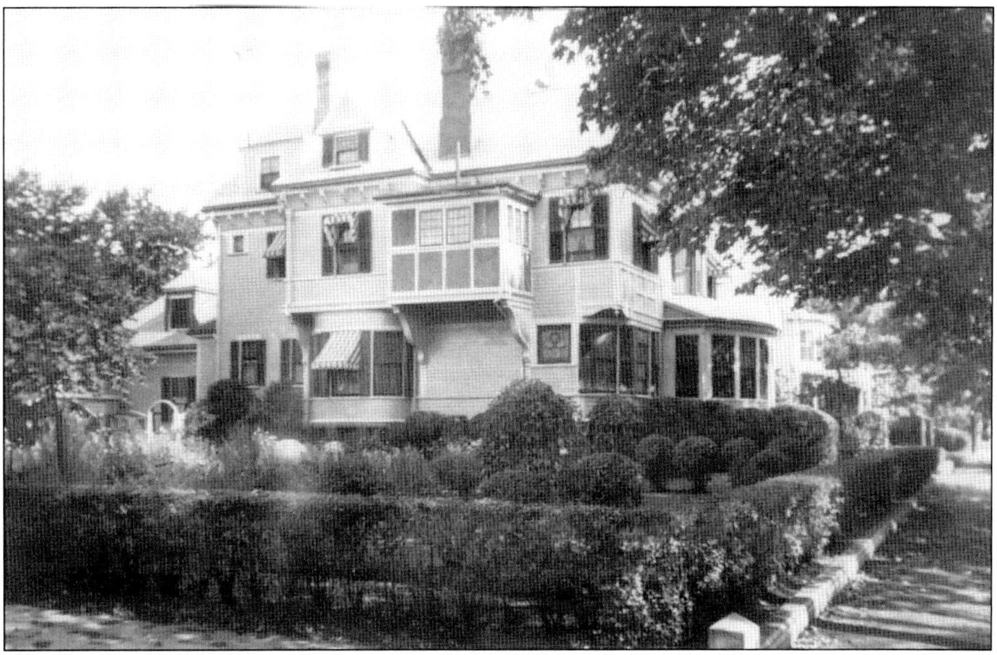

This image dates from around 1944 and shows the west side of the stately Queen Anne–style house built in the late 19th century by Peter Graffam at 181 Clifton Street.

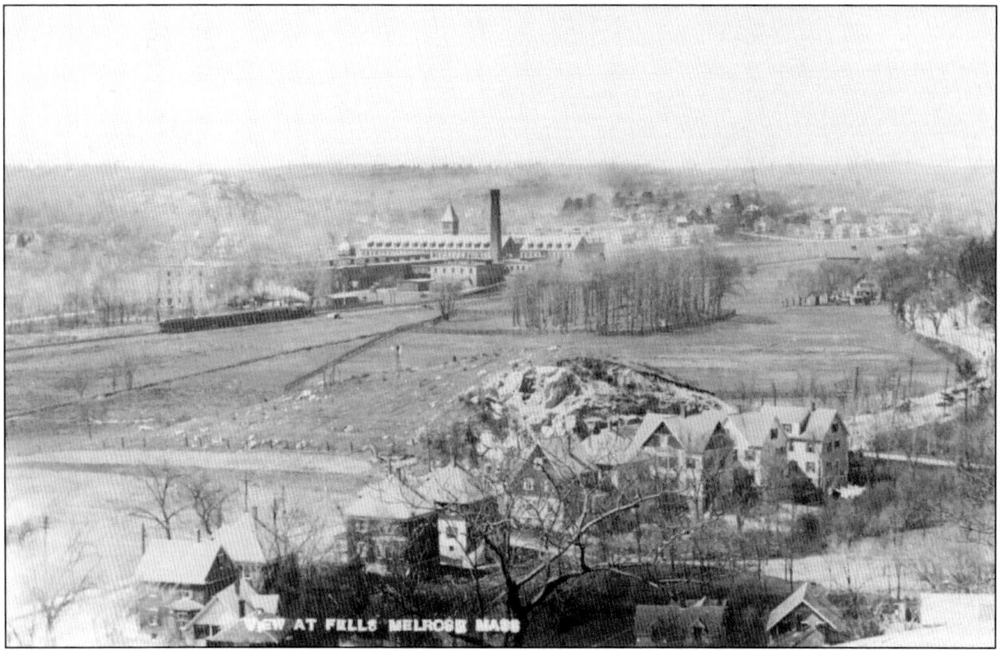

This view depicts the Boston Rubber Shoe Company mill on Washington Street on the Malden/Melrose line near Middlesex Fells. Main Street is to the right, and Island Hill is in the foreground. The area today is made up of Autumn Street, Wedgmere Road, and Fairlawn Street.

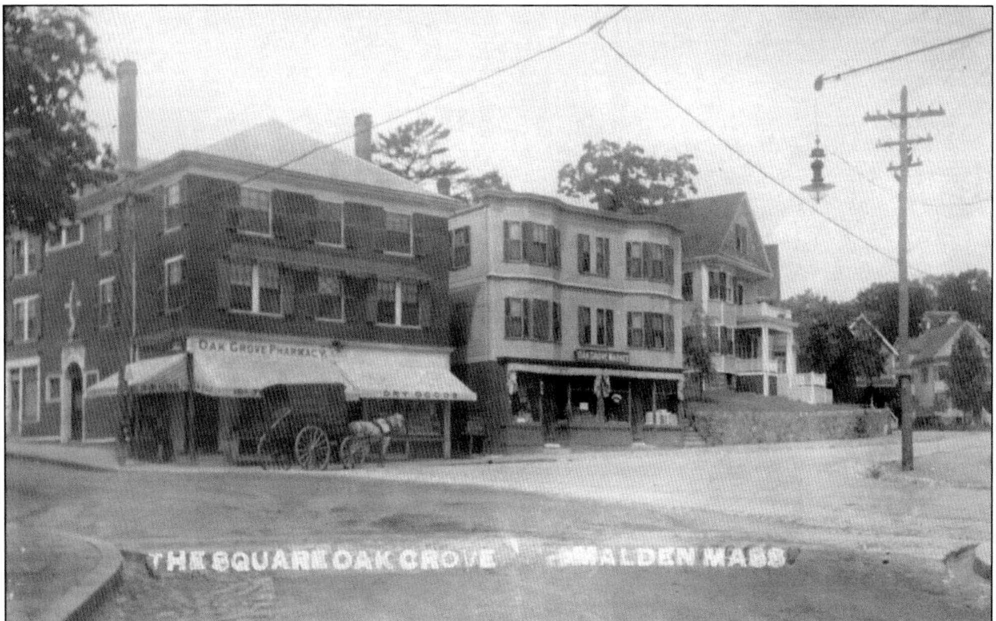

The Oak Grove section of Malden is predominantly a residential area. The Oak Grove Square pictured in this image is typical of Malden neighborhoods in the early 1900s.

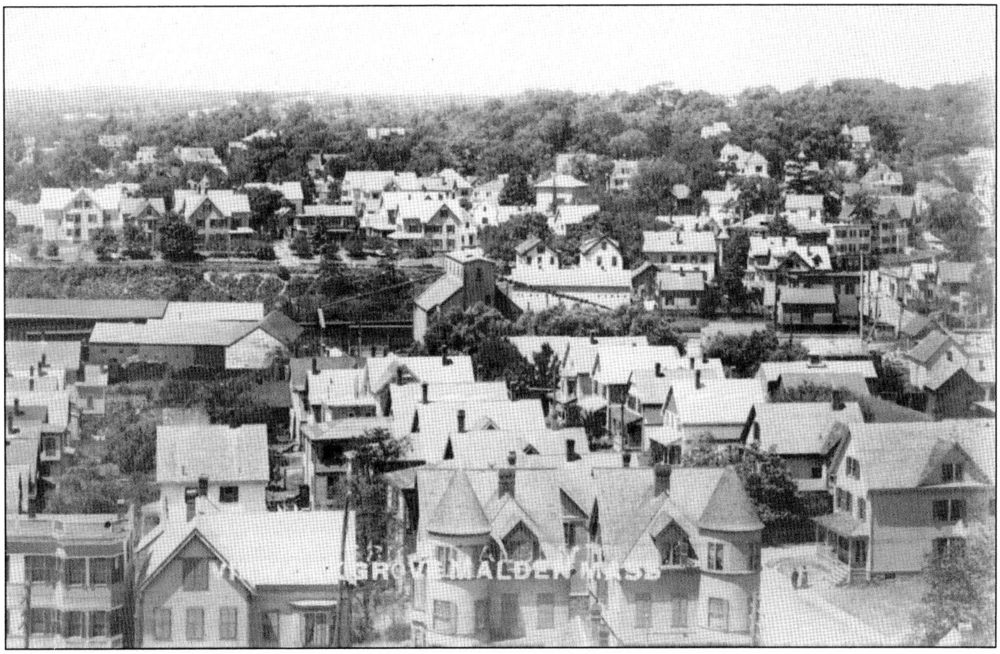

This panoramic view of Oak Grove depicts a number of residences. The commercial buildings in the center of this photograph are clustered along the tracks of the Boston & Maine Railroad, which runs north from Boston toward Melrose and beyond.

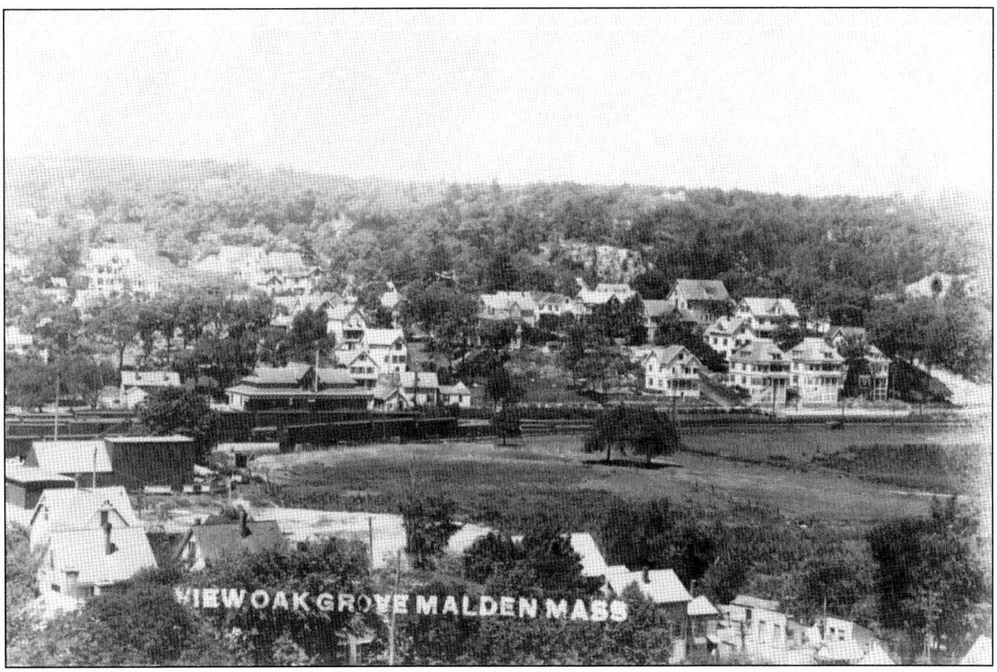

The Oak Grove Station on the Boston & Maine Railroad is in the center of this view. It was located where the Oak Grove "T" Station is now situated.

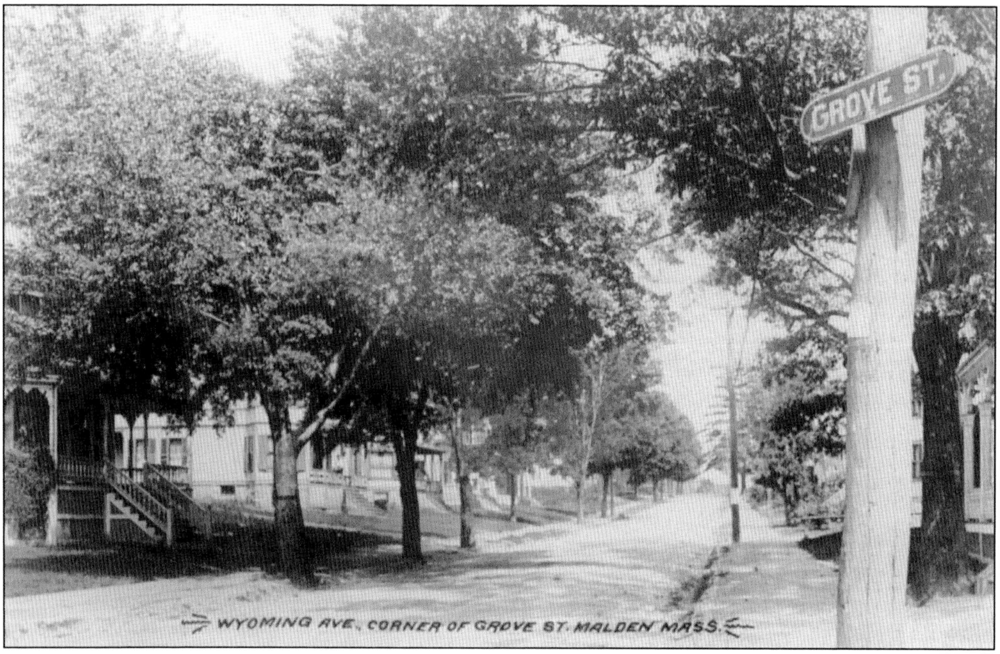

This view of Wyoming Avenue in the Oak Grove section was taken not far from Oak Grove Square at the corner of Grove Street.

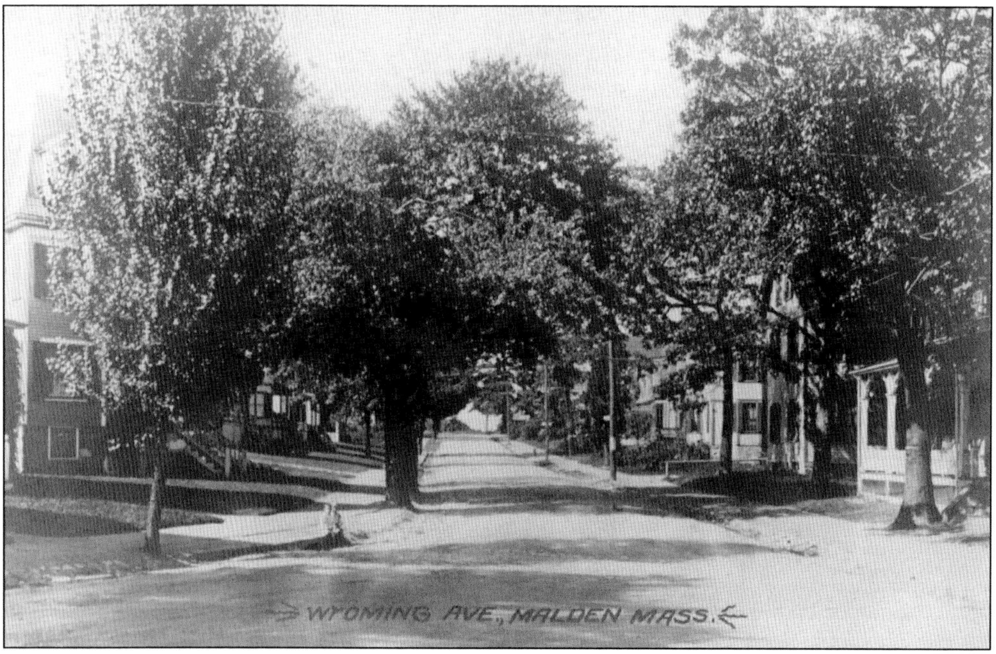

This c. 1908 real-photo postcard depicts Wyoming Avenue in summer and looks north from near Oak Grove Square. Note the two young children sitting on the curb.

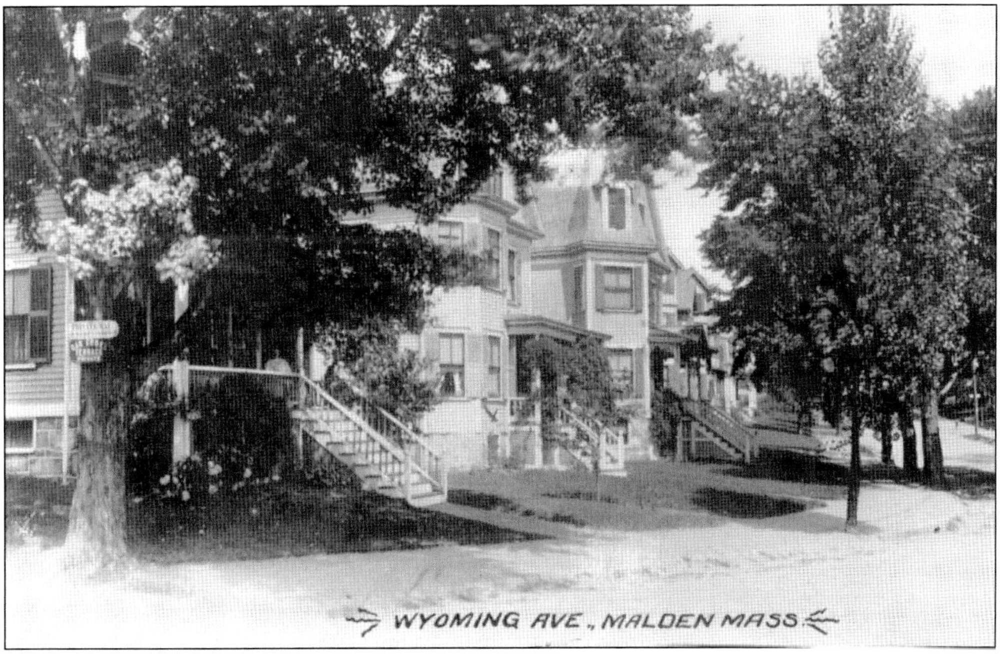

This is another view of Wyoming Avenue around 1908. This image shows the intersection of Wyoming Avenue and Oak Grove Terrace.

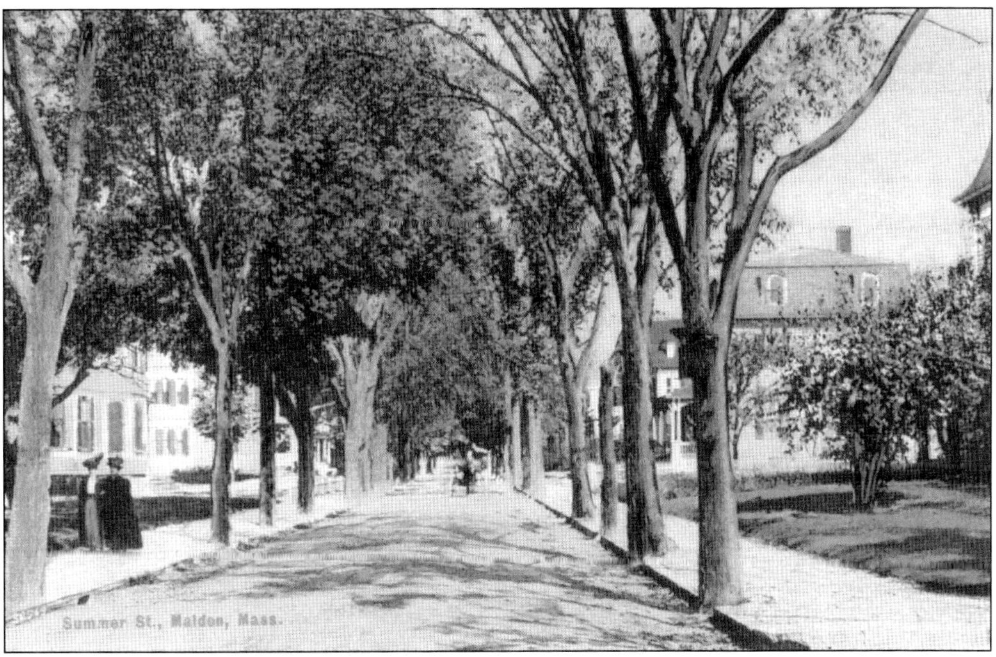

Summer Street in Malden's West End was known for its many fine residences, a number of which are depicted in this early postcard looking north toward Glenwood Street. Many of these fine homes have been preserved and may be seen today.

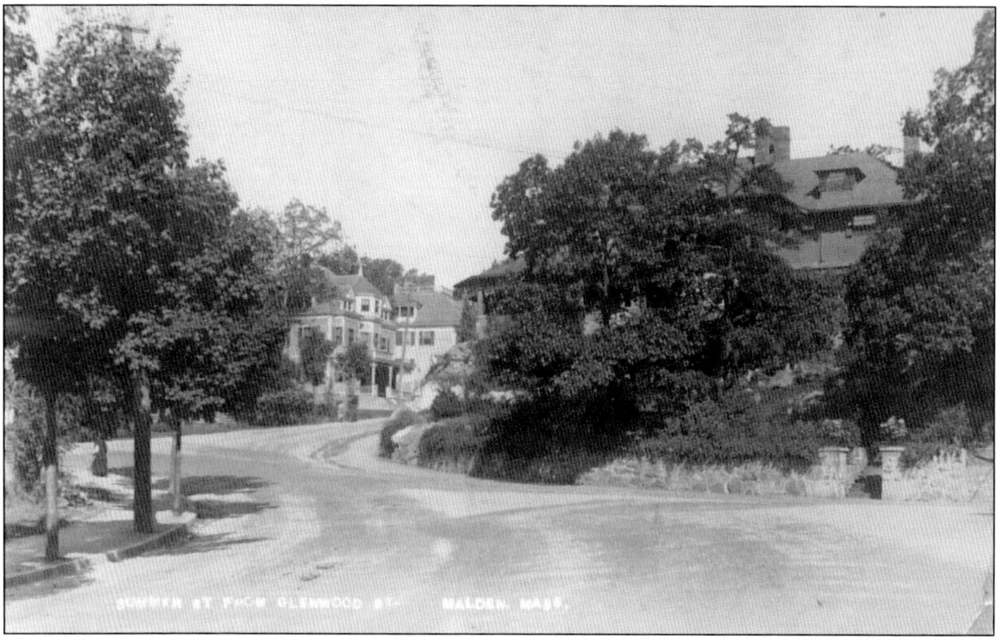

The large house seen at far right in this c. 1912 postcard is situated at the corner of Summer and Glenwood Streets. At the time, it was the residence of Eugene Nelson, a prominent Boston businessman.

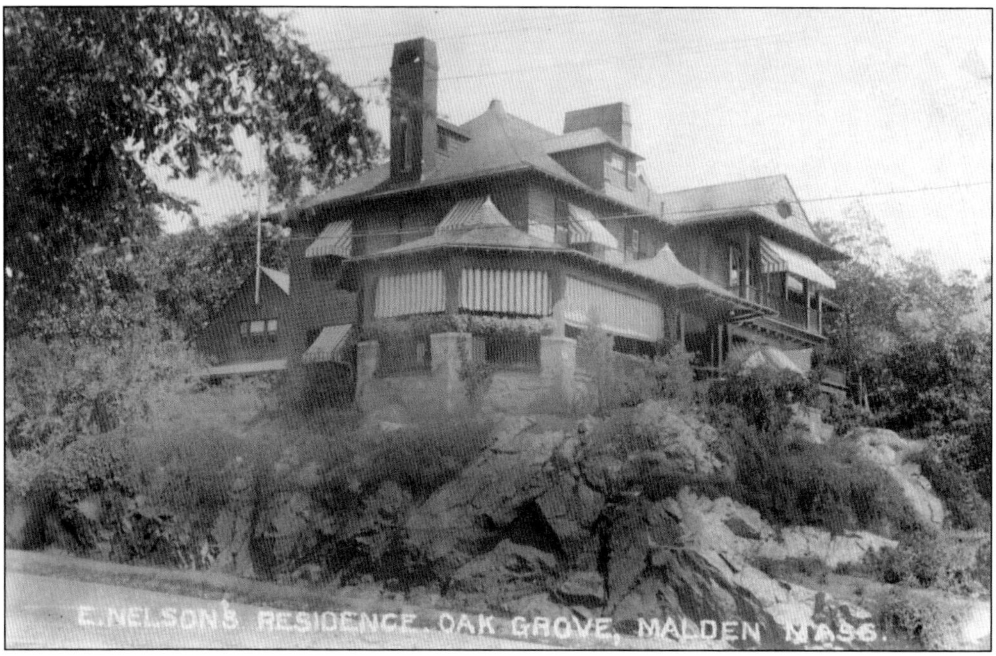

This postcard is identified by a caption at the bottom as the residence of Eugene Nelson. The same structure was later the home of Charles Neidner. The Charles Neidner and Sons Company had a national reputation for manufacturing quality linen fire hose. The house foundation was obviously built over an excavated ledge.

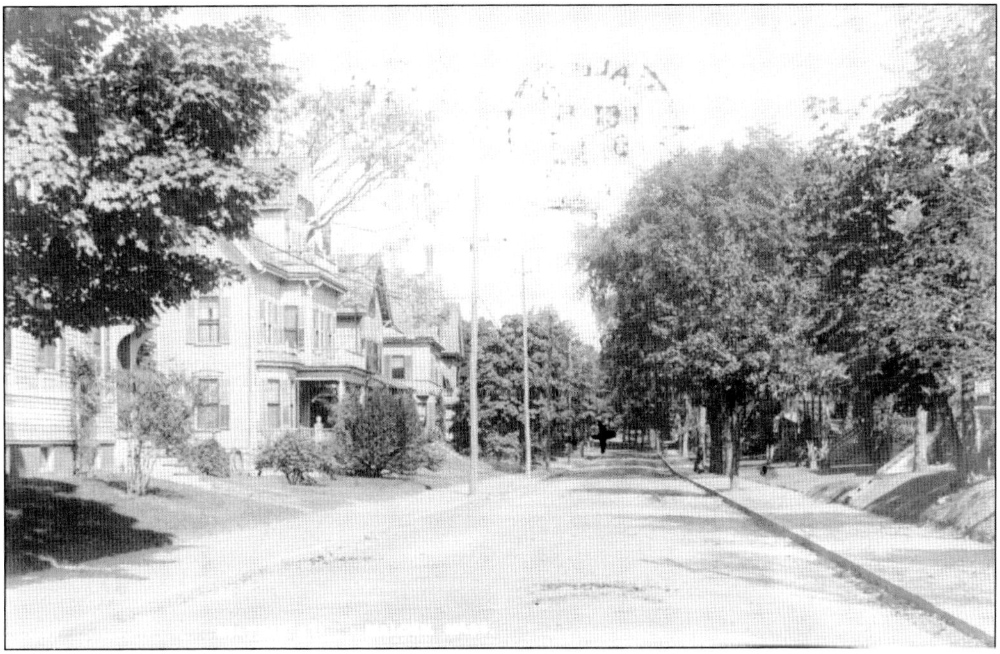

This image looking north from Clifton Street shows Beltran Street as it appeared in 1911. The "X" handwritten in ink on the front of this postcard was written by the sender to indicate her residence—a common addition on these old street photograph cards that depict houses.

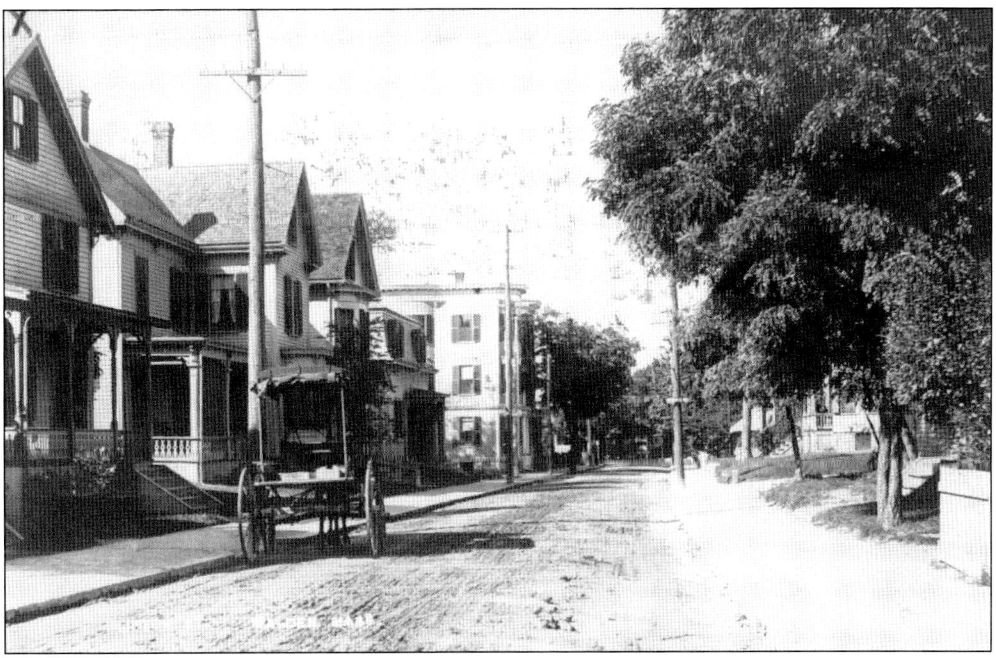

This view of Clifton Street is looking west toward Summer Street and features a horse and wagon, probably a delivery vehicle of a local merchant. Again, one can see an "X" inked over a house on the extreme left, added to indicate the sender's residence.

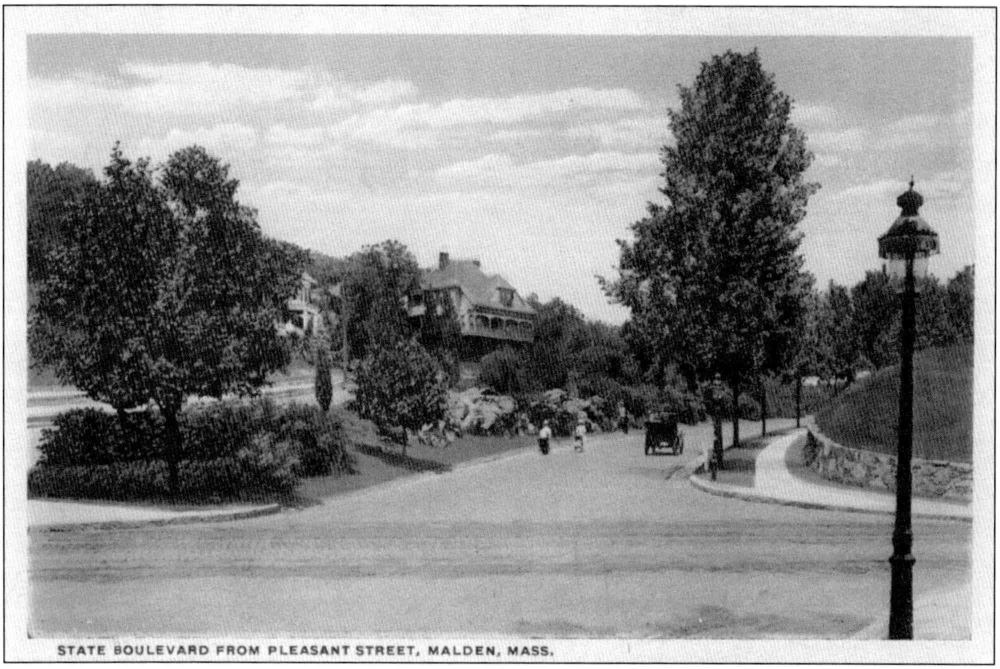

The State Boulevard (now known as Fellsway East) pictured in this postcard runs from Medford to Stoneham and provides access to the large Middlesex Fells shared by Malden, Medford, Melrose, and Stoneham.

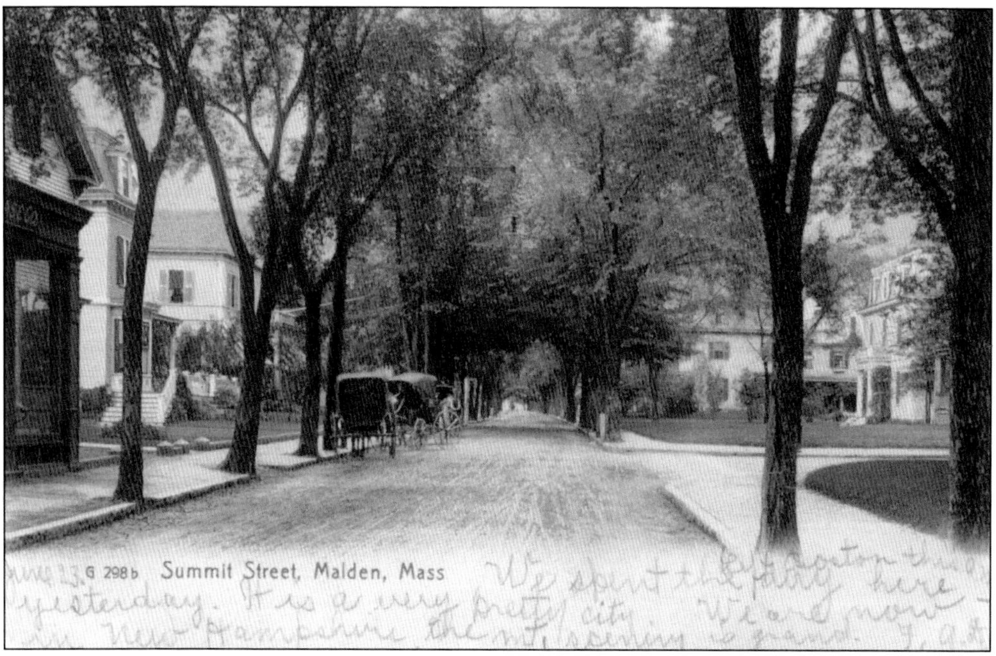

The R.G. Chase Company, nurserymen, located at 80 Summer Street at the time, is to the extreme left in this postcard, which is erroneously identified as a view of "Summit Street." This view of Summer Street again shows many fine residences. Lincoln Street is at right.

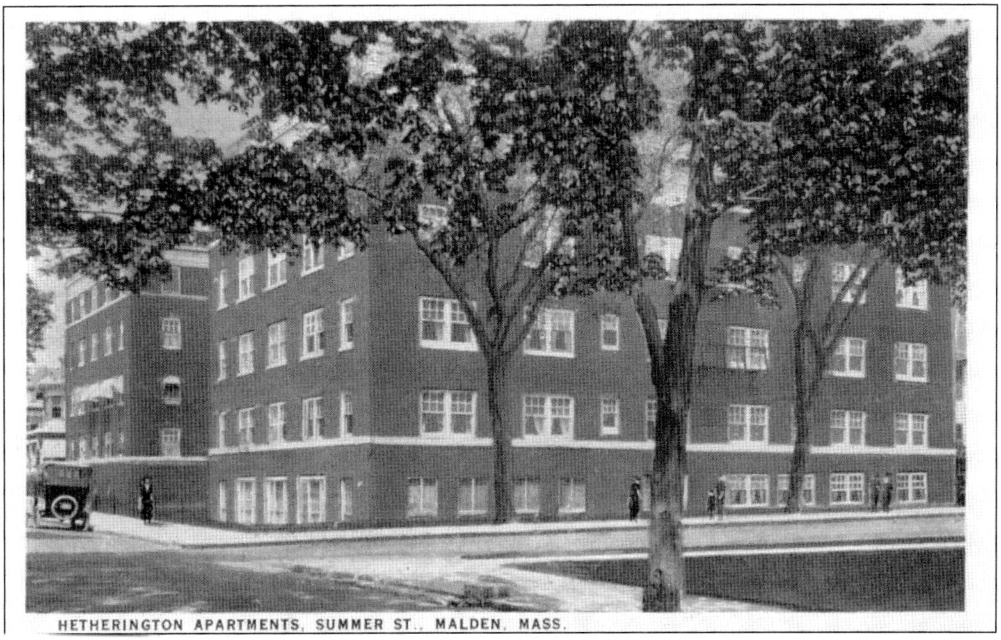

This early example of a linen postcard depicts the "New" (1921) Hetherington Apartments at 101–109 Summer Street, situated at the corner of Lincoln Street.

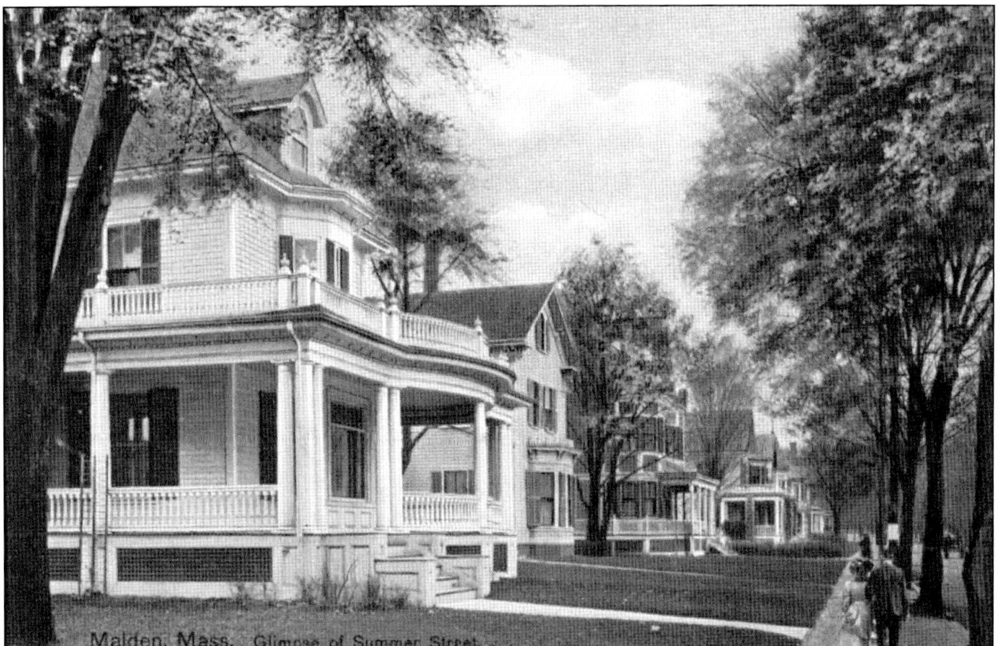

Another view of residences on Summer Street is presented in this card. The first house on the left is a superb example of the Victorian architecture in the West End of Malden.

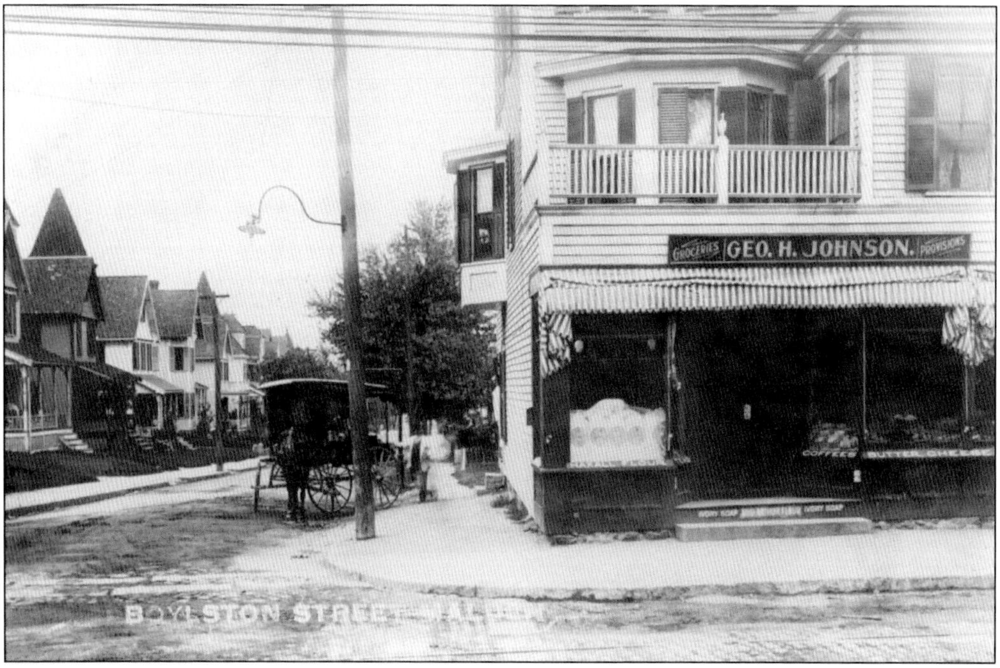

George H. Johnson operated a grocery and provisions store at the corner of Boylston and Bryant Streets in the Suffolk Square section of Malden. In this very clear photograph, note the signage as well as the horse wagon to the left that was used for deliveries.

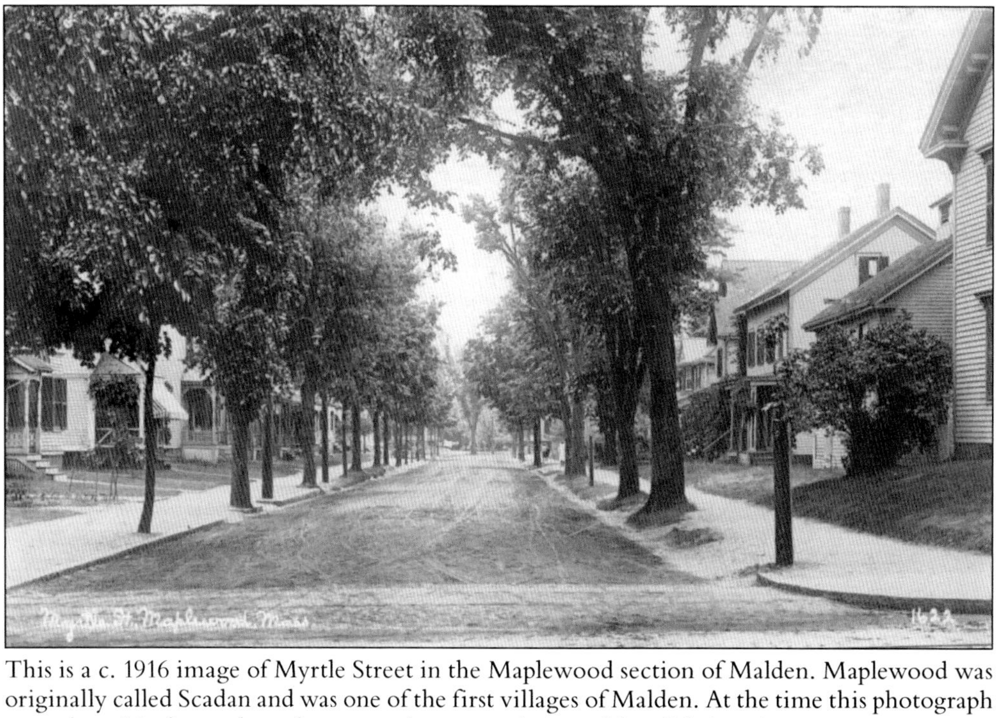

This is a c. 1916 image of Myrtle Street in the Maplewood section of Malden. Maplewood was originally called Scadan and was one of the first villages of Malden. At the time this photograph was taken, Maplewood was home to a large population of Swedish immigrants.

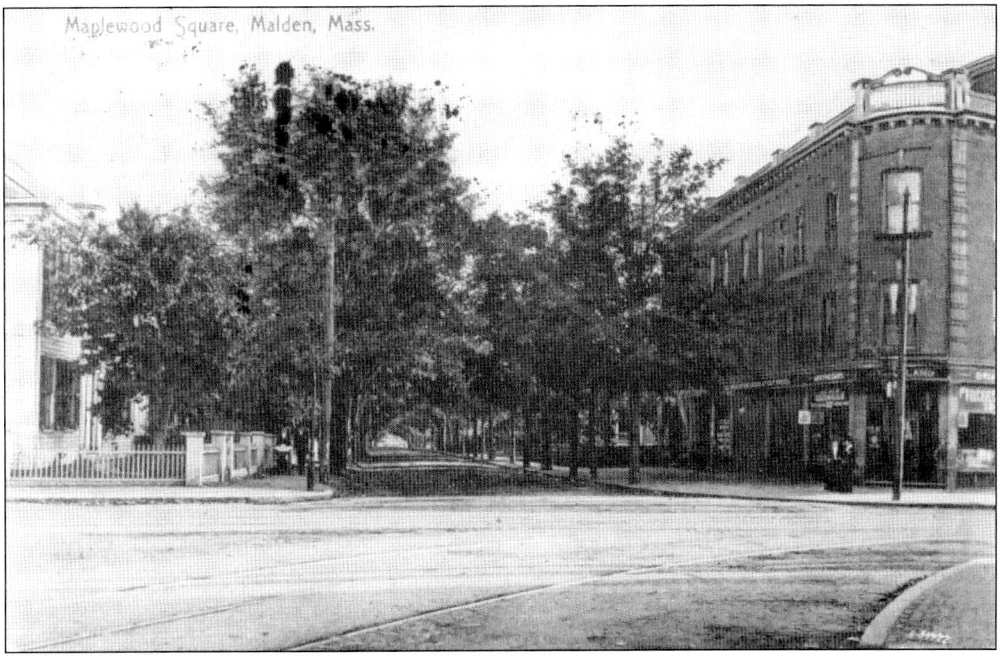

The tree-lined street in this photograph is Maplewood Street. The picture was taken at the intersection of Salem, Lebanon, and Maplewood Streets in Maplewood Square. The Knights of Phythias building, facing Salem Street, is seen to the right.

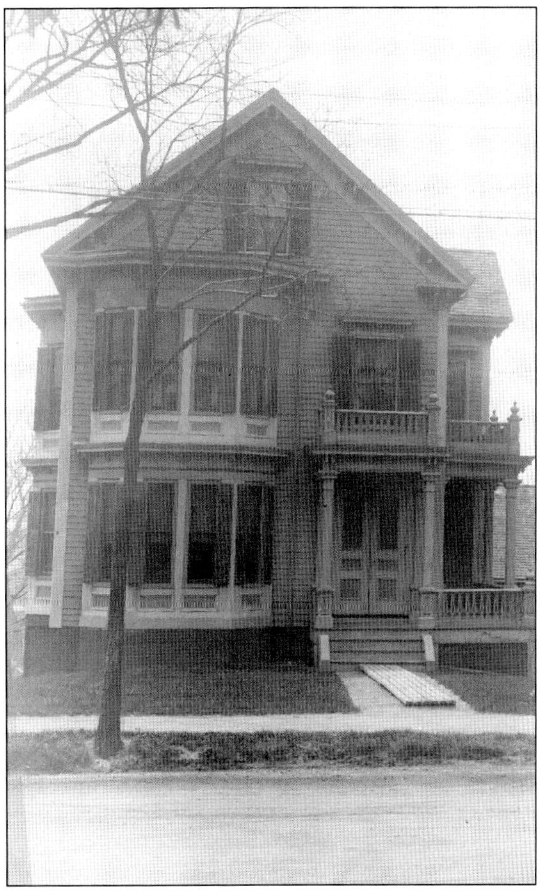

Often, real-photo postcards featuring a home were commissioned by a house owner or resident to send to friends and relatives. This example shows a house at 29 Webster Street in Maplewood.

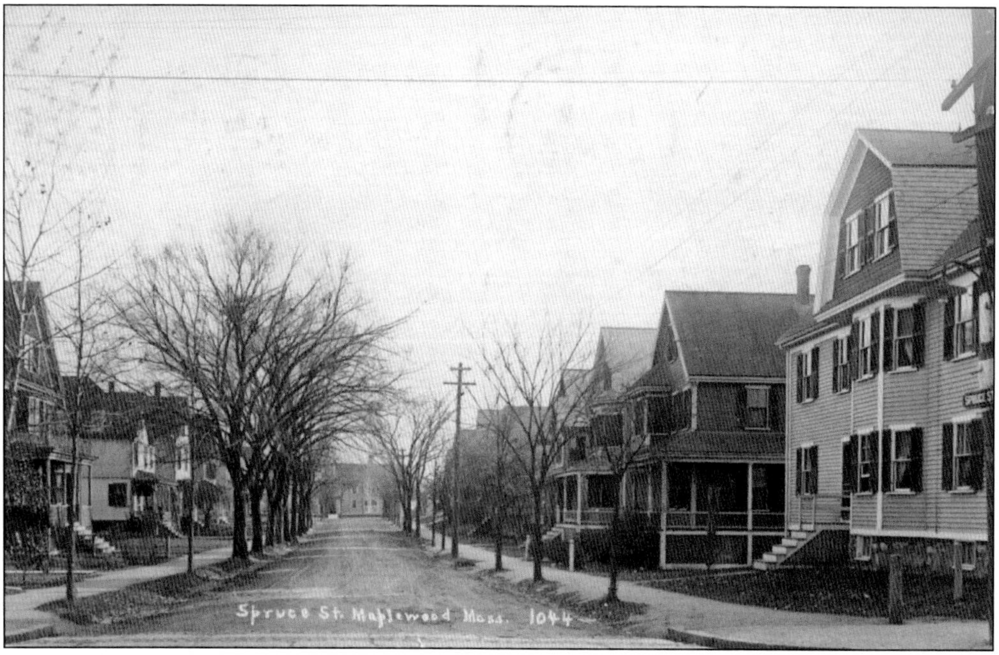

Spruce Street in Maplewood, seen in this view looking south toward Webster Street, has not changed a great deal since this real-photo postcard was printed around 1916. Maplewood contains a large number of single-family frame houses of the type shown here.

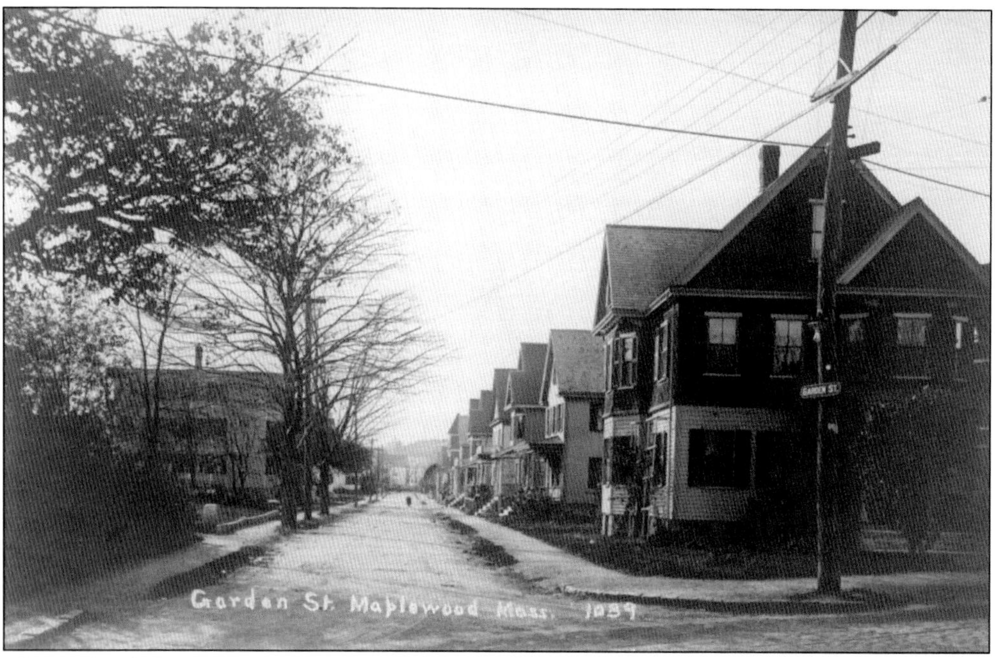

This undated photograph of Garden Street looks west toward Rockwell Street in the Maplewood neighborhood. The postcard was created around 1910.

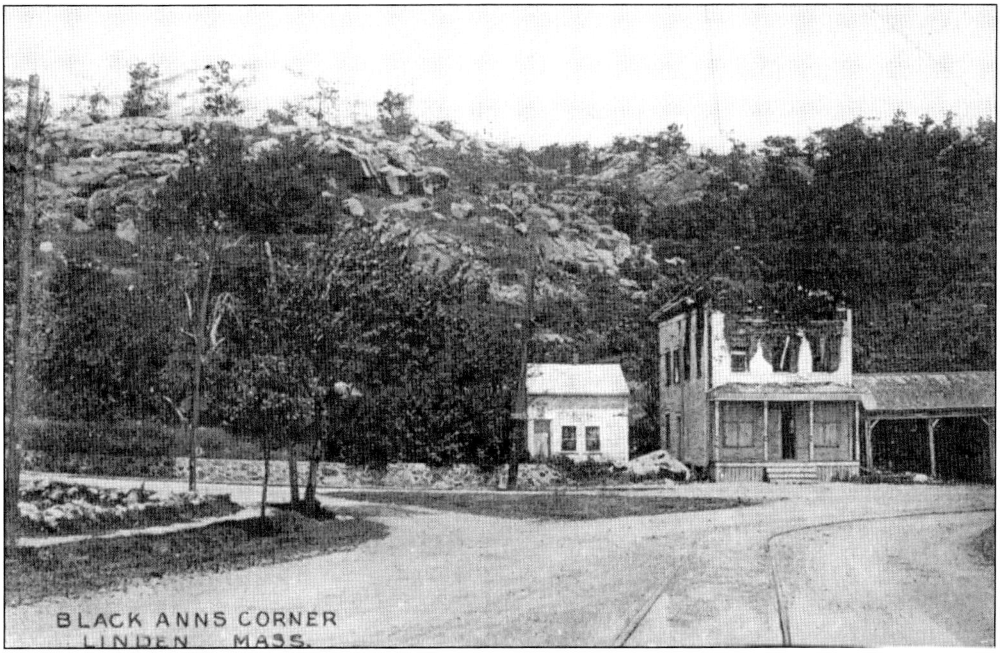

Black Ann's Corner is located at the intersection of Lynn and Salem Streets in the Linden section of Malden. "Black Ann" refers to the name of one Ann Welcome, who lived there in the 1700s.

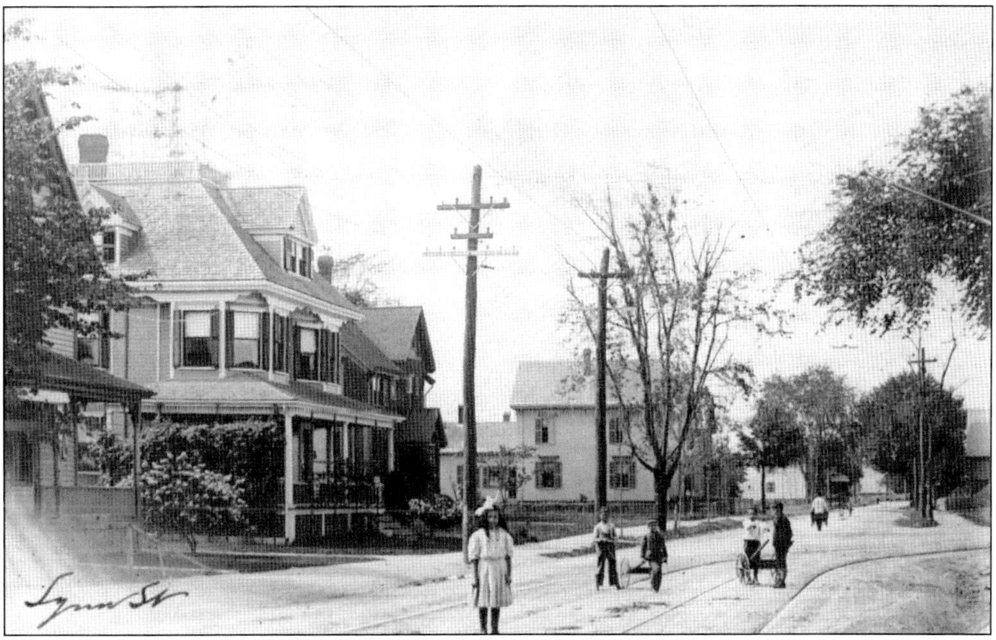

This is a c. 1909 view of Lynn Street in the Linden section of Malden. The children who pose for this photograph wear dress common to the period.

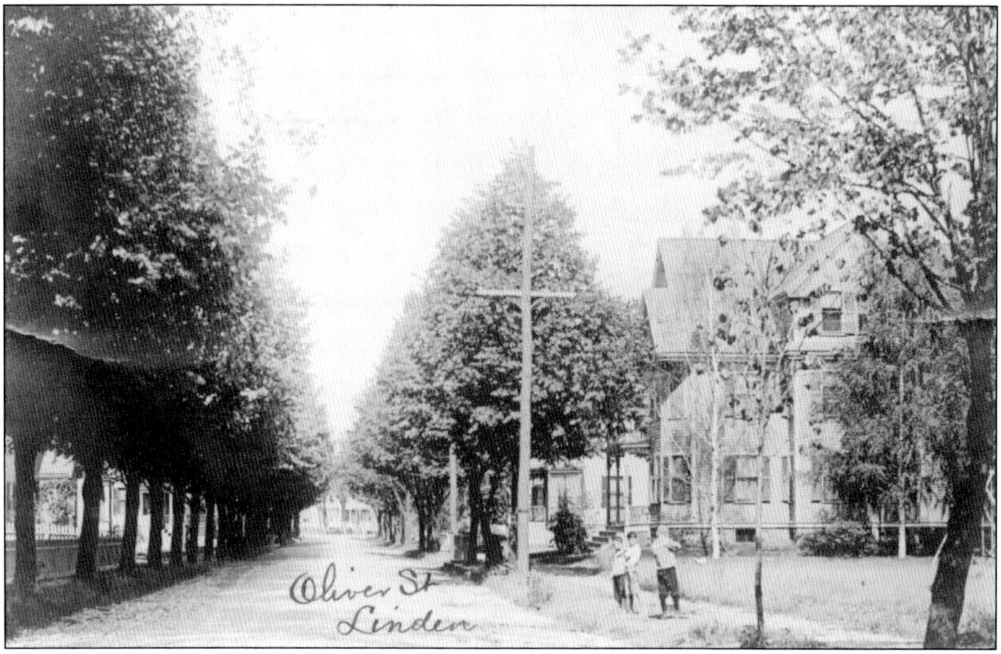

Oliver Street runs parallel to Lynn Street in Linden. This real-photo postcard again includes young children—in this case, young boys—with two of them attired in knickers.

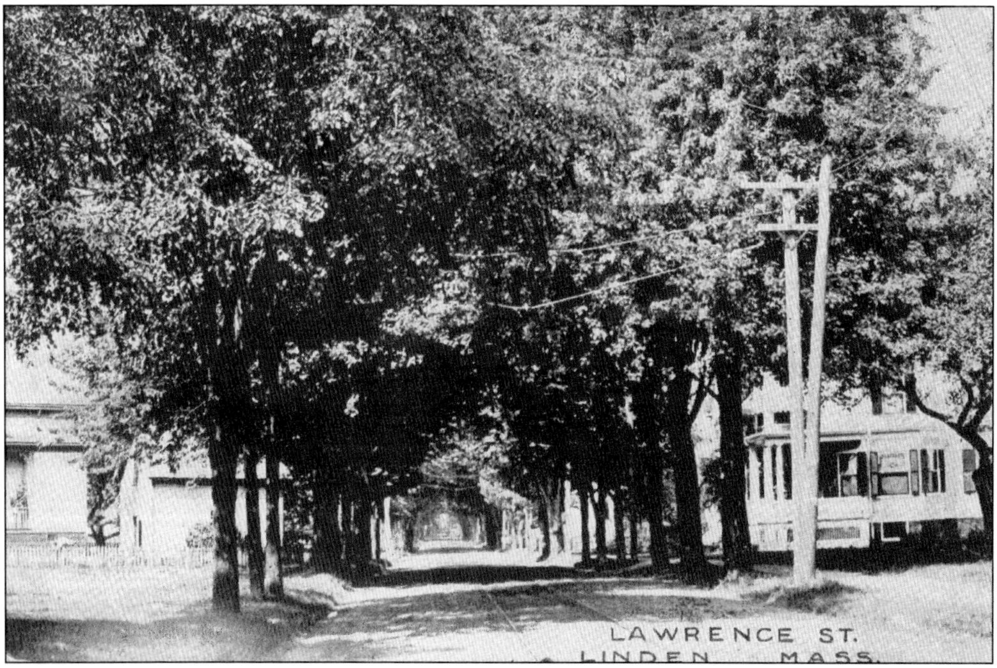

Lawrence Street, pictured here around 1910, is near to both Lynn and Oliver Streets in Linden and is located in a representative residential neighborhood.

Six

Parks

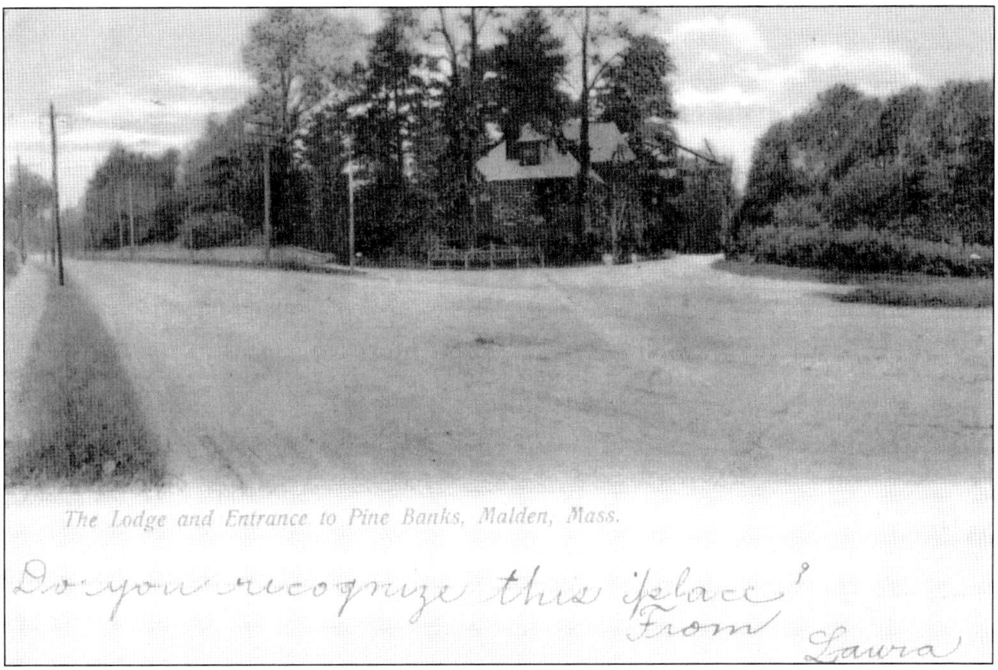

Although the city had converted from farming to industry and manufacture, the inhabitants always felt it beneficial to keep some open space. There are many parks of varying sizes scattered throughout Malden. At one point, the city could boast of seven parks laid out by the Frederick Law Olmsted or the Olmsted firms. Two parks in particular still stand out today as major attractions: Bell Rock, designed by Olmsted, and Pine Banks, which was given by Elisha Converse. This panoramic view looking north on Main Street shows the Pine Banks lodge and the entrance to Pine Banks Park on the Malden/Melrose border.

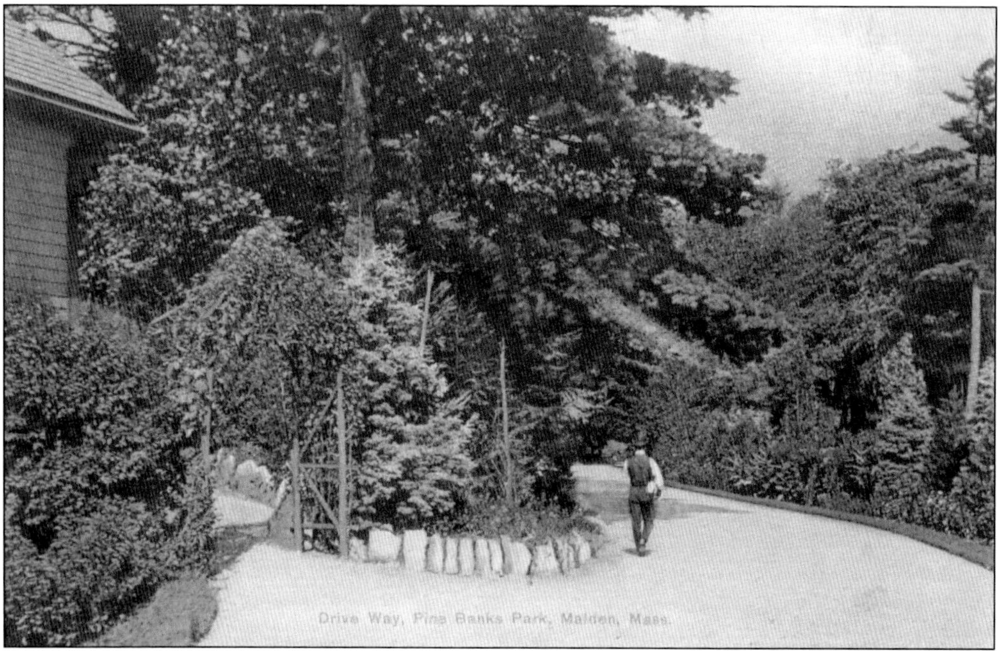

A view of the main entrance driveway at Pine Banks Park shows some of the flower beds that graced the entrance.

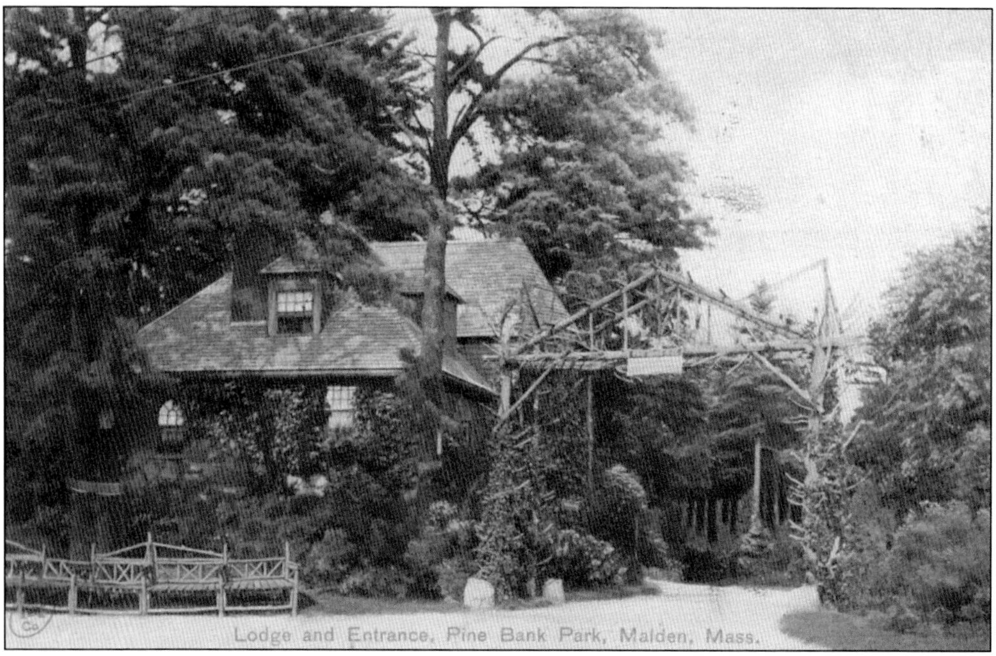

Elisha Converse built the Pine Banks lodge, shown beside the rustic entrance archway. The lodge was a Converse family retreat; today, it is the superintendent's residence and offices for the park.

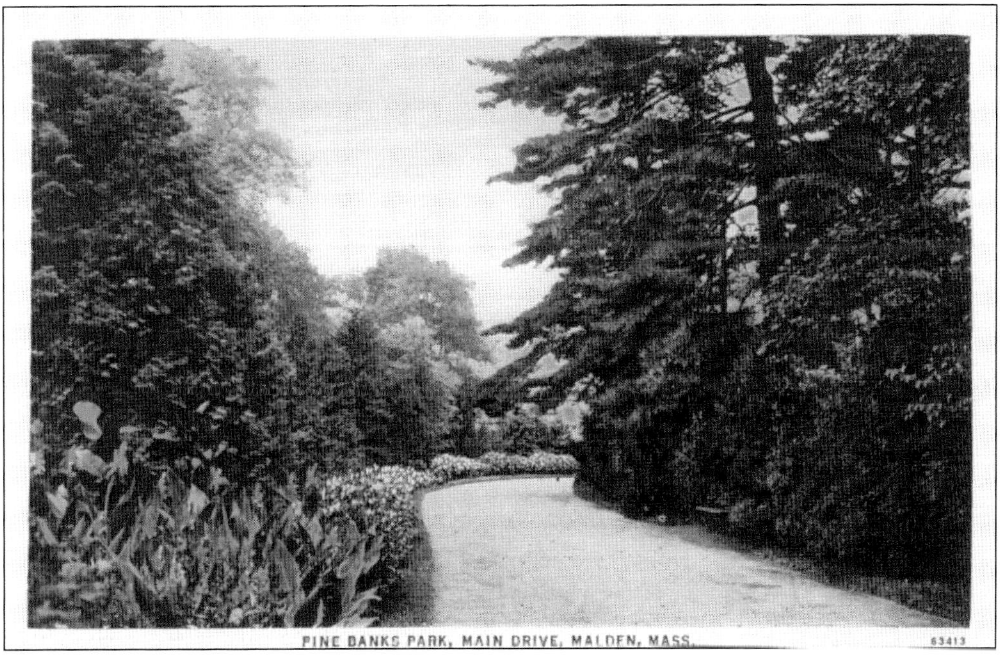

For many years, beautiful flower beds graced the entrance driveway at Pine Banks Park. Carriage roads similar to this one were laid out throughout the park.

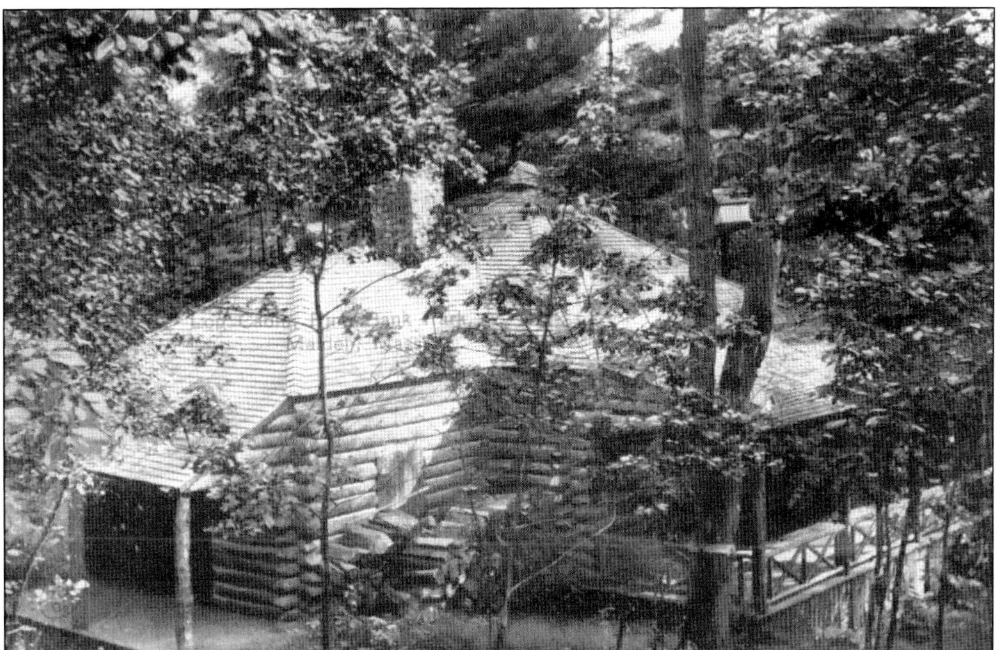

The rustic log cabin at Pine Banks Park was built by Elisha Converse. It was one of three log cabins erected at the same time at the park.

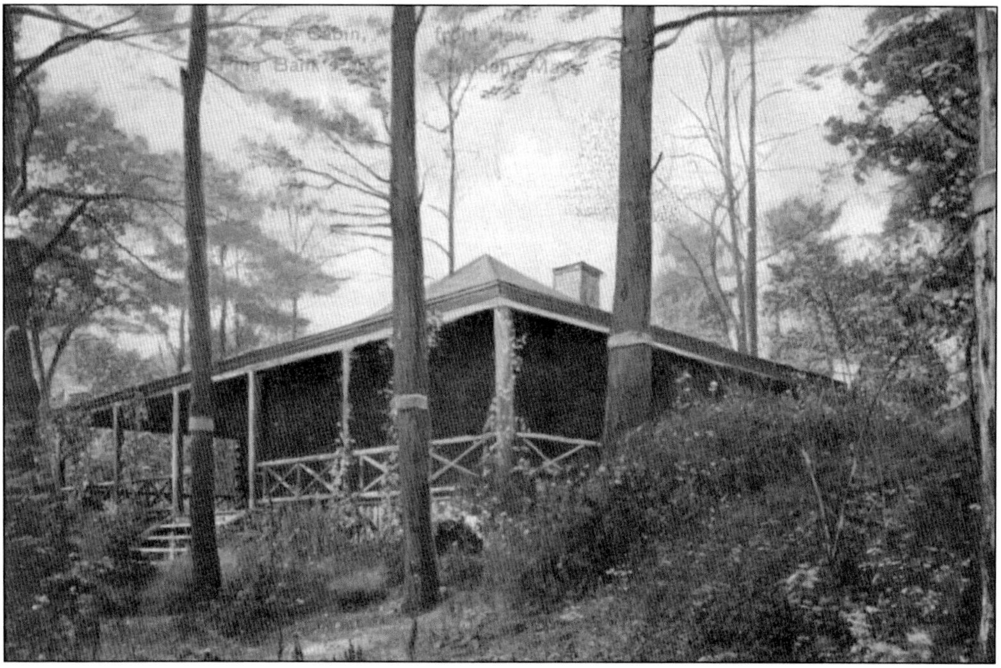

This is a front view of the log cabin at Pine Banks Park that was used as a family retreat for activities and lodging.

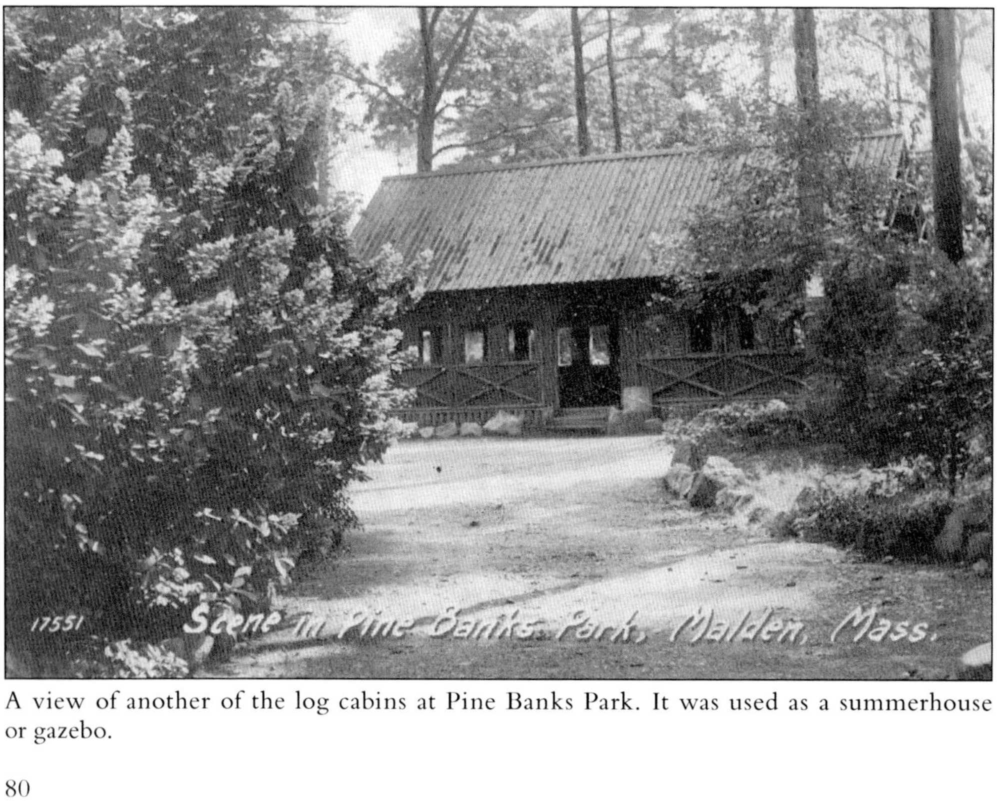

A view of another of the log cabins at Pine Banks Park. It was used as a summerhouse or gazebo.

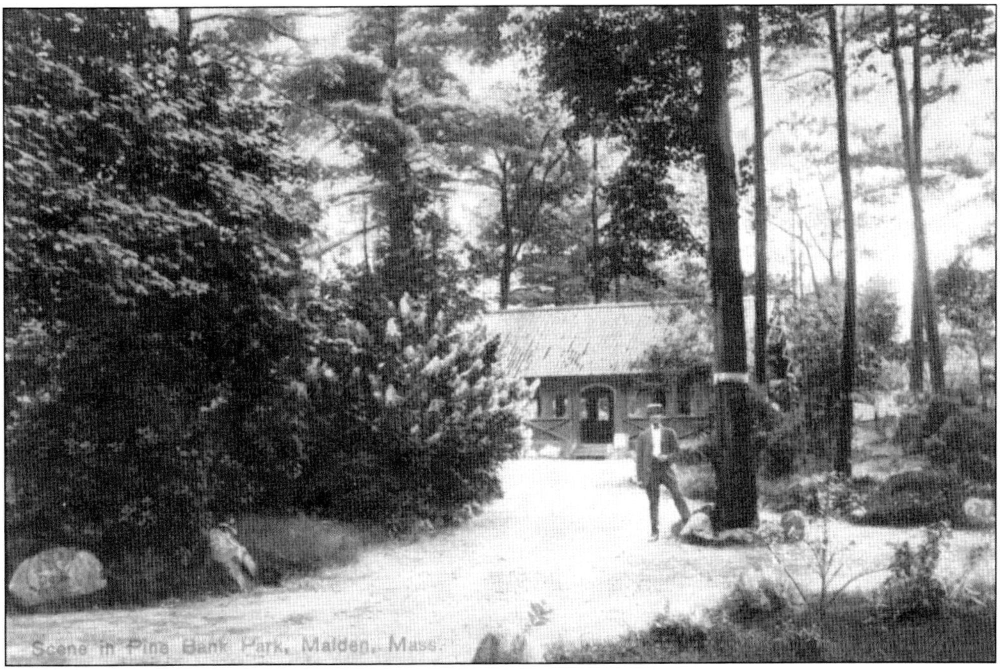

The summerhouse log cabin in Pine Banks Park is pictured here. Although this structure no longer stands, there are other picnic pavilions in the park today.

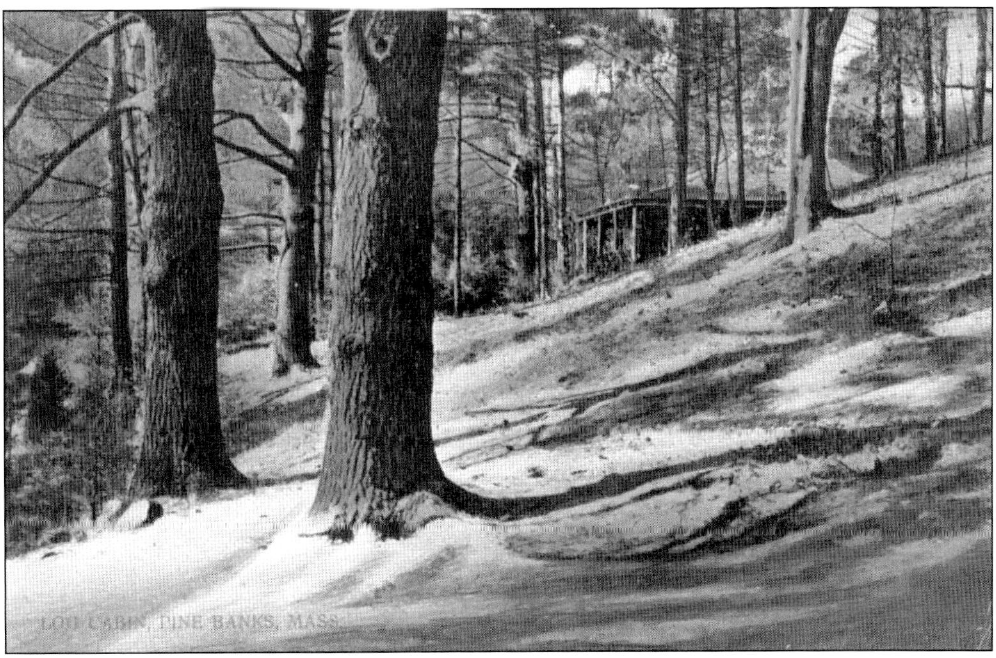

This is a view of the log cabin nestled among the pines in Pine Banks Park. This view illustrates the appropriateness of the park's name: Pine Banks.

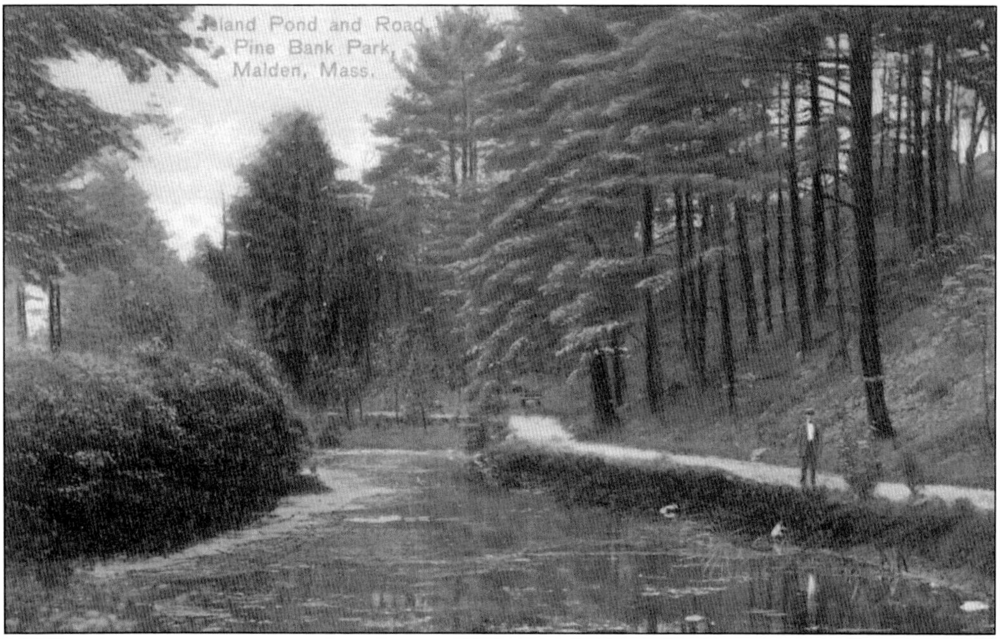

Pictured here is Island Pond in Pine Banks Park. Although no longer in existence, the pond originally had an island in the middle, hence the name Island Pond.

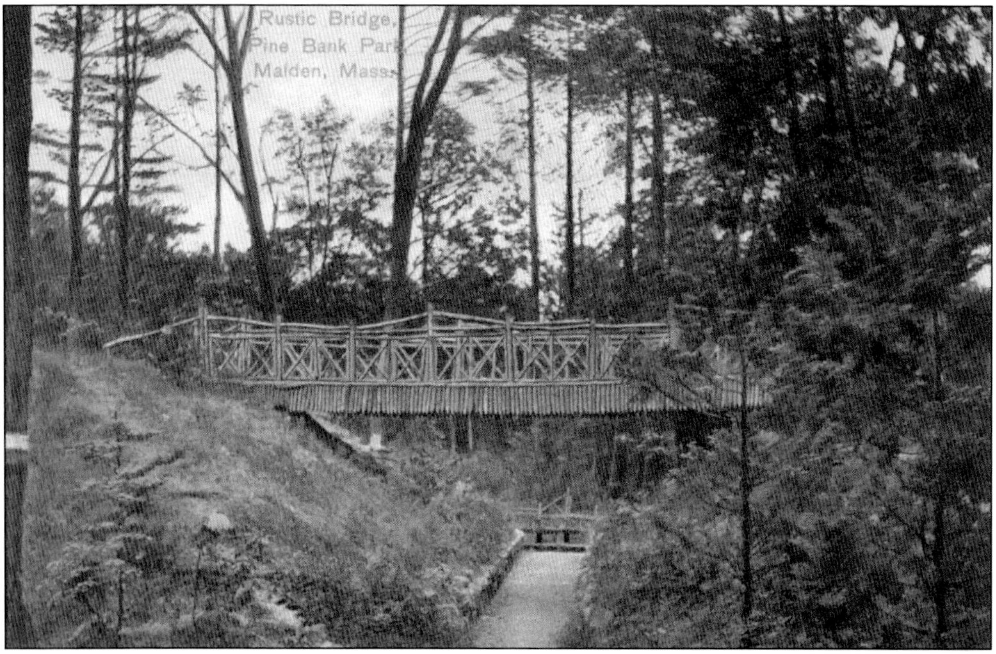

The rustic bridge at Pine Banks Park connected two geological formations called eskers. These eskers were formed by melting glaciers.

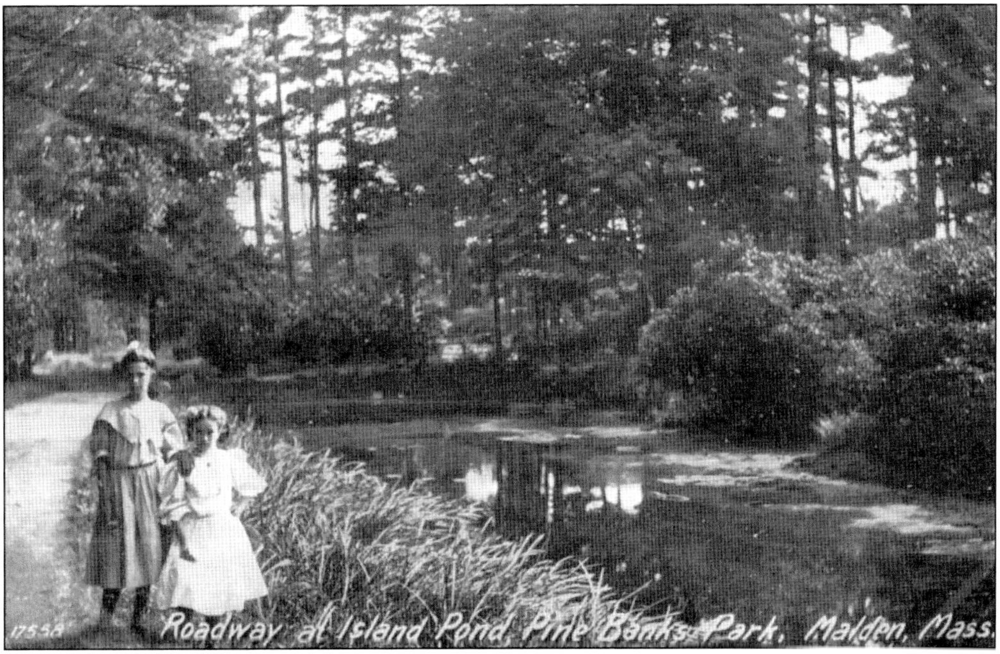

This image of the roadway at Island Pond shows the island at the right. Two young girls enjoy a day at the park by the pond.

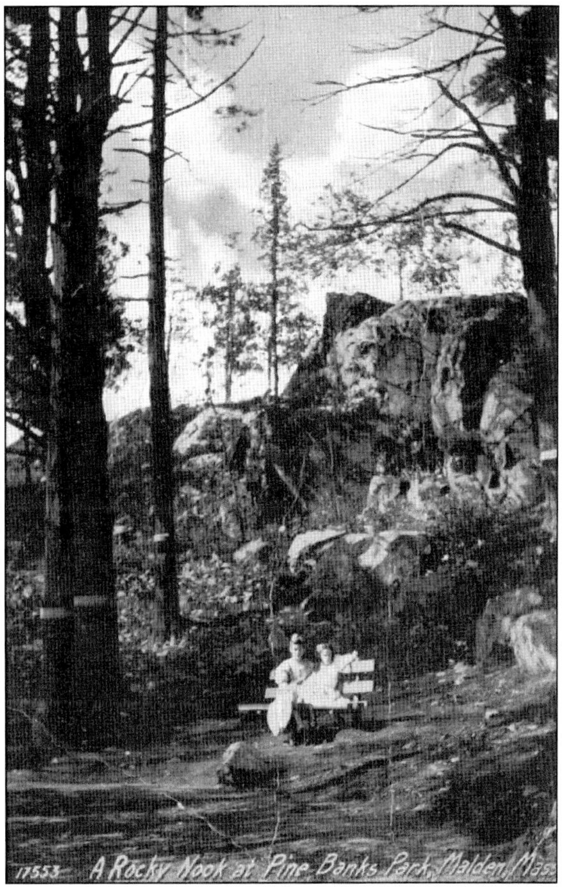

A rocky nook shows Mount Ephraim in the background. Mount Ephraim rises behind Island Pond in Pine Banks Park.

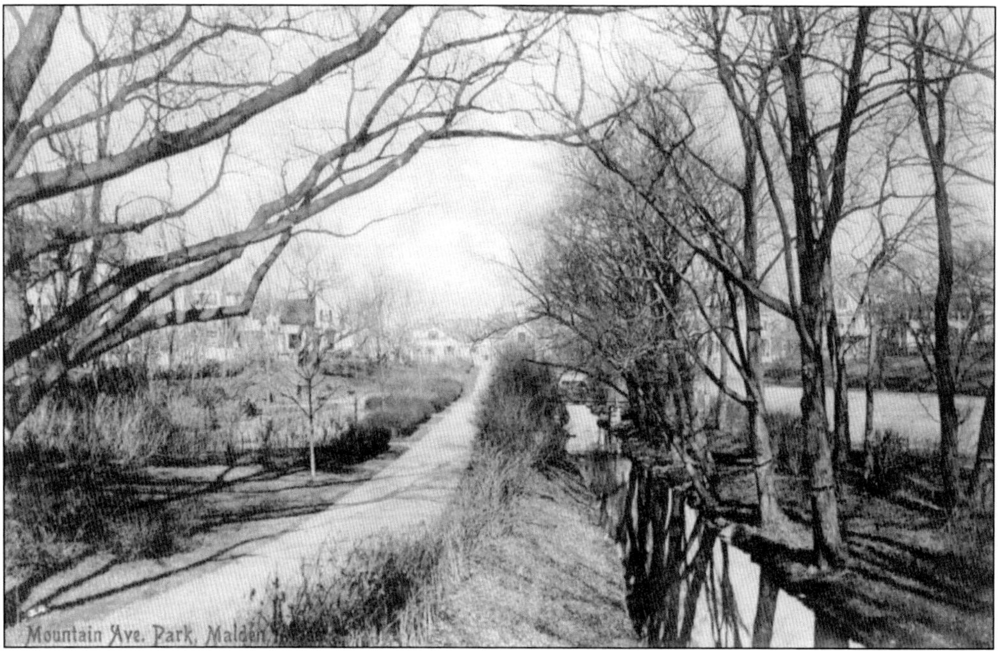

This view of Coytemore Lea Park is looking north toward Clifton Street. Today, the Three Mile Brook, also known as Spot Pond Brook, pictured in the center of this view, runs underground in a culvert. There are still traces of the walkway in the park.

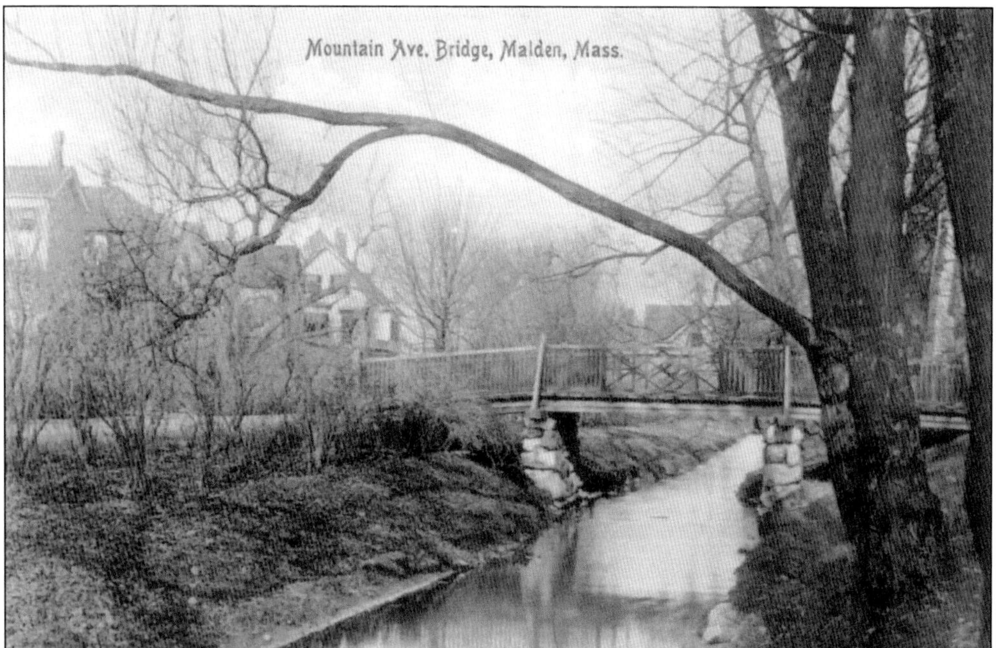

The ornamental bridge spans the Three Mile Brook, or Spot Pond Brook, in Coytemore Lea. This brook, coming from Spot Pond, helped spawn early industry in this area, including Barrett's Dye House and Odiorne's nail rolling mill.

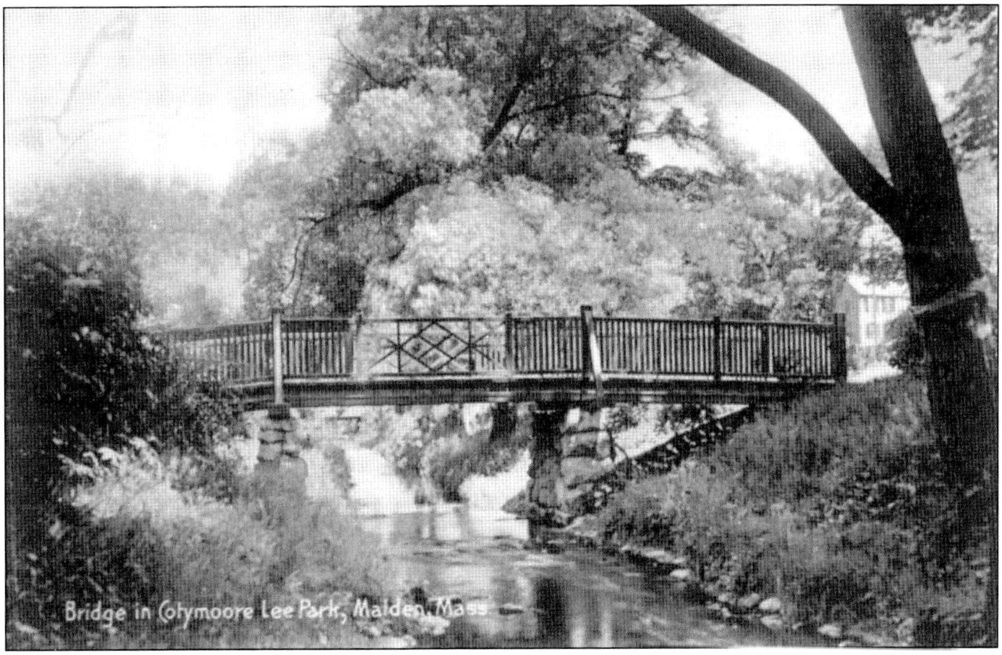

Seen here is a close-up view of the ornamental bridge in Coytemore Lea. The park was designed by noted landscape architect Frederick Law Olmsted. The park was originally the site of Thomas Coytmore's gristmill, operating in the 1600s; it was one of the first businesses in Malden.

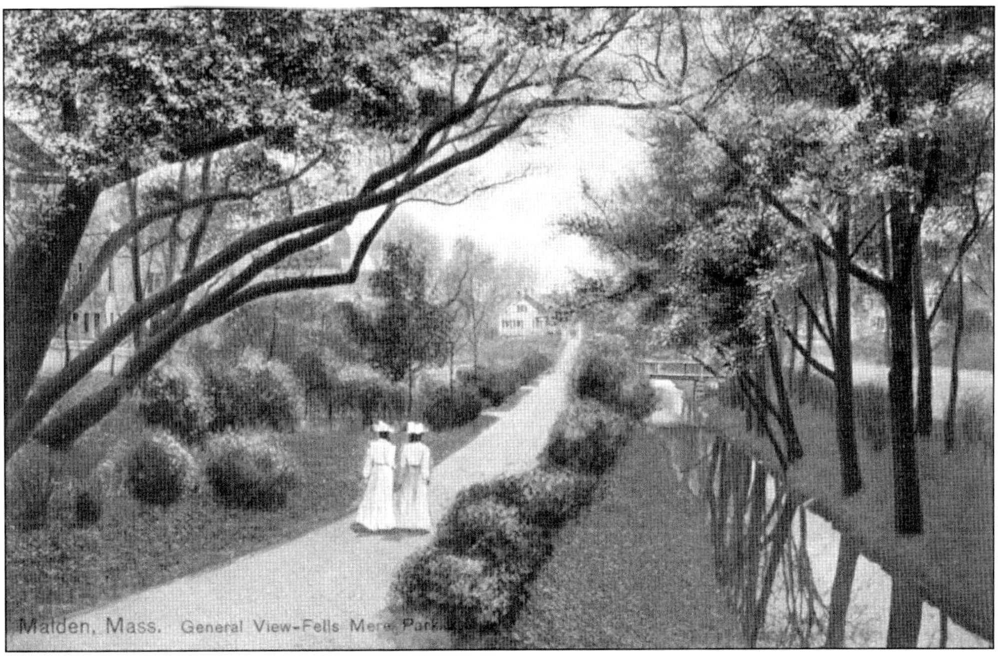

This view of the path and bridge in Coytemore Lea looks toward Clifton Street. By the time this image was captured, many of the early industries utilizing the brook had disappeared.

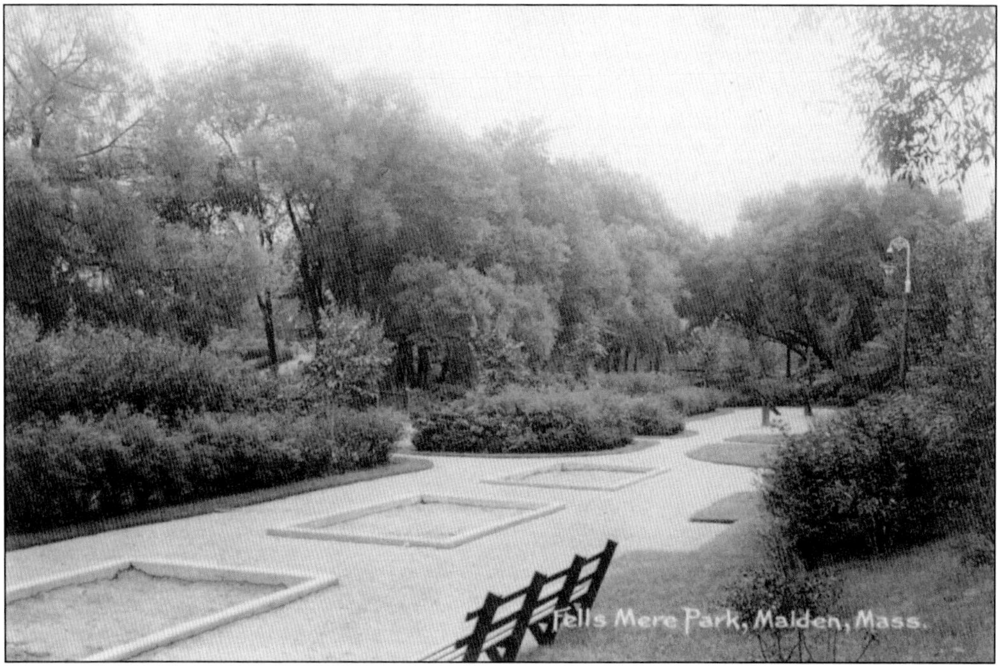

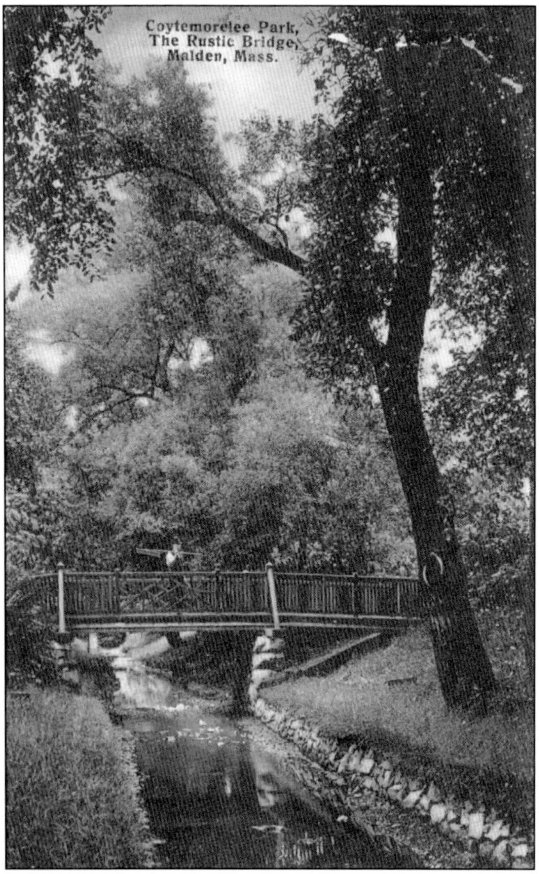

The erroneously titled postcard reads, "Fells Mere Park," but this is actually the sandboxes at Coytemore Lea Park. It is not uncommon to find mistitled postcards.

This is another view of the ornamental bridge and the Spot Pond Brook in Coytemore Lea Park. The brook originally ran through to Malden Square, forming a mill pond at the site of the present Dowling Building before emptying into the Malden River.

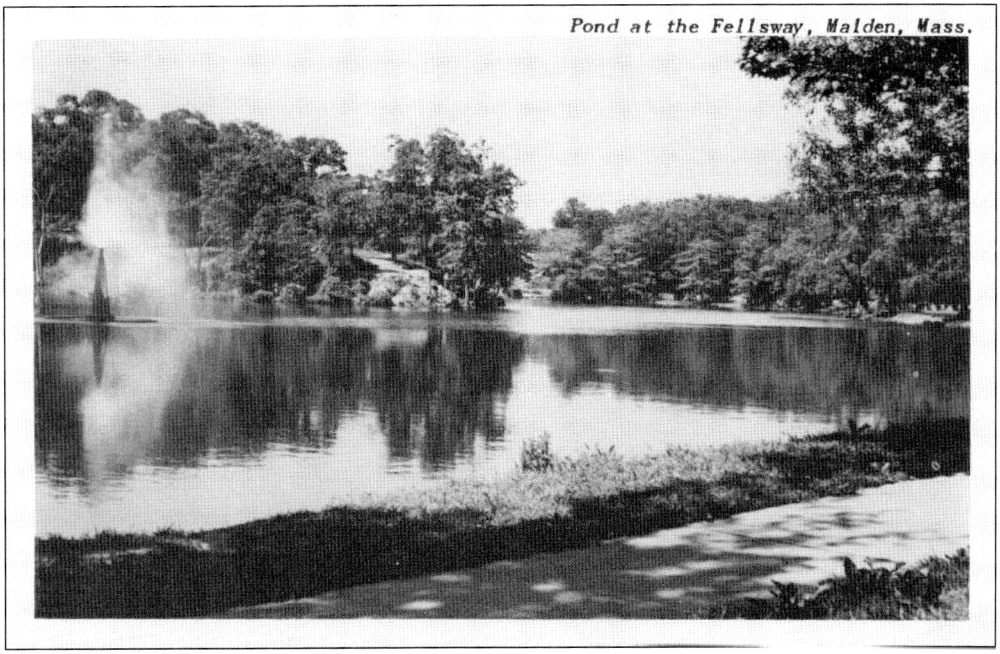

Fellsmere Park and pond once served as a reservoir for the Boston Rubber Shoe Company. The land for the park was donated by Elisha Converse. Converse enlarged the pond to serve as a reservoir for his shoe factory after the original factory was destroyed by fire in 1875. There was a pipe connecting the reservoir to his factory in Edgeworth.

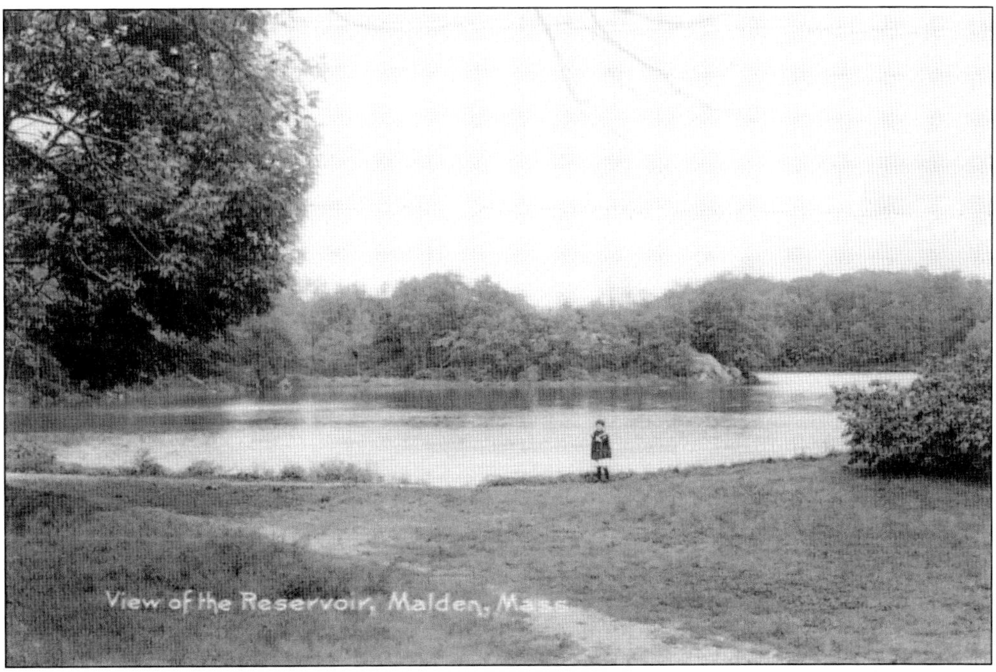

Fellsmere Park and the pond, located along the Fellsway East between Murray Hill Road and Savin Street, were designed by noted landscape architect Frederick Law Olmsted.

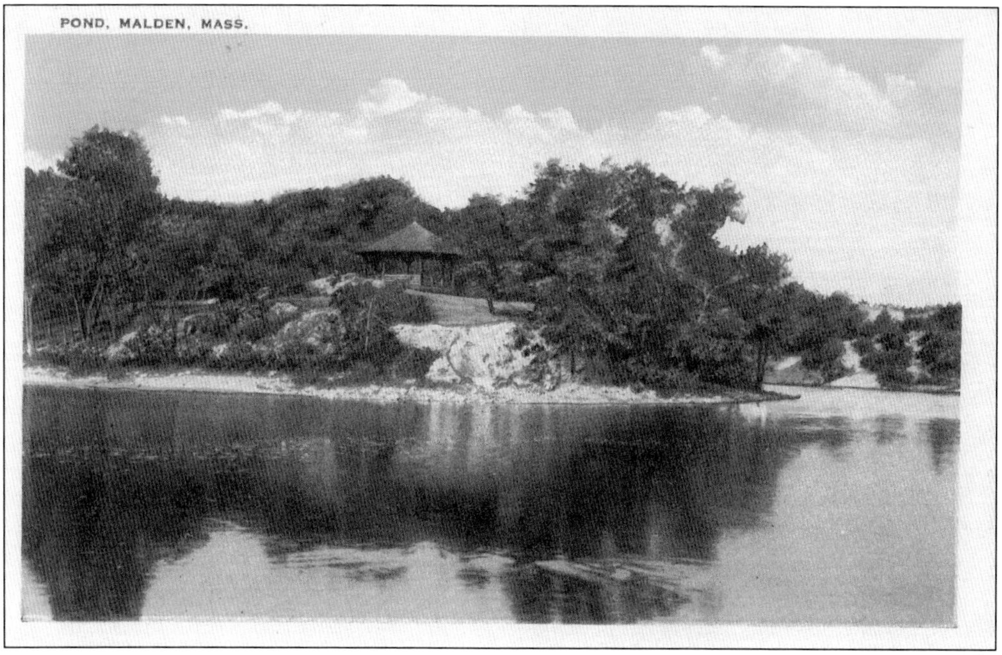

A bandstand, or gazebo, once adorned the nubble overlooking the pond at Fellsmere Park. The pond has been used for various recreational purposes, including swimming, boating, and fishing derbies.

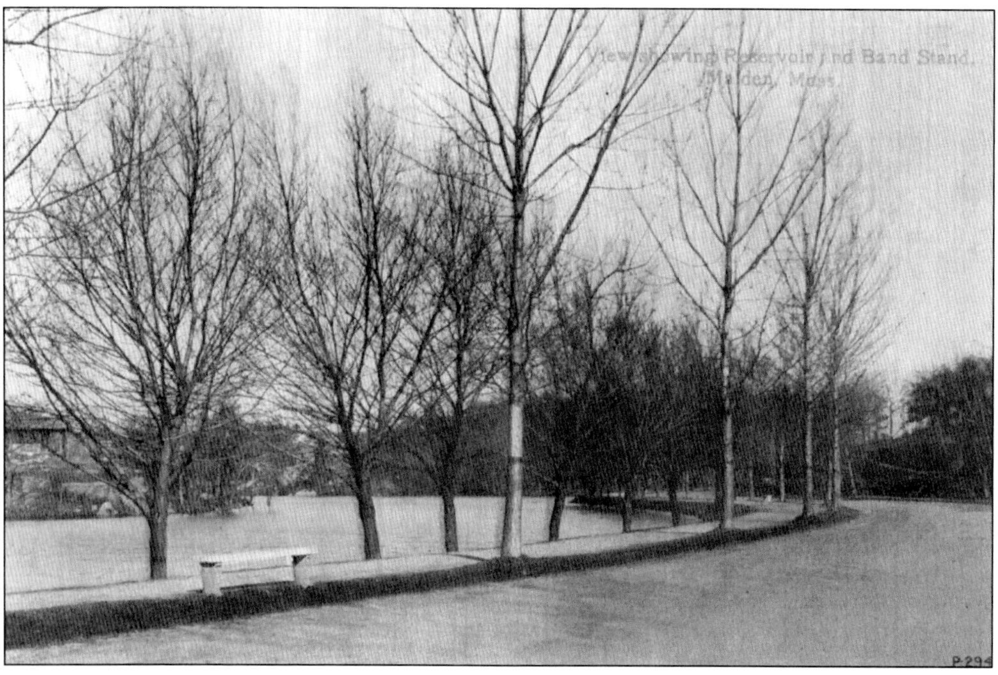

This is a view of the Fellsway East as it winds along the Fellsmere Park.

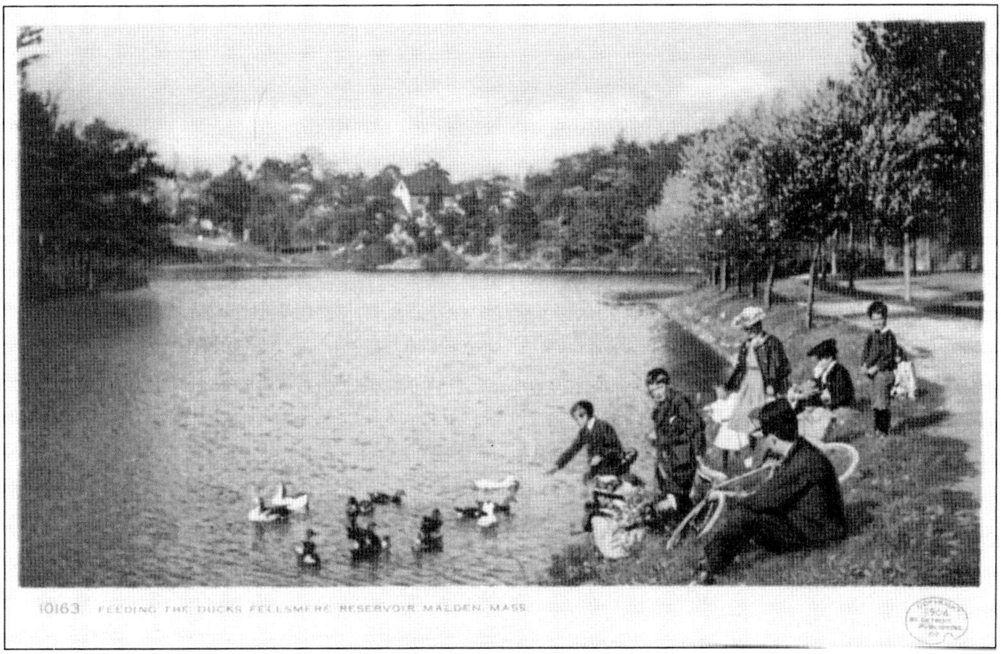

Feeding the ducks at Fellsmere Pond remains a popular pastime of Malden residents. In recent years, swans and other water fowl have taken up residence at the pond.

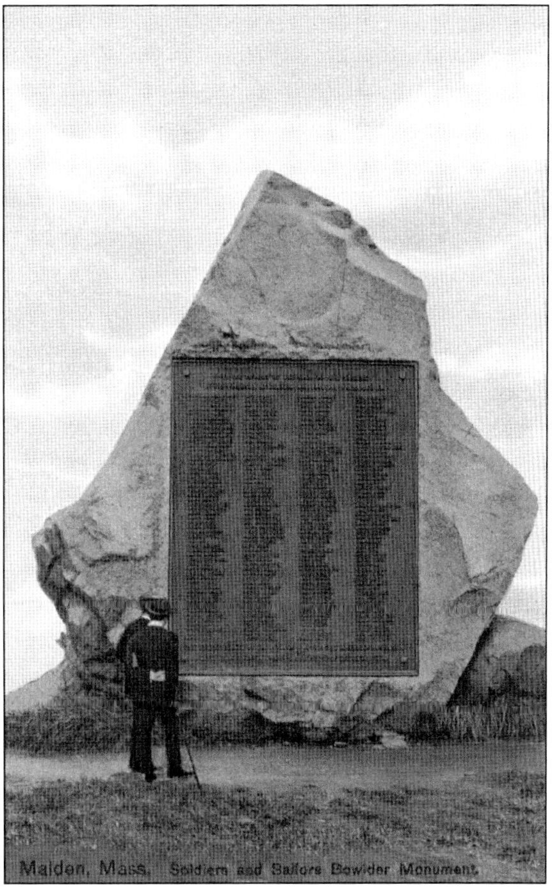

The Soldiers and Sailors Memorial boulder was located in Bell Rock Memorial Park. The boulder was removed and replaced by *The Flag Defenders* sculpture. Bell Rock Memorial Park is located on Main Street between Wigglesworth Street and Ellis Street.

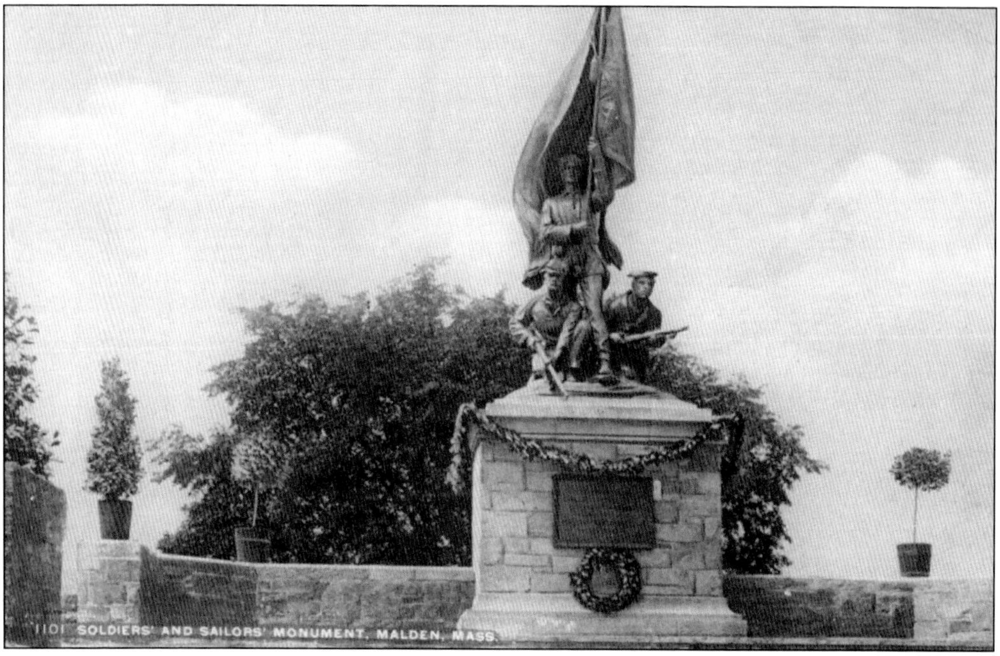

The Flag Defenders was designed by noted sculptor Bela Lyon Pratt and dedicated to Malden soldiers and sailors in the Civil War in October 1910. The park is also the home to a memorial to Rev. Michael Wigglesworth and, more recently, a World War II memorial.

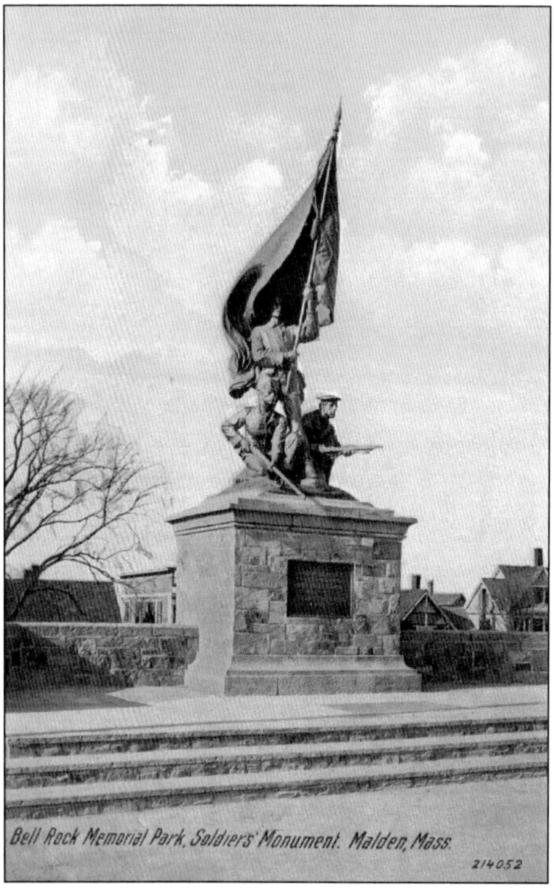

The Flag Defenders sculpture in Bell Rock Memorial Park consists of a flag bearer and a soldier and a sailor defending the flag bearer. The park was designed by Frederick Law Olmsted.

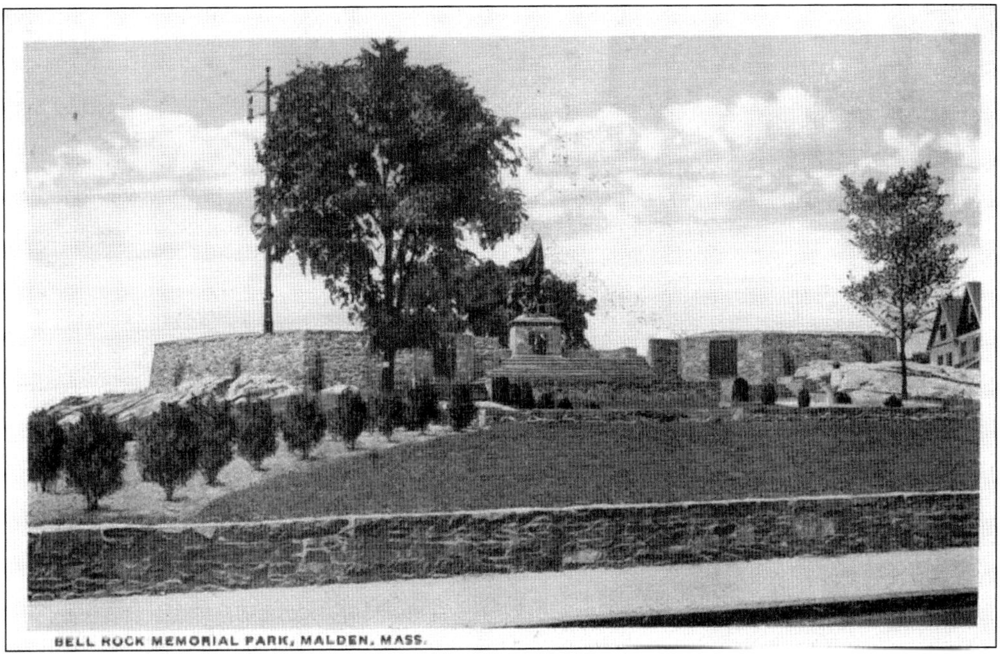

A wide view of Bell Rock Memorial Park shows the landscaping and *The Flag Defenders* sculpture. There is a large light mast that once illuminated the plaza around the sculpture to the left.

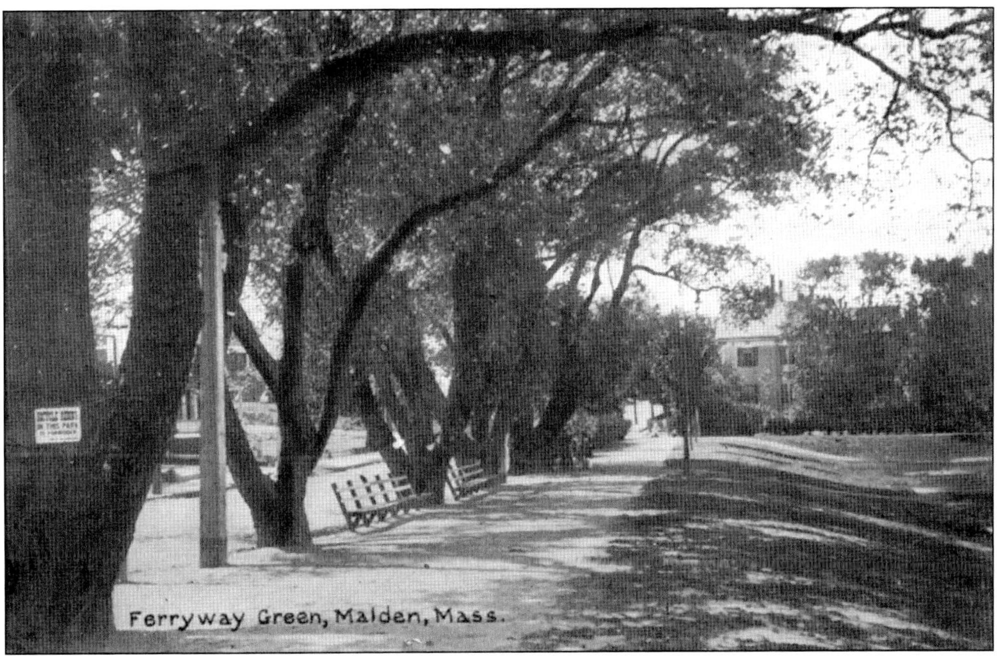

Ferryway Green was originally called Hitchings Field. This view is looking south along Ferry Street. This is another park also designed by Frederick Law Olmsted. It is now the site of the Ferryway School.

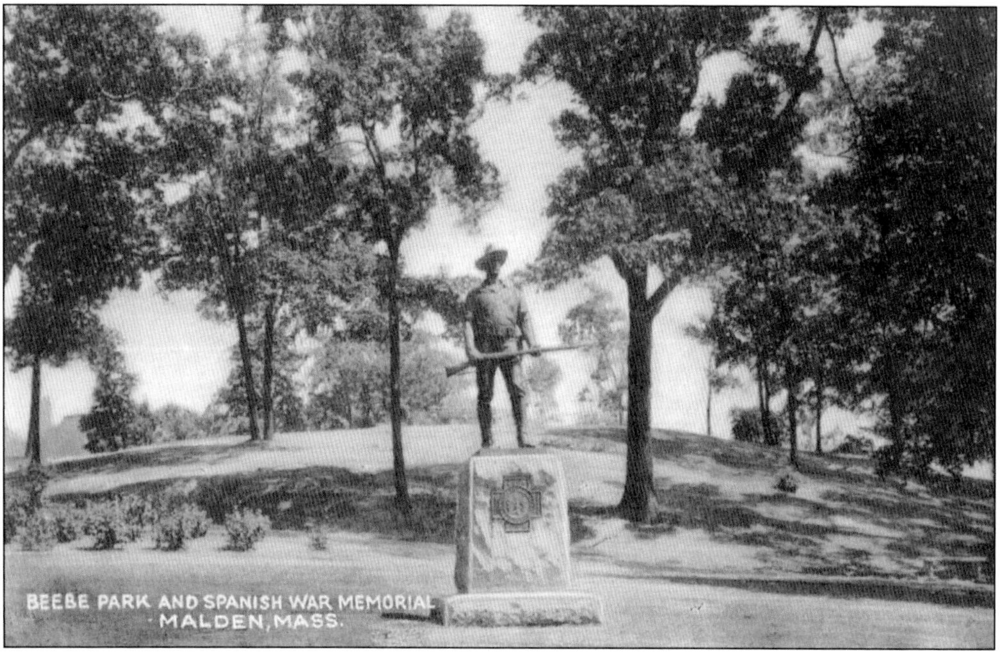

The Spanish-American War memorial, *The Hiker*, is seen in Wallace Park, commonly referred to as Beebe Park, at the corner of Highland Avenue and Pleasant Street. *The Hiker* was created by Theo Alice Ruggles Kitson in 1906 to commemorate American soldiers who fought in the Spanish-American War; a number of copies were erected across the United States.

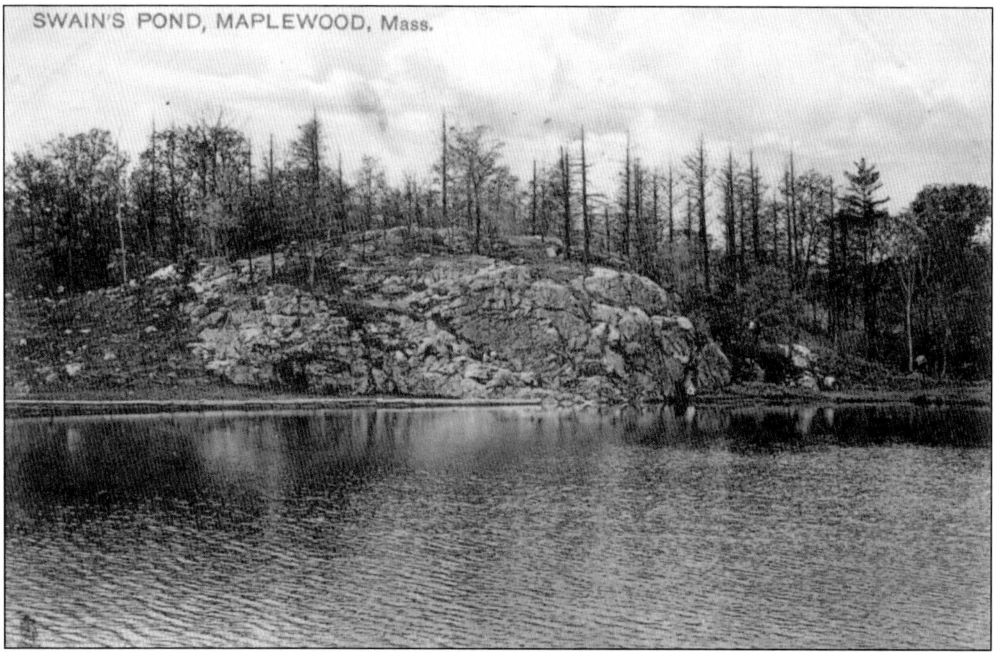

Swain's Pond was originally part of the Maplewood section of Malden. After Melrose separated in 1850, it was considered part of Melrose.

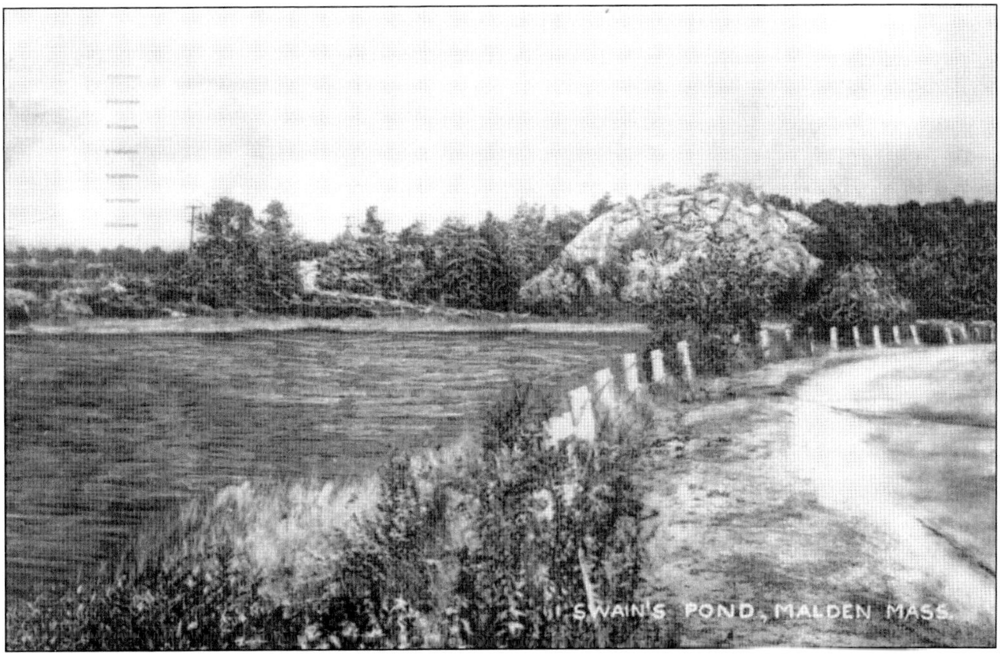

The road to the right of Swain's Pond leads to Lebanon Street in Malden. The area was originally farmland.

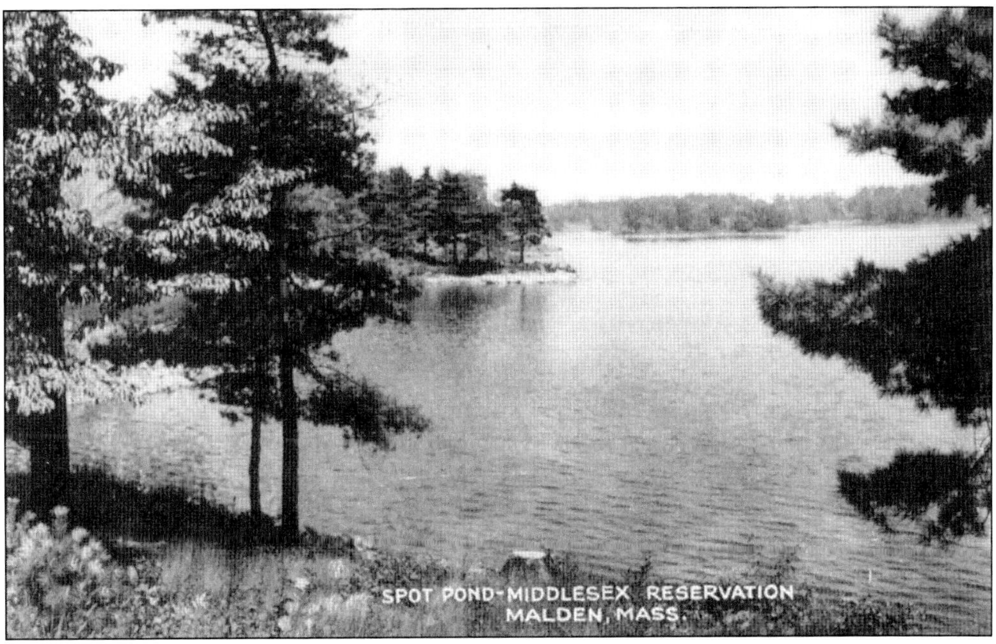

The title of the postcard claims it to be Malden, but Spot Pond today is part of Stoneham. The pond served as a water supply for Malden for many years. It is located in the Middlesex Fells, which includes Malden, Melrose, Stoneham, Medford, and Winchester.

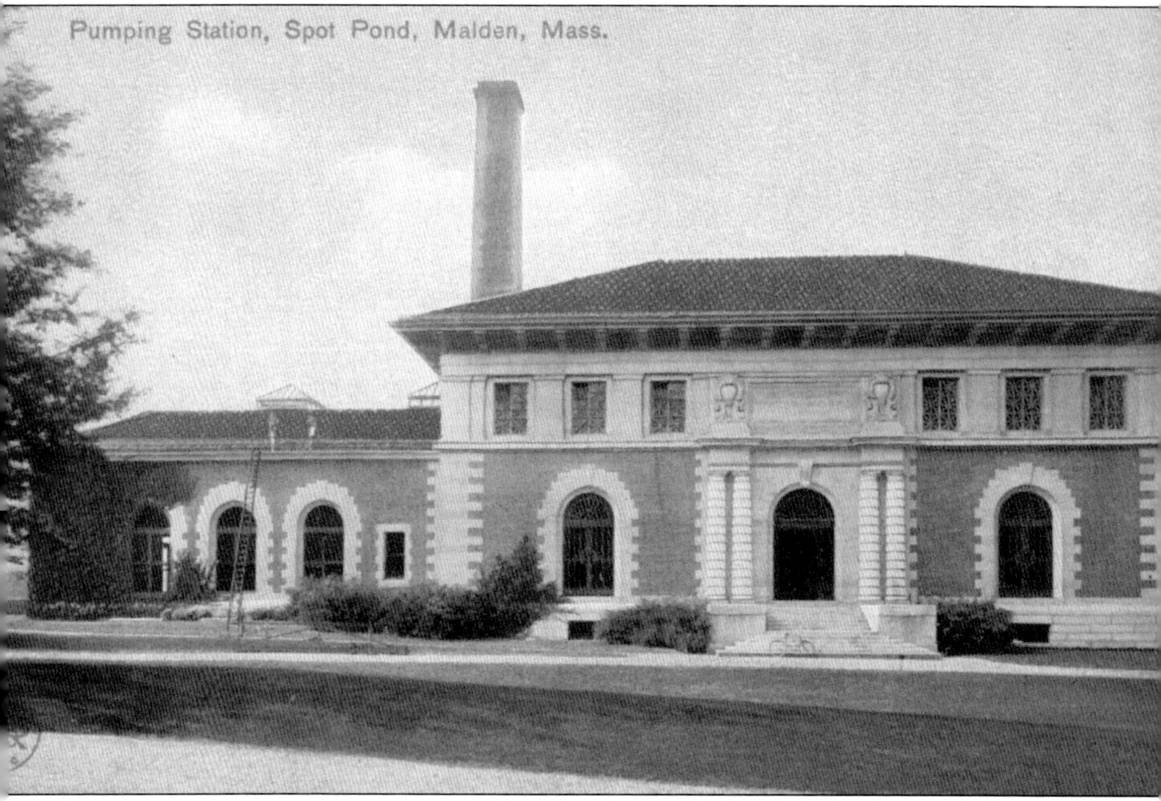

Pictured is the pumping station at Spot Pond. For many years, the water from Spot Pond served the city of Malden and other communities, through the pumping station, as its drinking source.

Seven

Public Buildings and Places

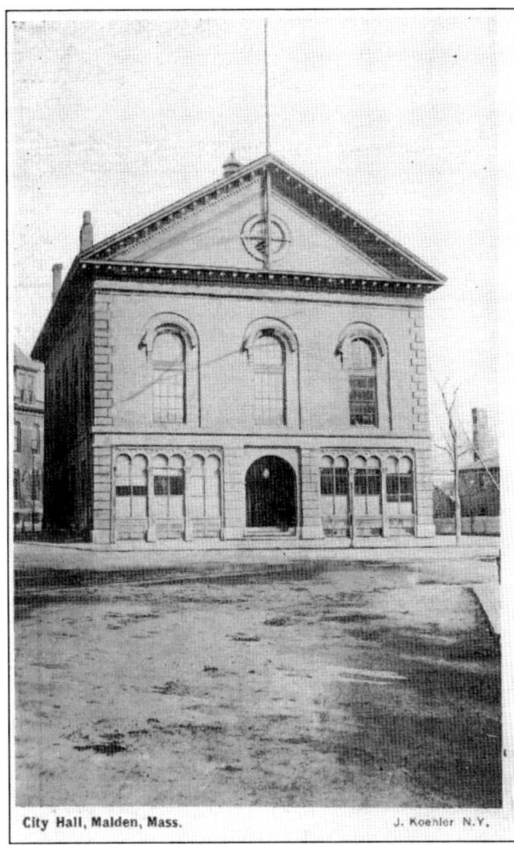

This view shows the Malden City Hall, built in 1857 and originally called the town house. It was built by Jonathan Clark on Main Street, roughly opposite Pleasant Street, and was torn down in the late 1970s. By the turn of the 20th century, Malden had become a fairly large city. It boasted a city hall, a police station, multiple fire stations, a hospital, YMCA, hotels, fraternal lodges, and more. The opulence of the architecture of these buildings reflects Malden's wealth during this period and can still be seen on those structures that remain.

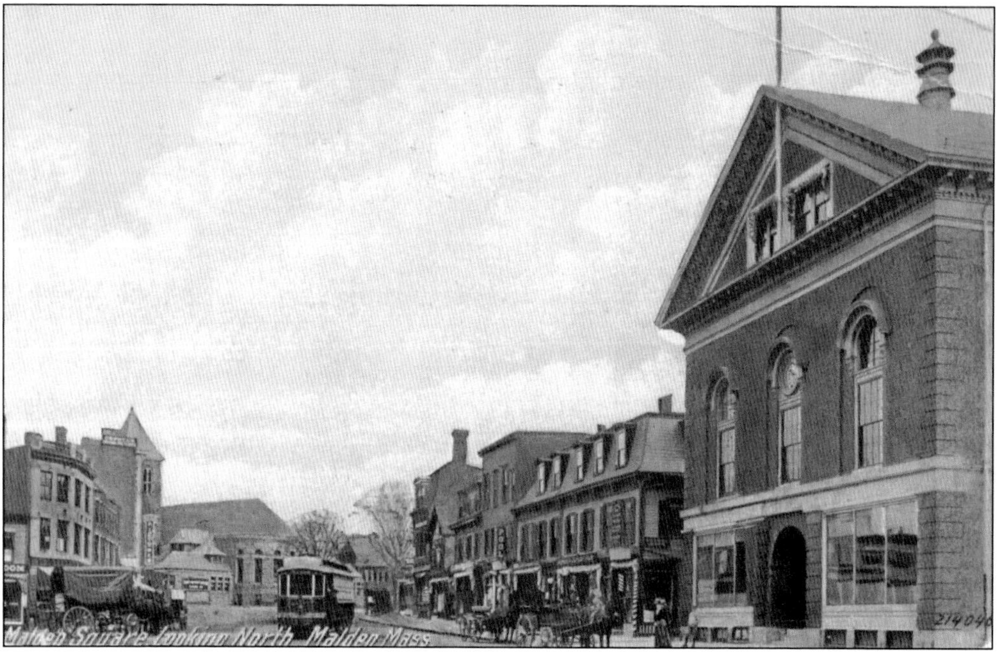

A busy Malden Square features the old city hall to the right. A number of architectural and cosmetic changes have been made to the city hall in comparison to the previous image. By the turn of the 20th century, Malden had become a fairly large city. The opulent architecture of these buildings reflects Malden's wealth during this period.

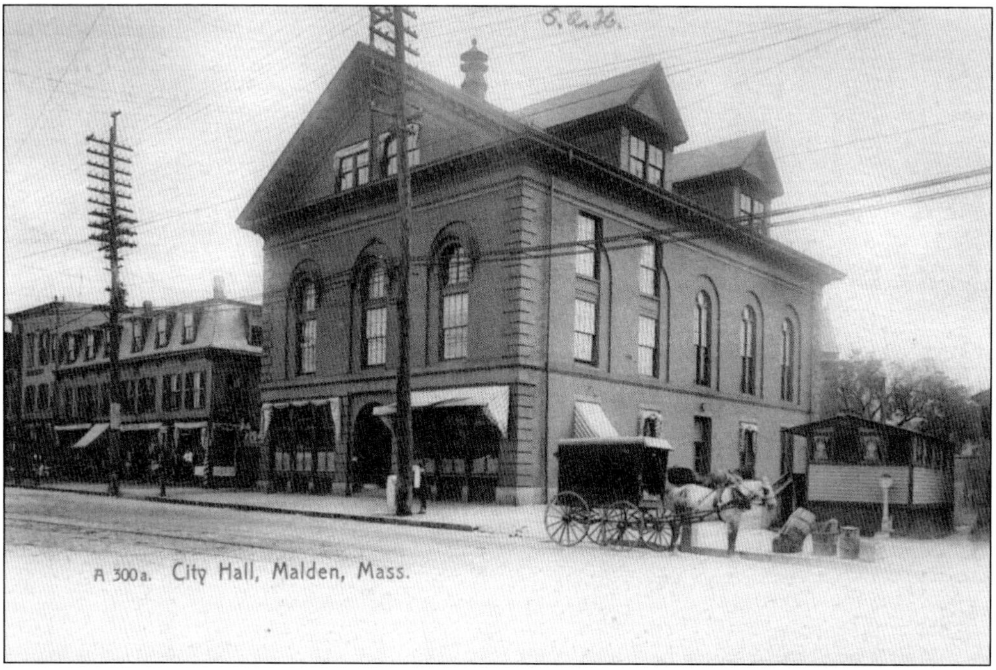

This view of old city hall shows the facade facing Main Street. A horse-drawn merchant cart to the right reflects an earlier time.

This c. 1917 view shows Chemical No. 3 House and Engine, located on Mountain Avenue near Summer Street. The building later housed an emergency ambulance unit. It is presently a private residence.

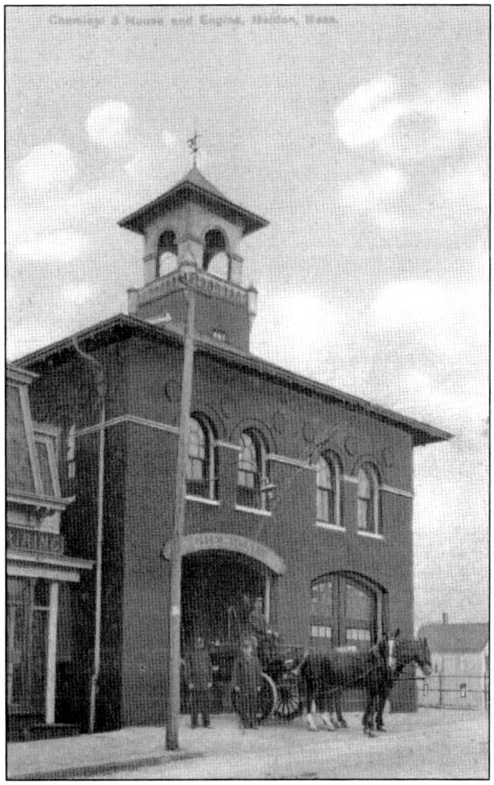

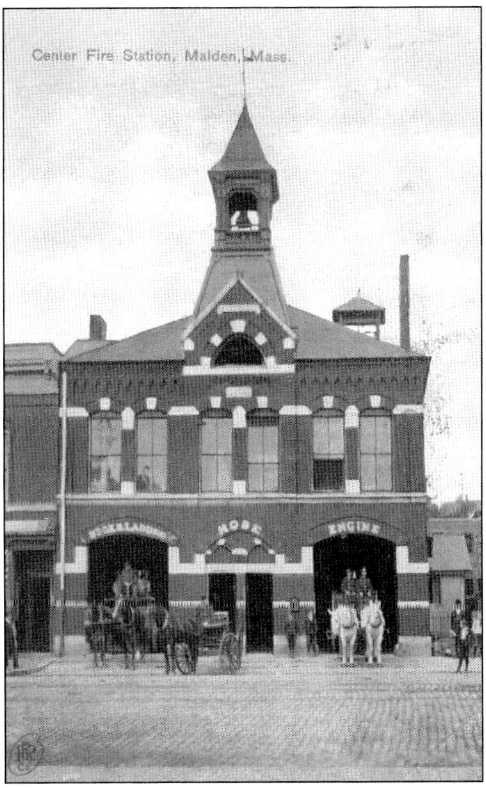

Seen here is a c. 1911 view of the Central Fire Station, which was located on Main Street in Malden Square. The fire house contained three horse-drawn units: a hook and ladder, a hose wagon, and an engine. It was built in 1875 and located where Exchange Street now intersects with Main Street.

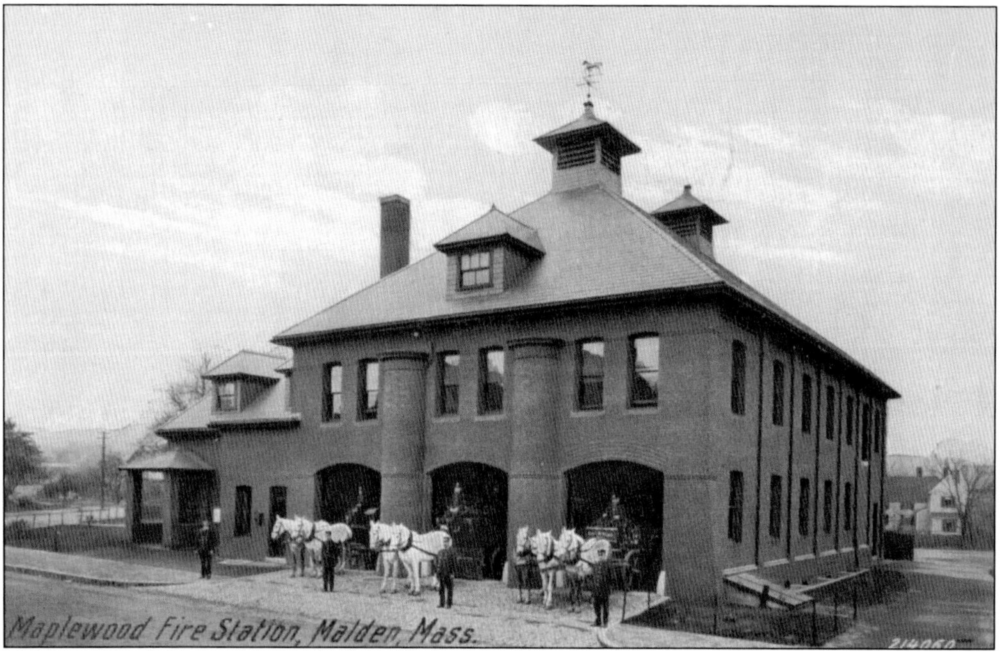

Pictured is Maplewood Fire Station on Laurel Street around 1913. The building has recently been remodeled for reuse by the Mystic Valley Regional Charter School.

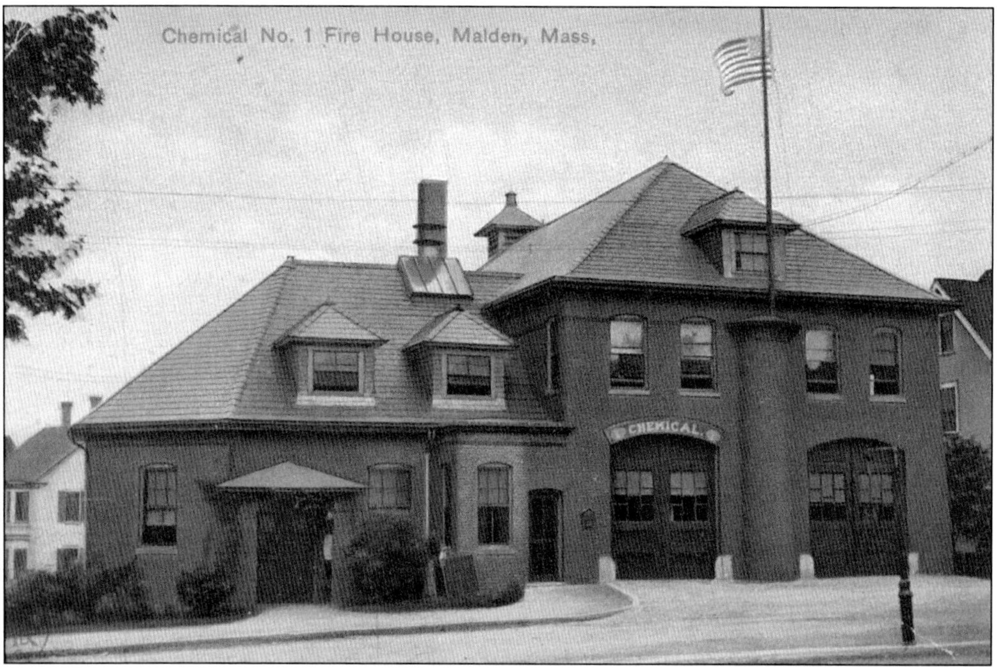

This view shows Chemical No. 1, located on Ashland Street in the Belmont Hill section of Malden. It has been converted to a private residence.

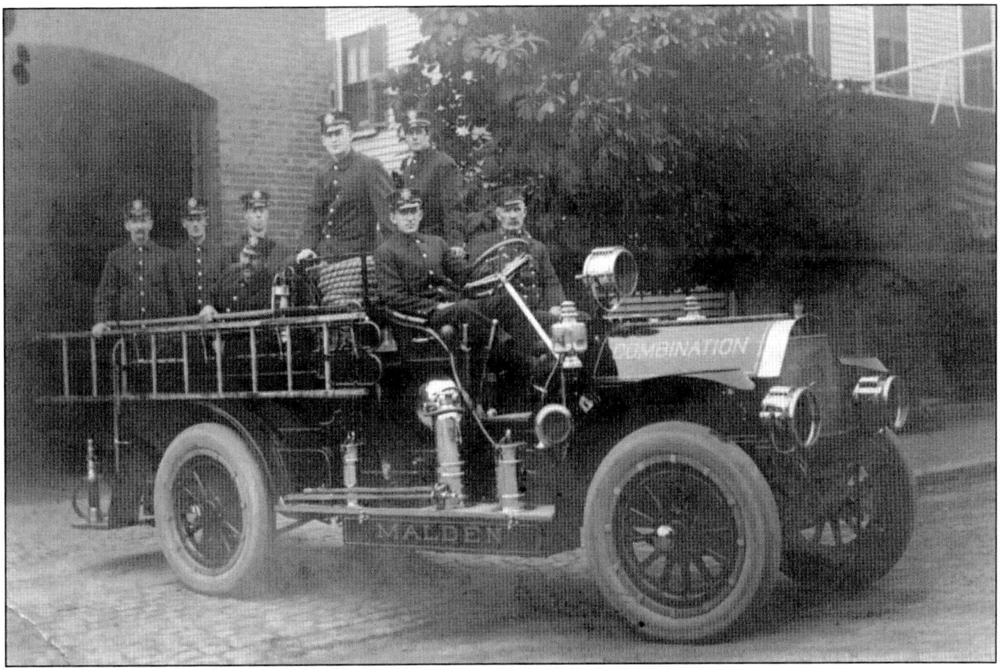

This c. 1910 postcard depicts the very first motorized fire engine used by the Malden Fire Department. October 1918 saw the last use of horses in the Malden Fire Department.

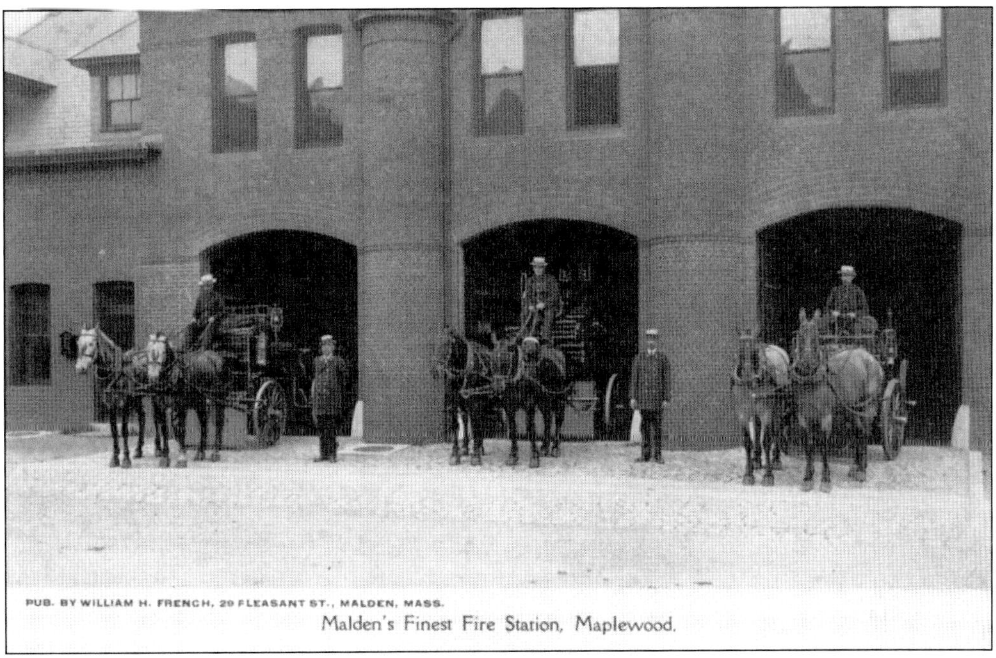

This close-up view shows the Maplewood Fire Station located at the corner of Laurel and Granite Streets.

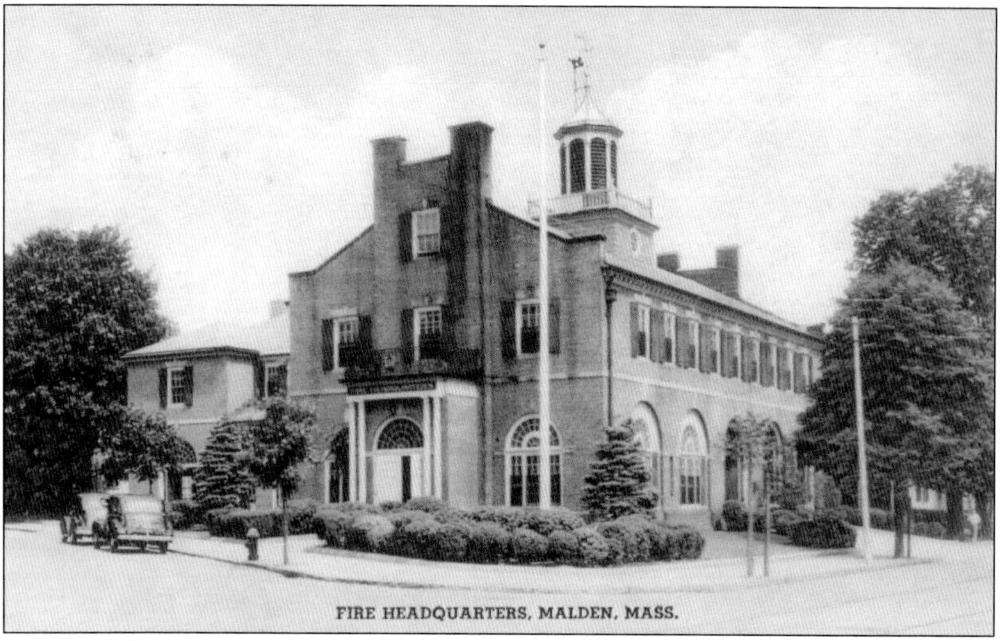

The Central Fire Station replaced the Central Fire House on Main Street in 1919. Located on Salem Street, opposite the high school, it is still in use today.

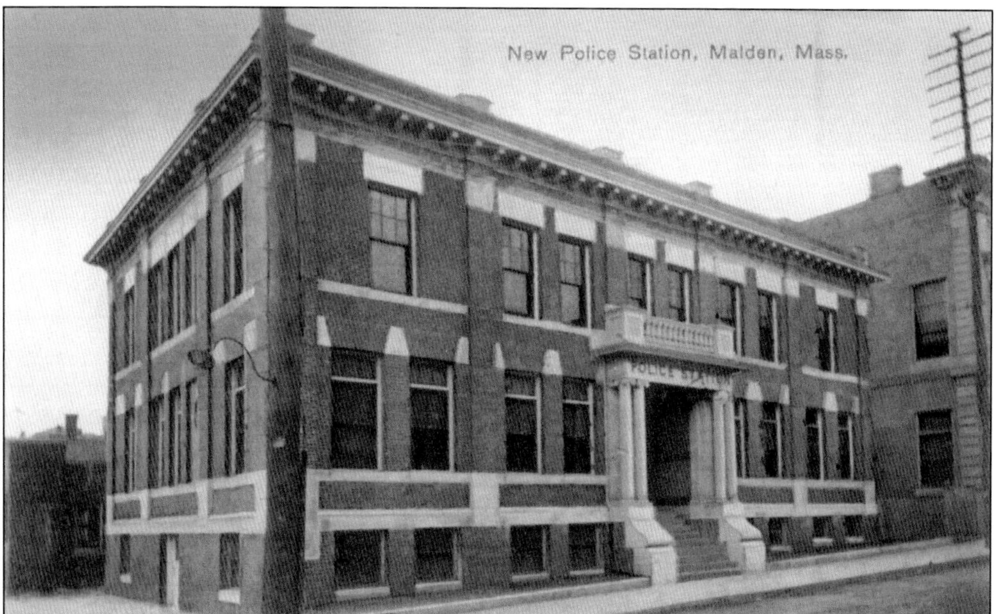

The "new" Malden Police Station, pictured here around 1910, was located on Middlesex Street at Exchange Street. It was razed in the late 1970s.

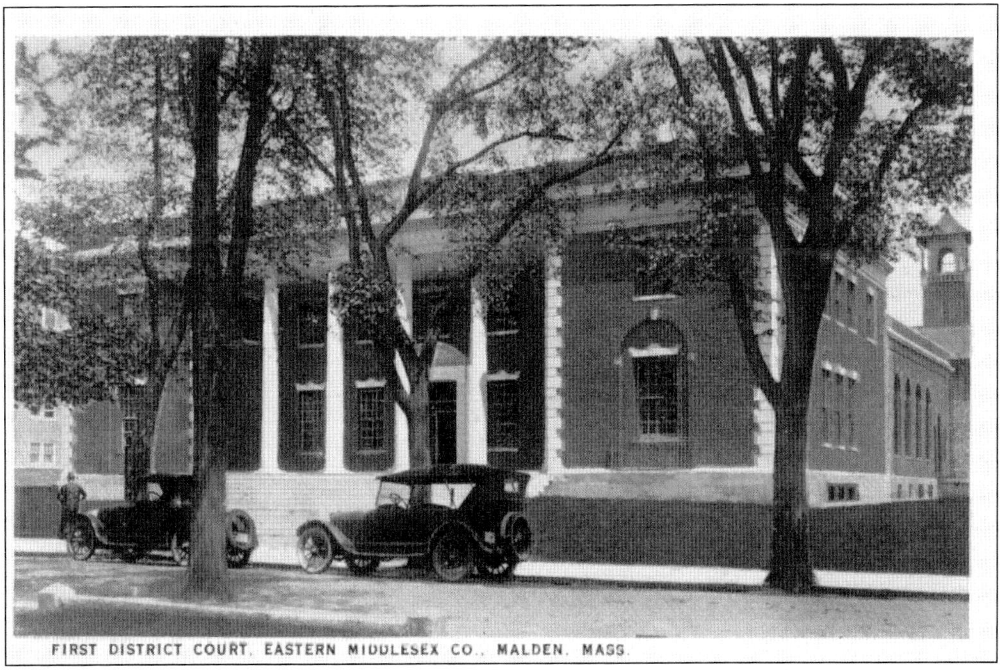

The First District Court of Eastern Middlesex is located at the corner of Summer Street and Mountain Avenue. It still serves as the courthouse today.

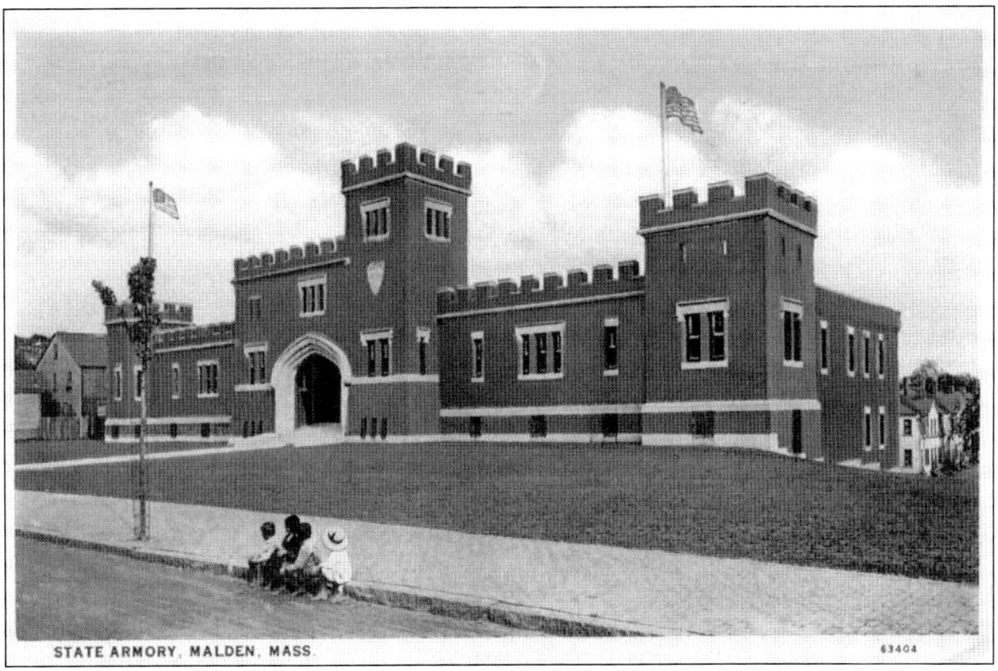

The State Armory was located at 150 Mountain Avenue and housed Companies K and L of the 182 Infantry Regiment, Massachusetts Volunteer Militia. The armory is presently the home of the Malden YMCA, which preserved its original facade.

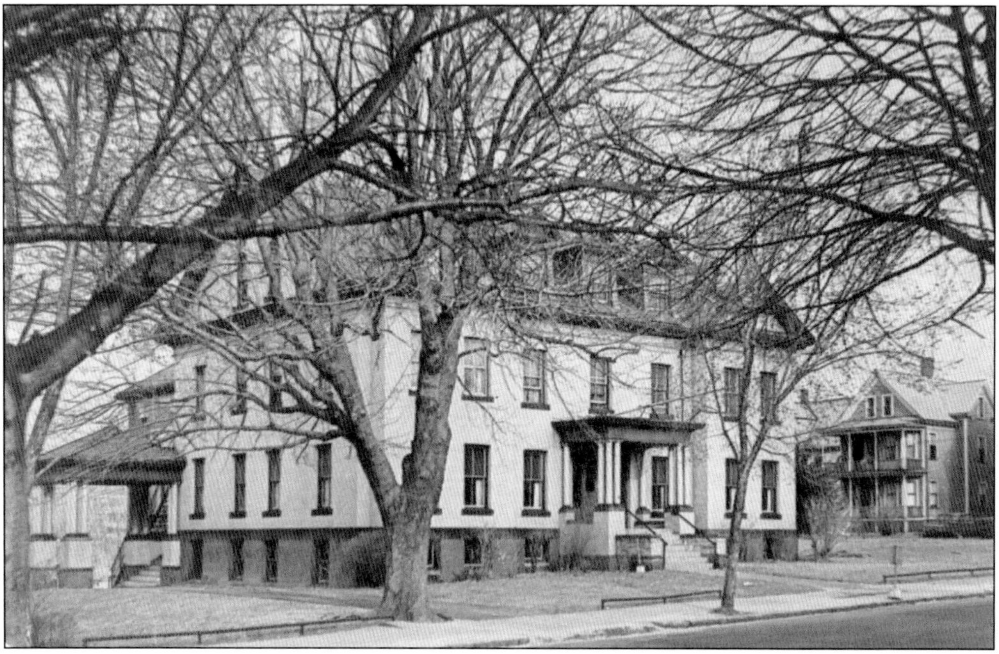

The Malden Home for Aged Persons at 578 Main Street appears in this c. 1955 view. The building now houses medical offices. Its yellow brick facade differed from the red brick of nearby buildings.

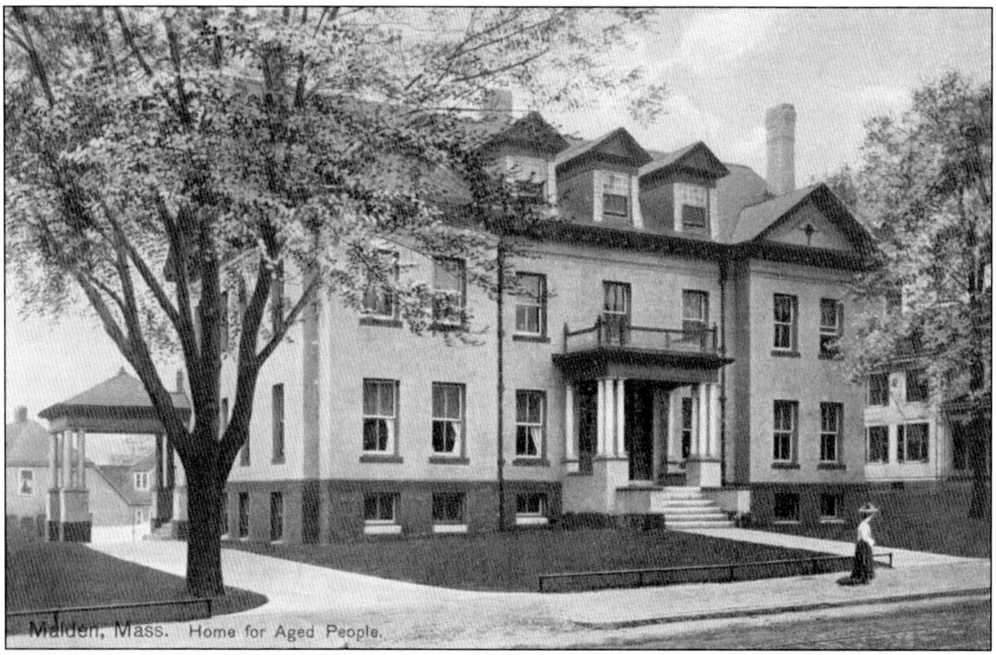

This earlier view of the Malden Home for Aged Persons was taken around 1908. For many years, it cared for Malden's aged population. It was converted for other uses in the early 1990s.

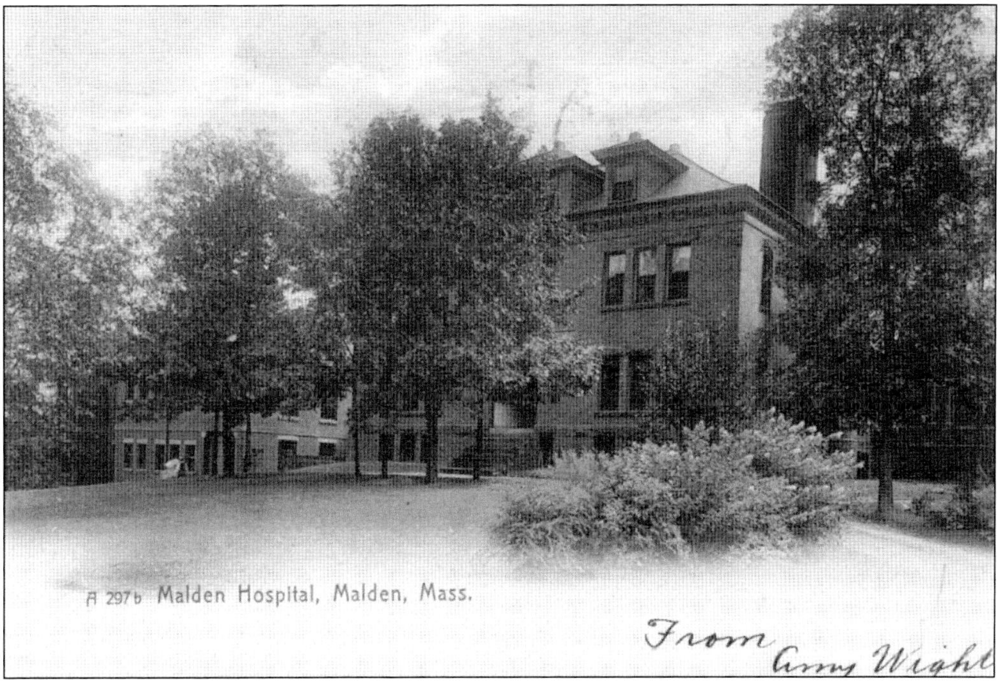

The main building of the Malden Hospital is pictured in this c. 1907 postcard. The hospital stood on a hill that overlooks Fellsmere Pond in the West End of Malden.

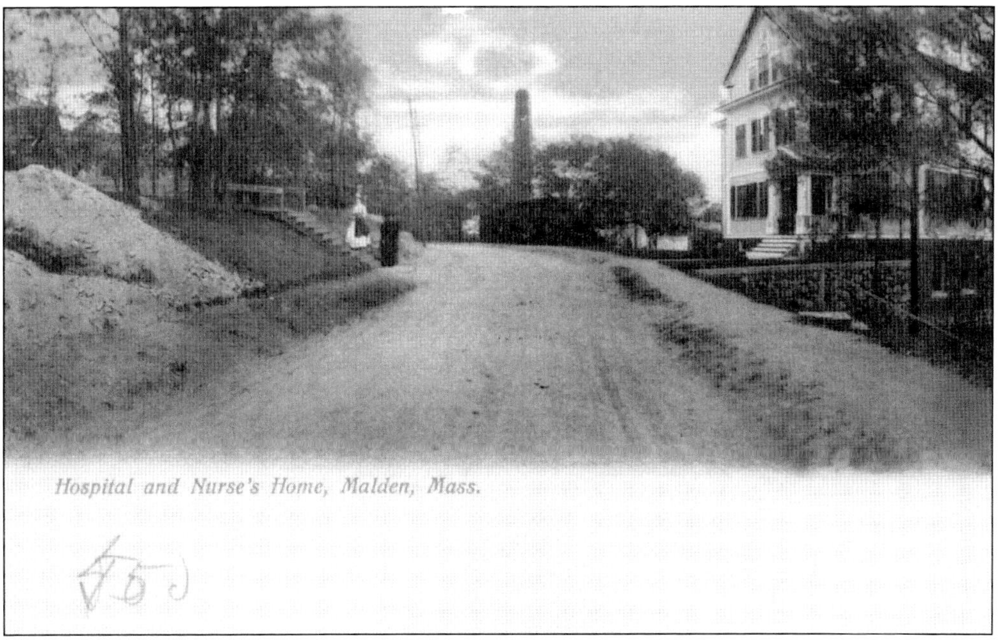

The Malden Hospital included a nursing school that trained registered nurses and was noted for its excellent professional reputation. This pre–World War I image is of the student nurses' home on the hospital grounds.

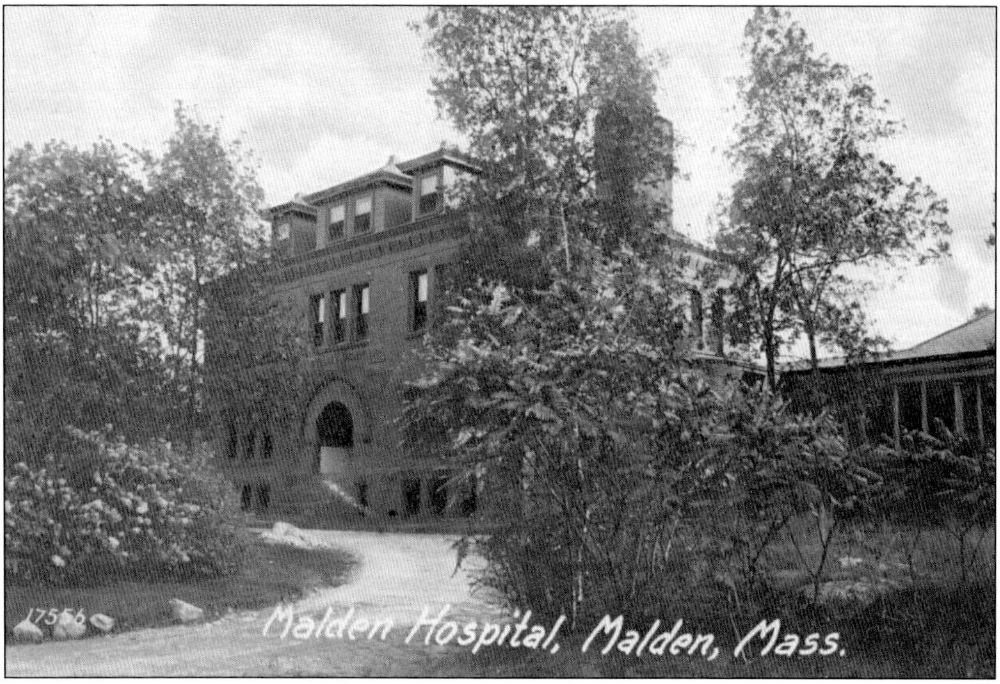

This is an early view of the first Malden Hospital. It was built on woodlands donated by Elisha Converse.

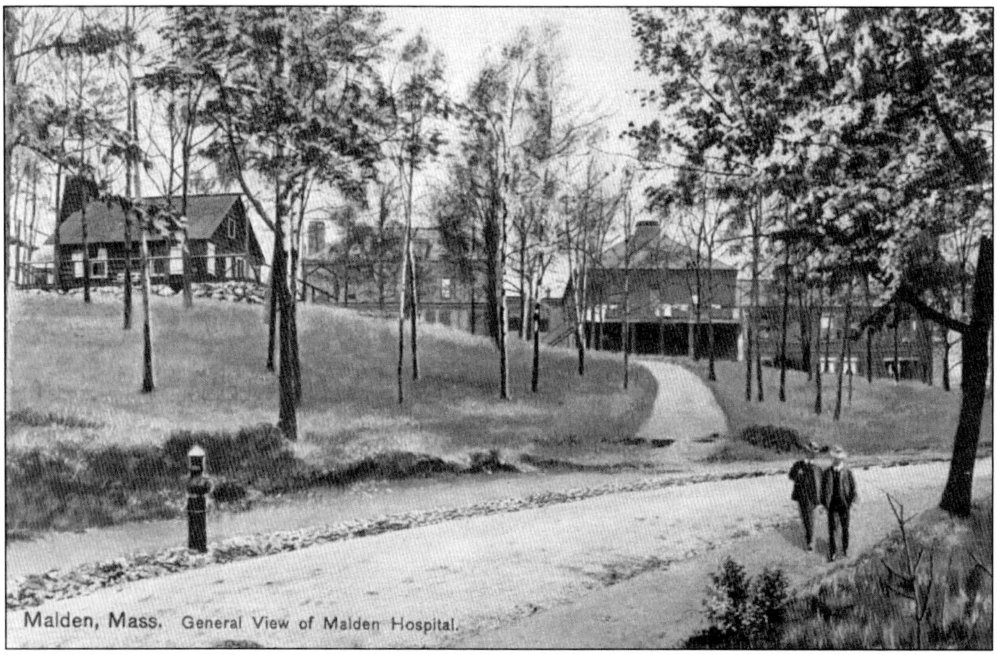

In this view of the hospital, the log cabin at left was used as an early isolation unit, housing consumptives and others.

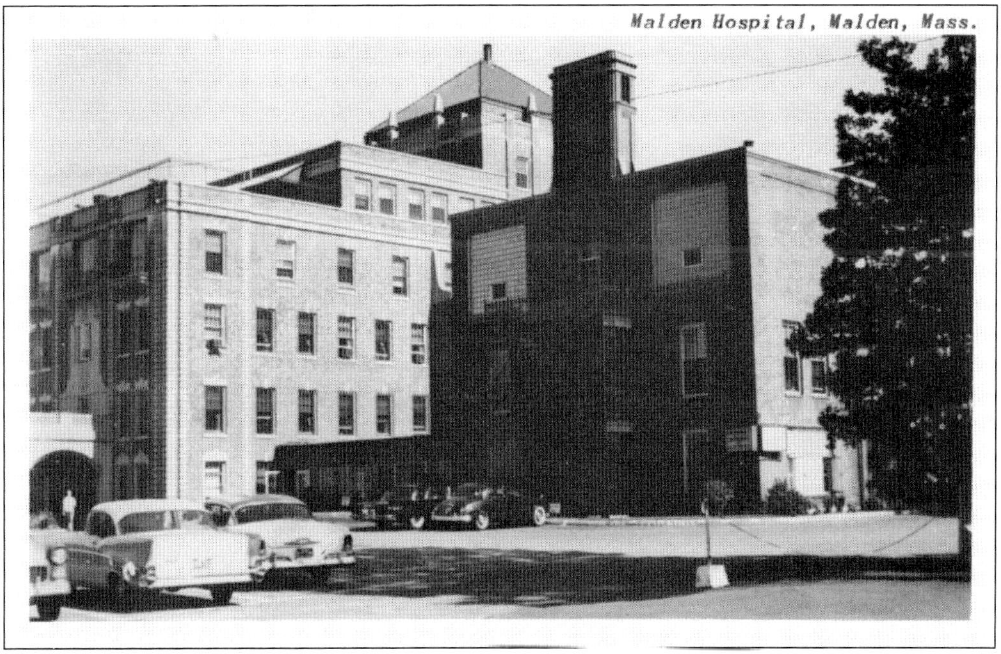

This view of Malden Hospital was captured around 1955. The 1930 building is at left, a later addition sits at right.

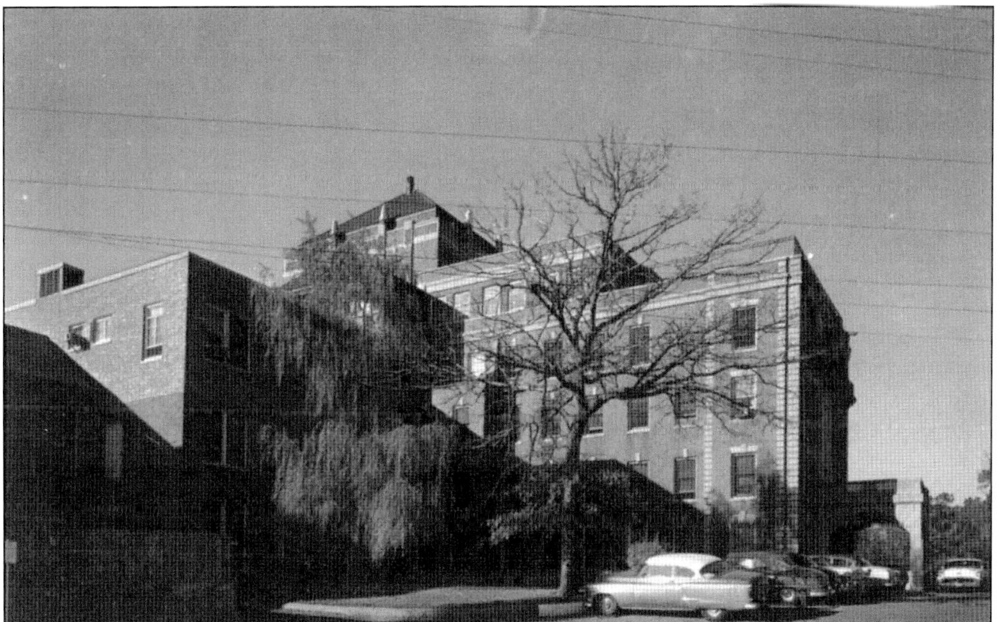
This c. 1955 view of Malden Hospital shows its main entrance. It also documents the hospital's growth over a number of years from its early beginnings.

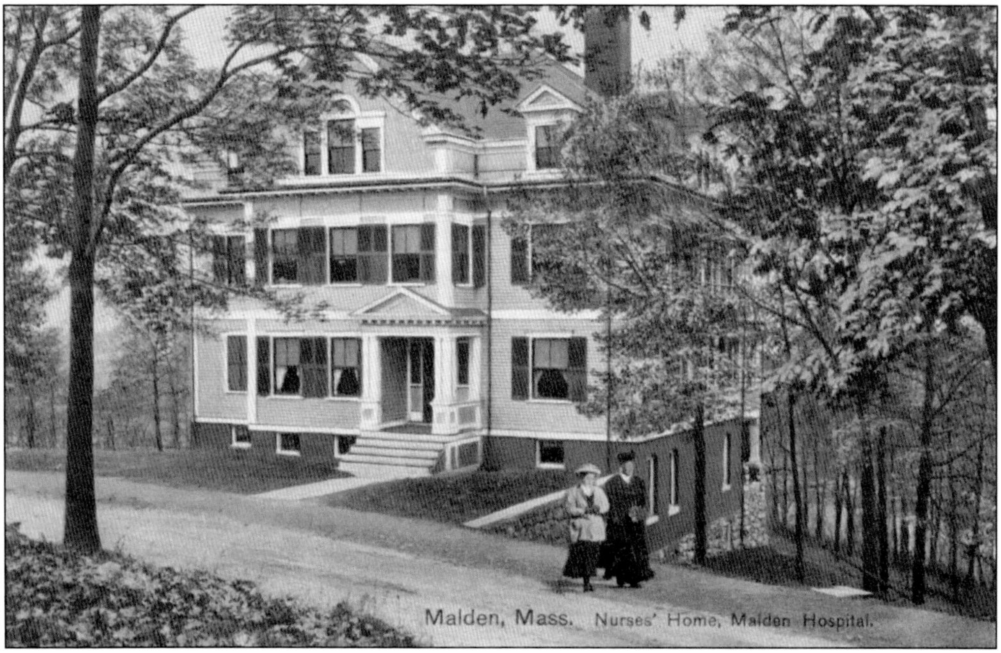

Here is a later view of the nurses' home at Malden Hospital. The hospital ran a school of nursing for many years. The nurses received a nursing diploma administered through the hospital itself. The registered nurses from the Malden Hospital School of Nursing number in the thousands.

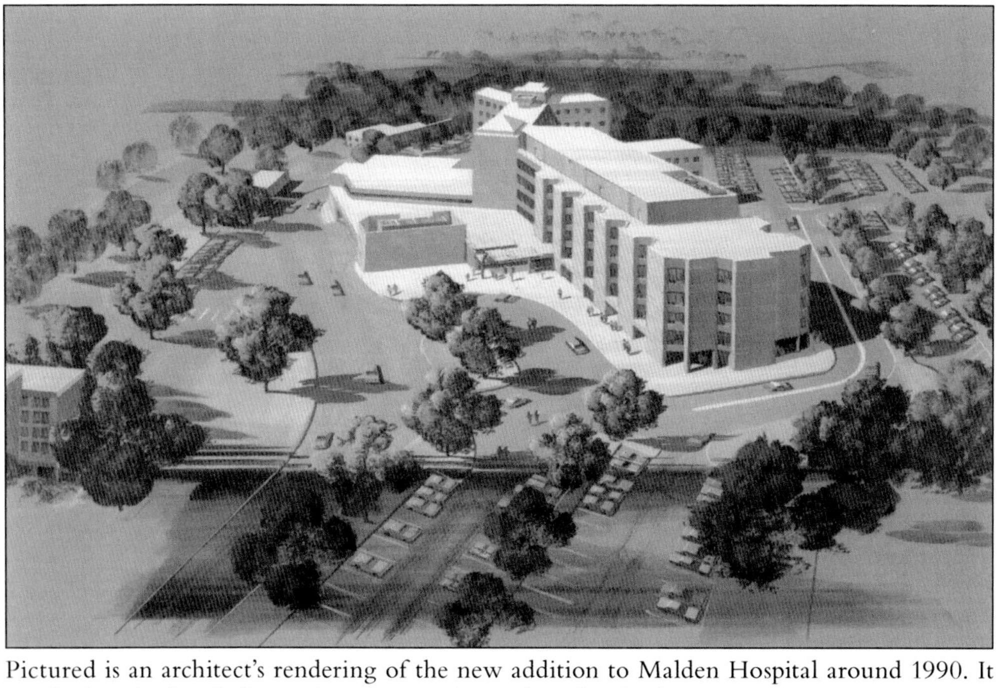

Pictured is an architect's rendering of the new addition to Malden Hospital around 1990. It emphasizes the hospital's continued expansion and modernization.

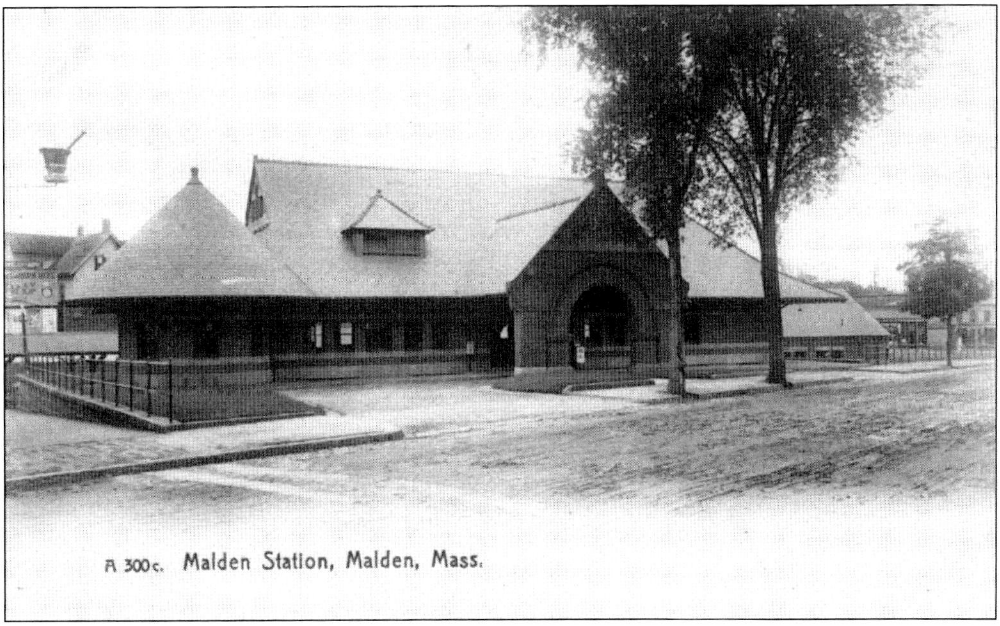

The Malden Station of the Boston & Maine Railroad is seen here as it appeared on Summer Street around 1910. The porte cochere at the front of the station was later enclosed. The building has since been converted to a restaurant.

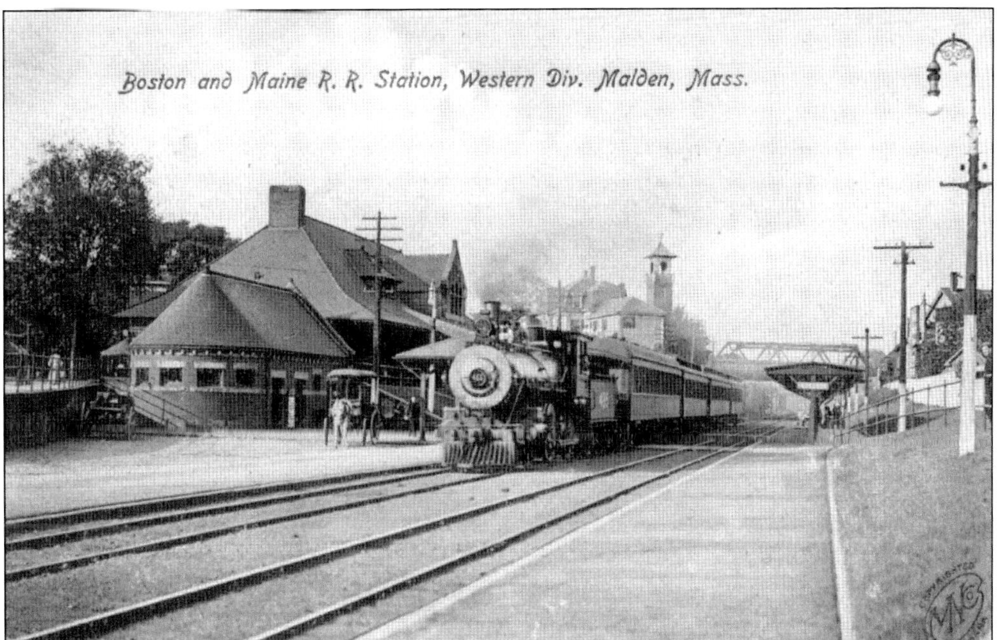

A Boston-bound train pulls into the Malden Station in this view. The hose-drying tower of the Mountain Avenue firehouse appears in the background.

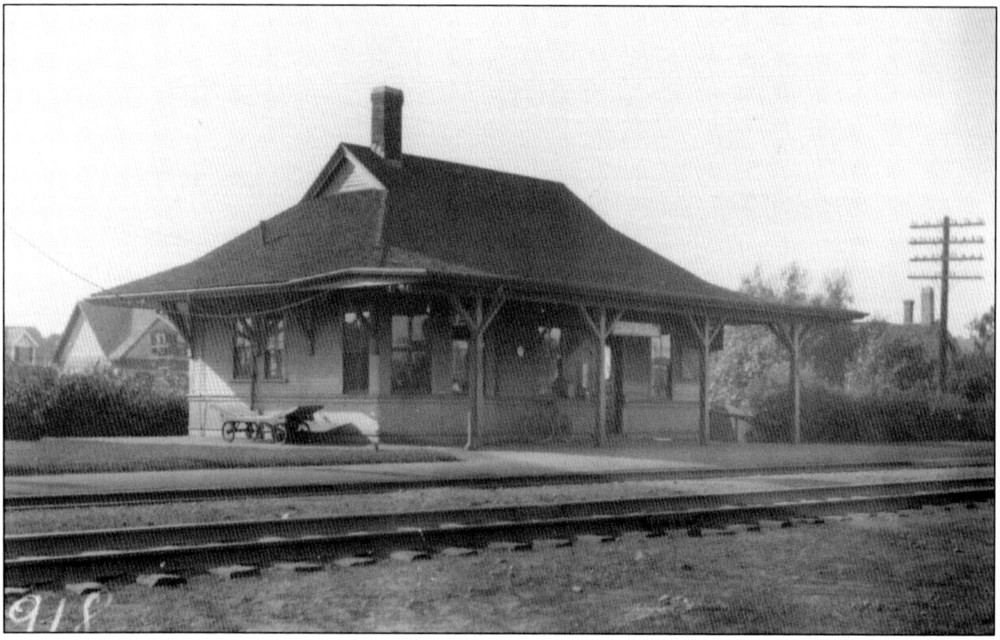

Edgeworth Station on the Boston & Maine Railroad was located between Avon and Medford Streets. This was a convenient stop for workers at the Converse rubber factory.

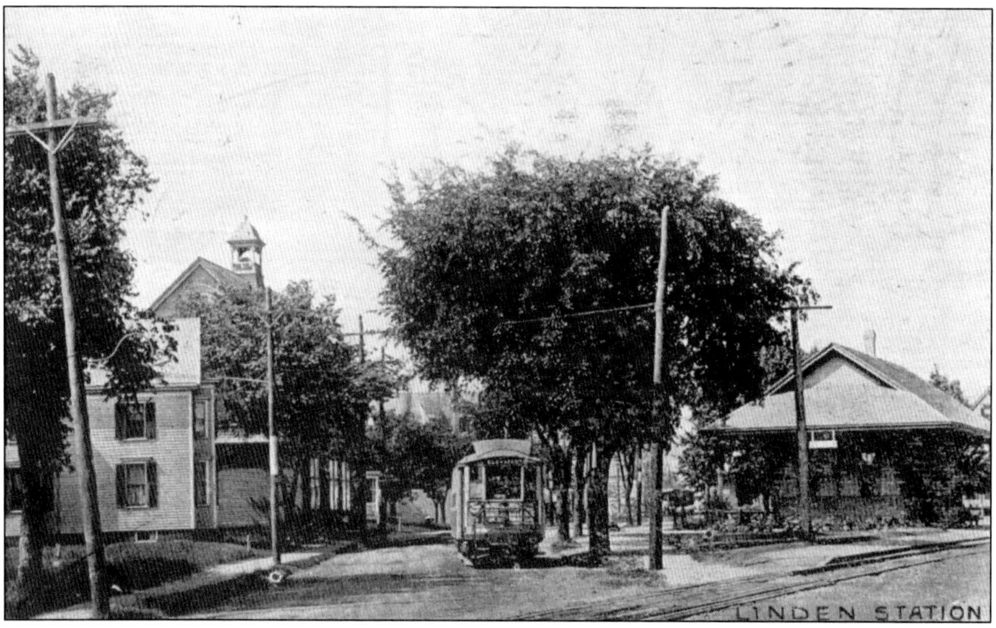

The Boston Elevated Railway semi-convertible car arrives at the end of the Sullivan Square–Linden Square line on Lynn Street around 1906. Linden Station on the Saugus Branch Railroad is on the right. Eliot Paul immortalized this station in the title of his memoir, *Linden on the Saugus Branch.*

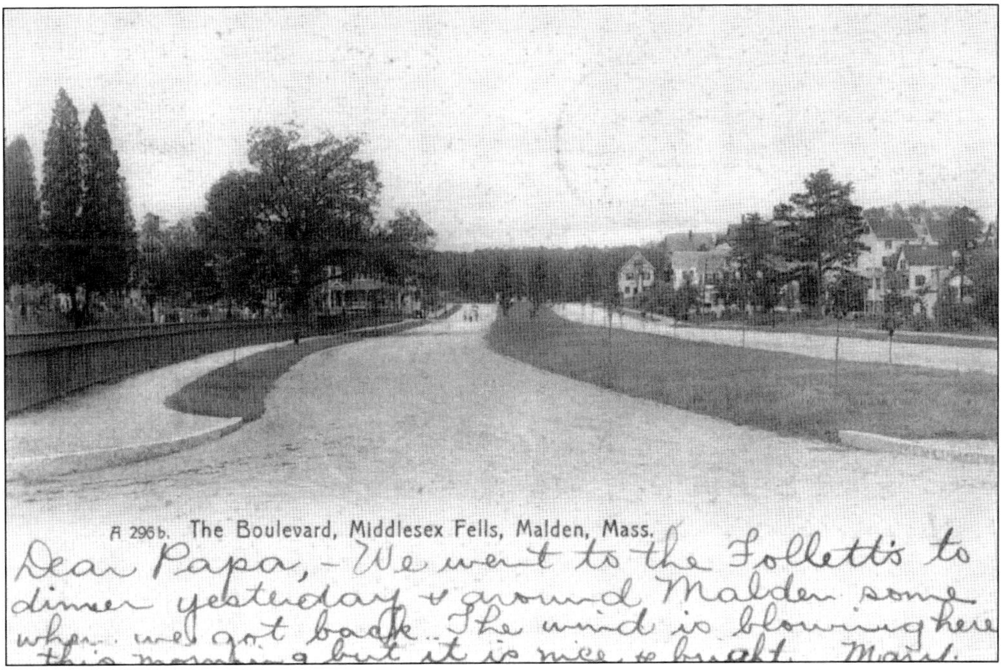

The Fellsway East is seen in this view shortly after its construction. St. Mary's Cemetery, seen at left, dates to the 1850s and is the burial ground of many Irish immigrants.

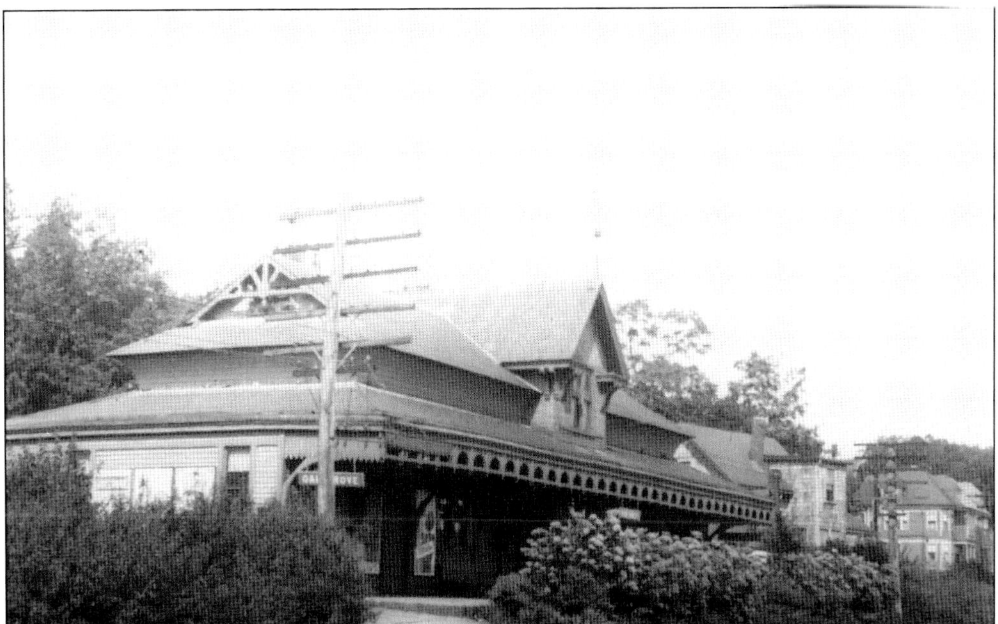

The Oak Grove depot of the Boston & Maine Railroad on Washington Street is seen in this view. The station was razed in 1974 for the MBTA Oak Grove Station.

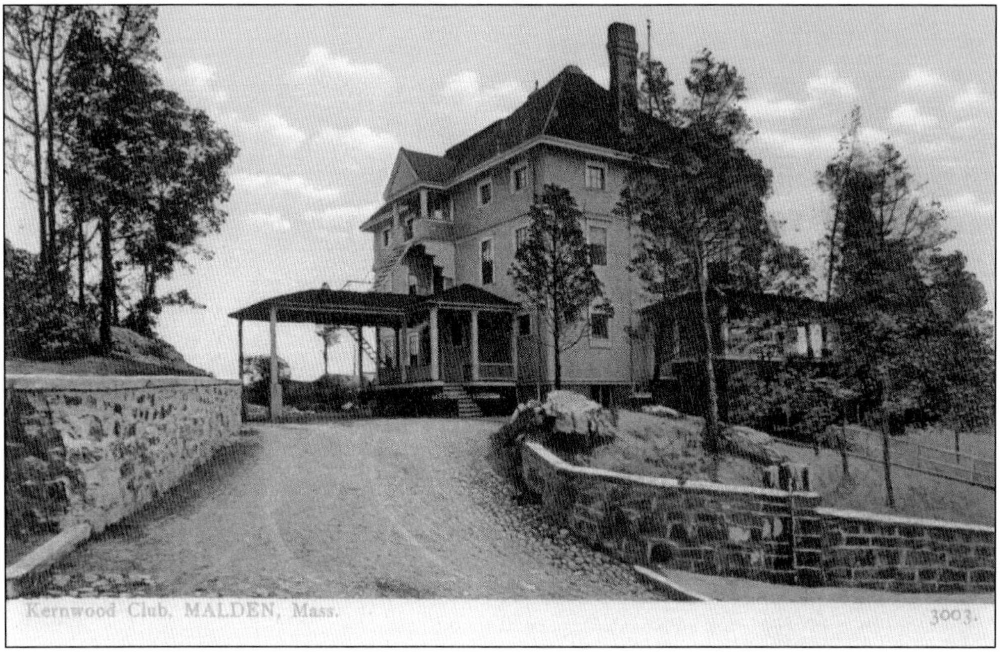

The Kernwood Club on Alpine Street, founded in 1889, was one of Malden's two social clubs; the other was the Malden Club. The site is presently an apartment building.

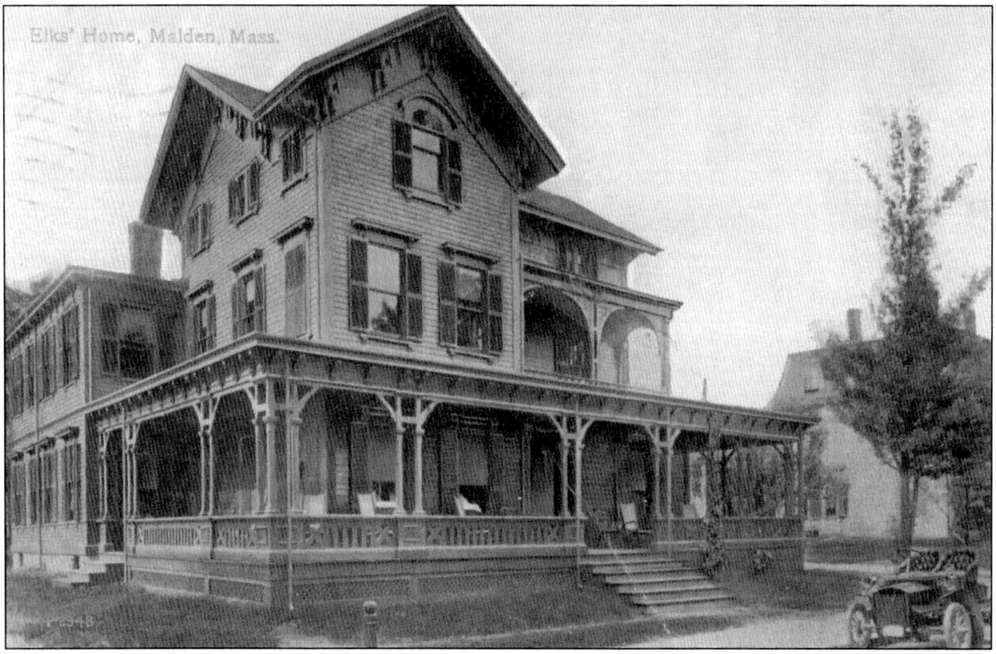

The original Elks Home on Florence Street is seen in this view. The Elks Club built its present clubhouse on this same site.

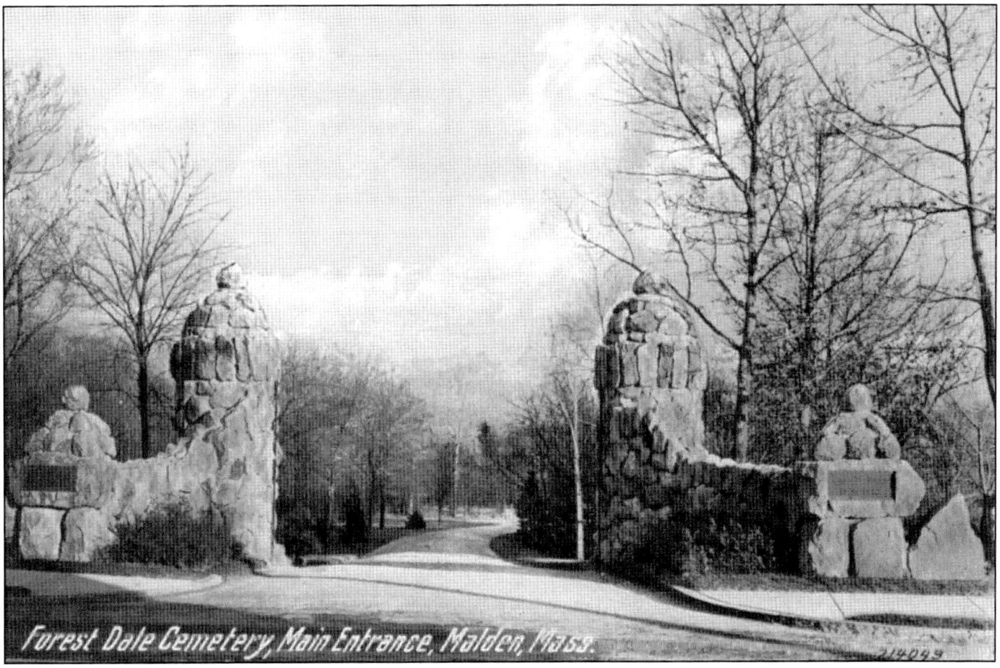

The Main Street gates of Forest Dale Cemetery are seen in this view looking east. The cemetery was opened in 1885. Forest Dale, the fourth city cemetery in Malden, was designed as a garden-type cemetery.

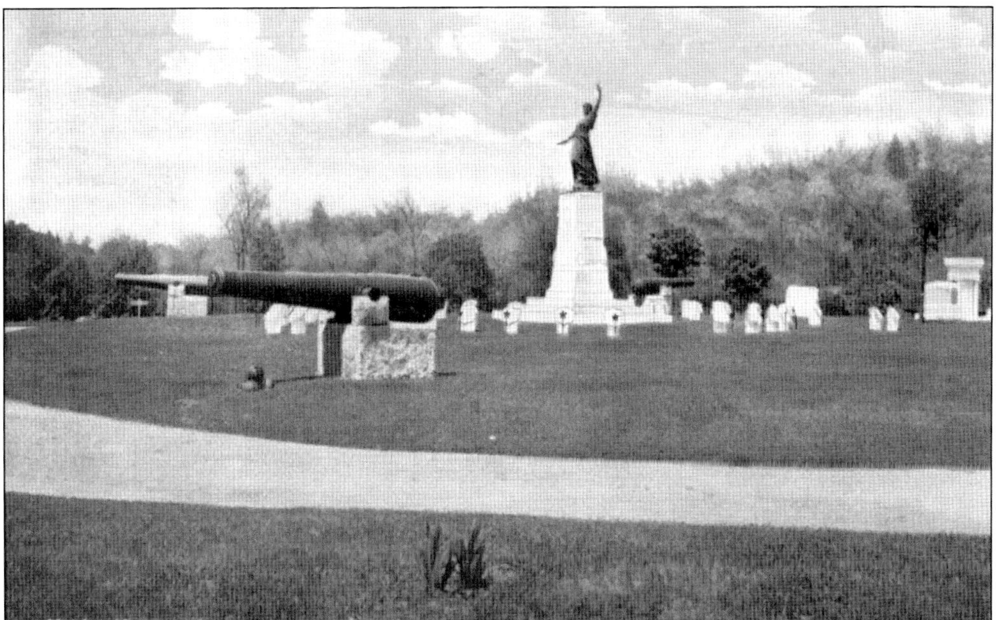

The Soldiers and Sailors Monument in Forest Dale Cemetery was erected in 1894 by the City of Malden at the request of Post No. 40 of the Grand Army of the Republic to honor those who fought in the Civil War and are buried here.

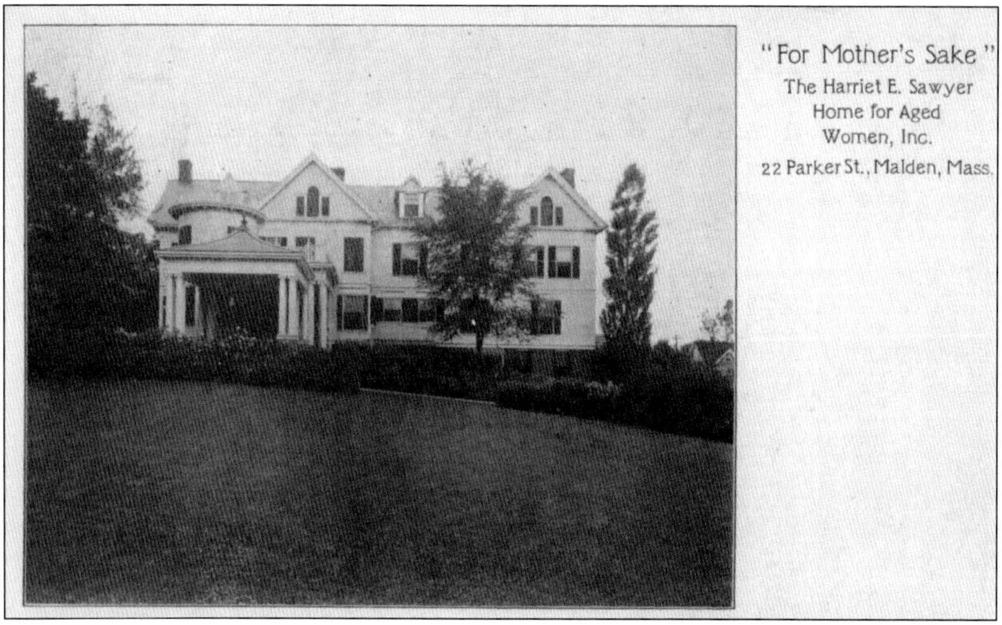

The Joshua Millett mansion at the corner of Parker and Ferry Streets became the Harriet Sawyer Home for Aged Women after Millett's death. The original home of a businessman, it was an upper-class Victorian house containing many modern features and ornament of the time.

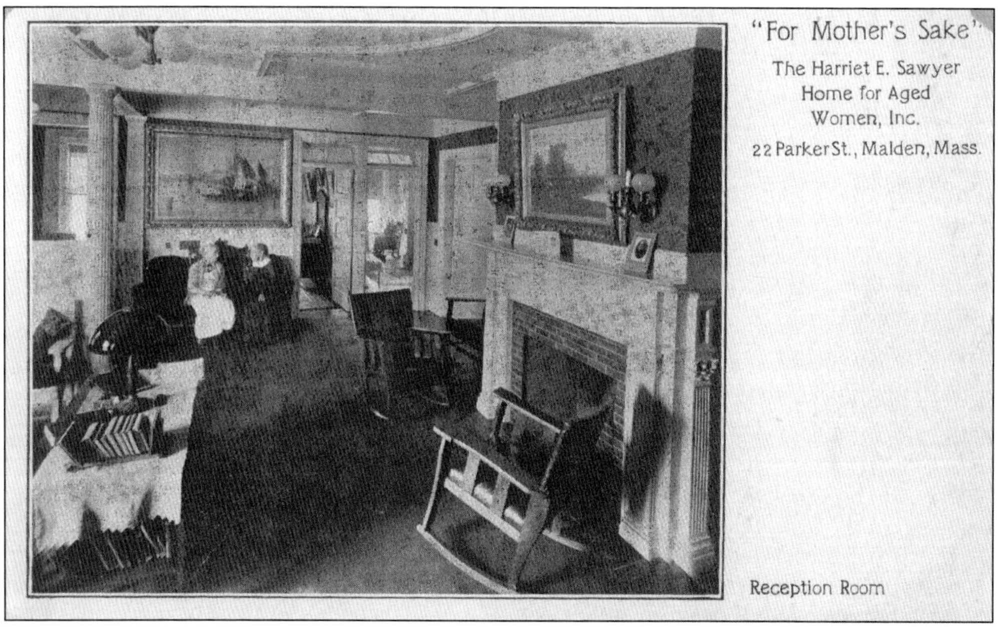

The parlor, or reception room, in the Harriet Sawyer home shows the comfort of the space for the women residents.

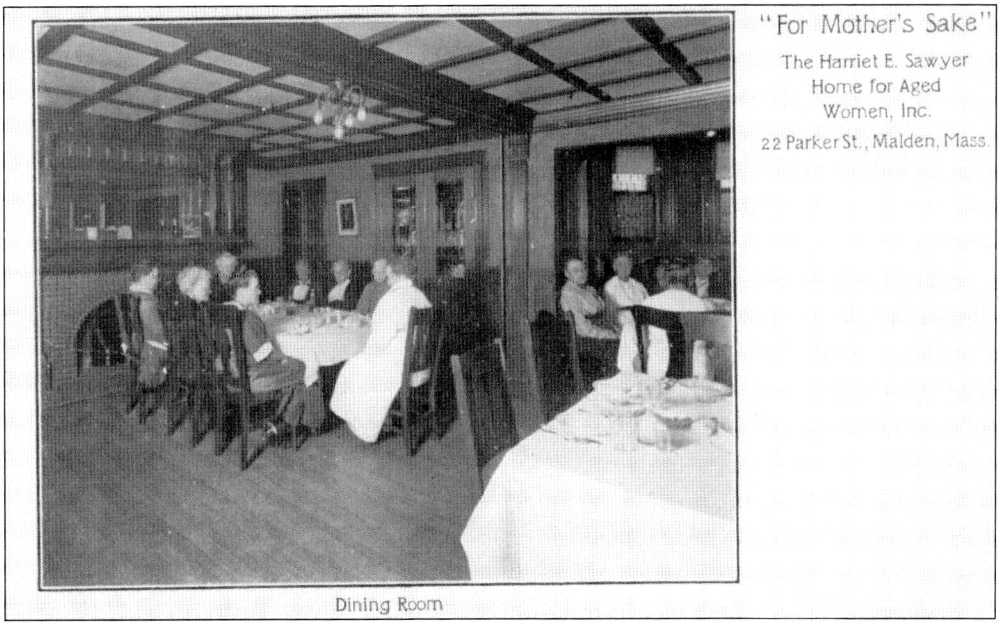

The dining room of the Harriet Sawyer home reflects the opulence of the entire interior.

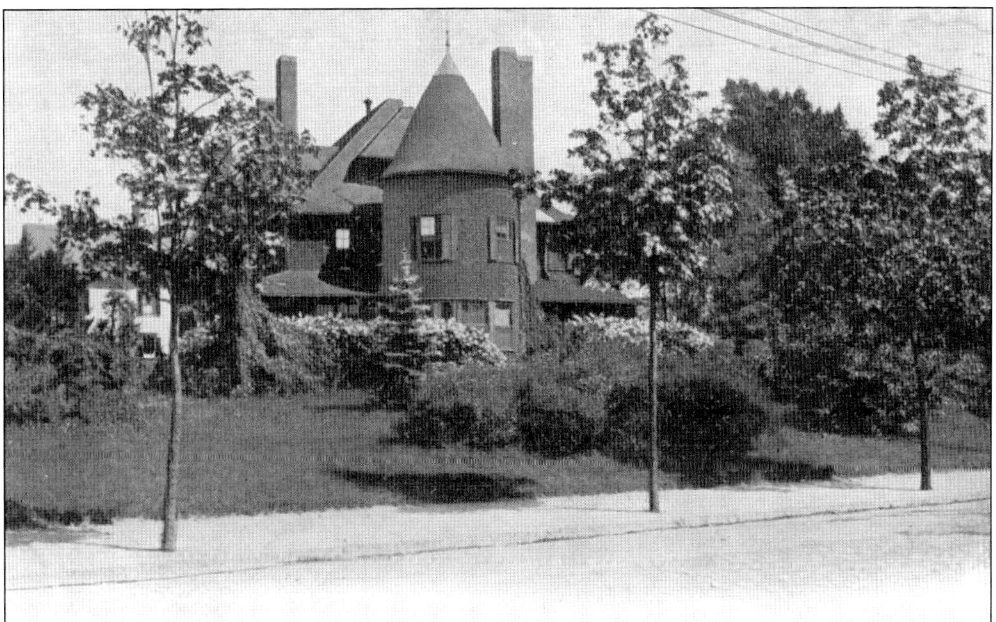

The Harry Converse mansion, situated on the corner of Main and Appleton Streets, was the home of Col. Harry Converse, Elisha Converse's son. After he moved, the home was converted to the Choate Home sanatorium.

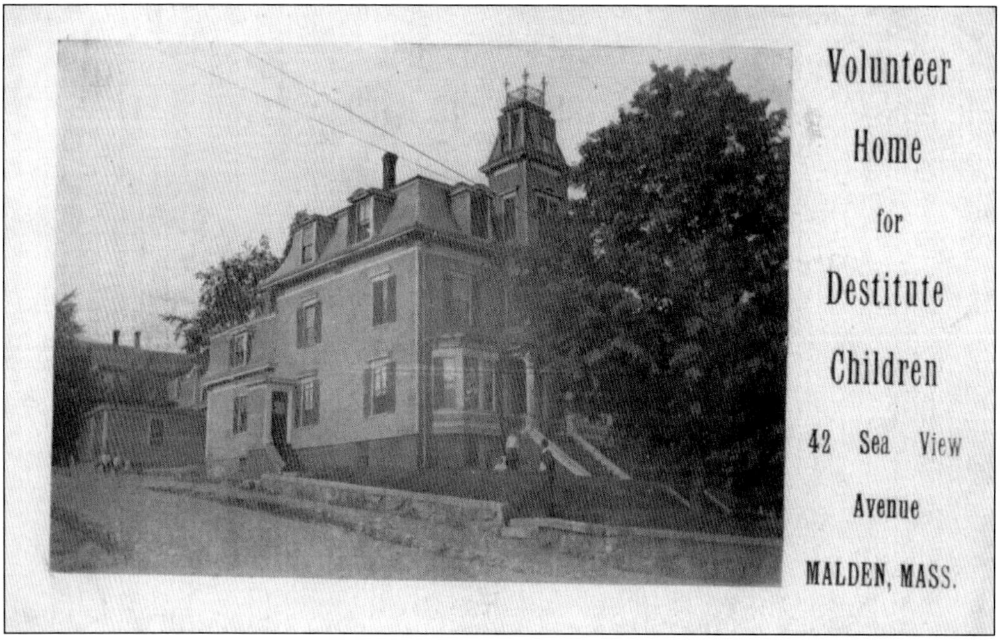

The Volunteer Home for Destitute Children was located on Sea View Avenue in the Maplewood section of Malden. It is a private home today.

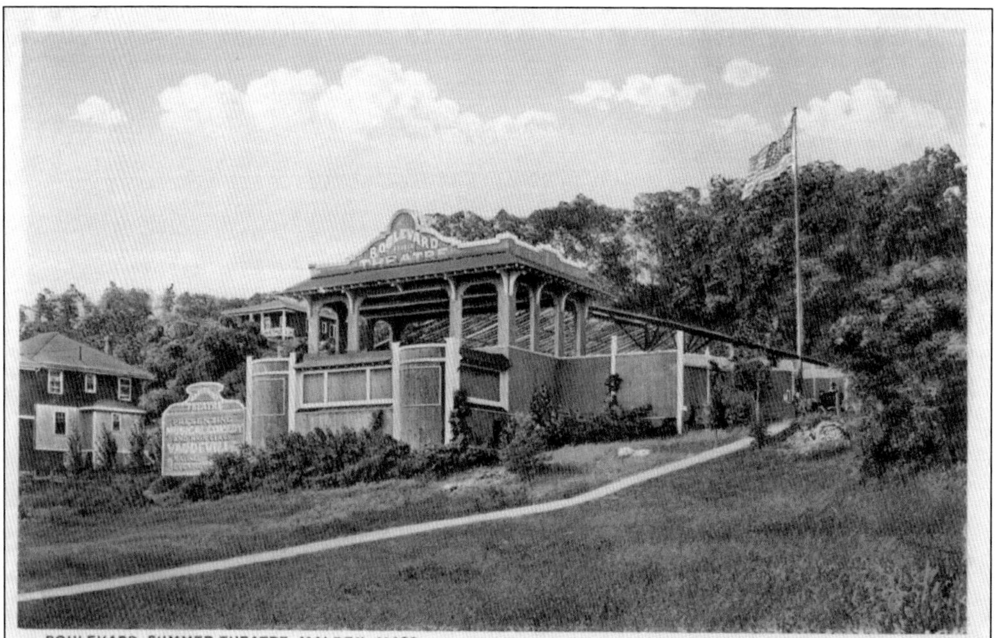

The Boulevard Theatre was located on the Fellsway near the Malden/Medford line. It presented vaudeville acts and plays.

Eight

Camp Woodman

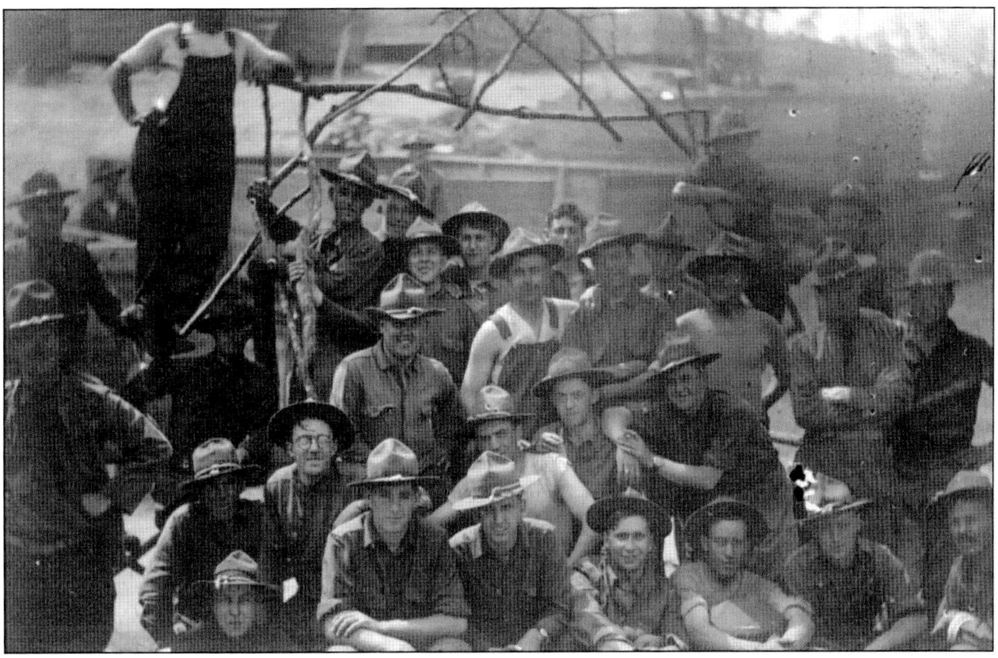

This is a group portrait of a platoon of enlisted men of Company L, 5th Massachusetts National Guard, encamped at Amerige Field in July and August 1917. During World War I, Amerige Field was used as a base for military personnel and was known as Camp Woodman. Located at the corner of Savin Street and Fellsway East, it housed approximately 250 men of Company L.

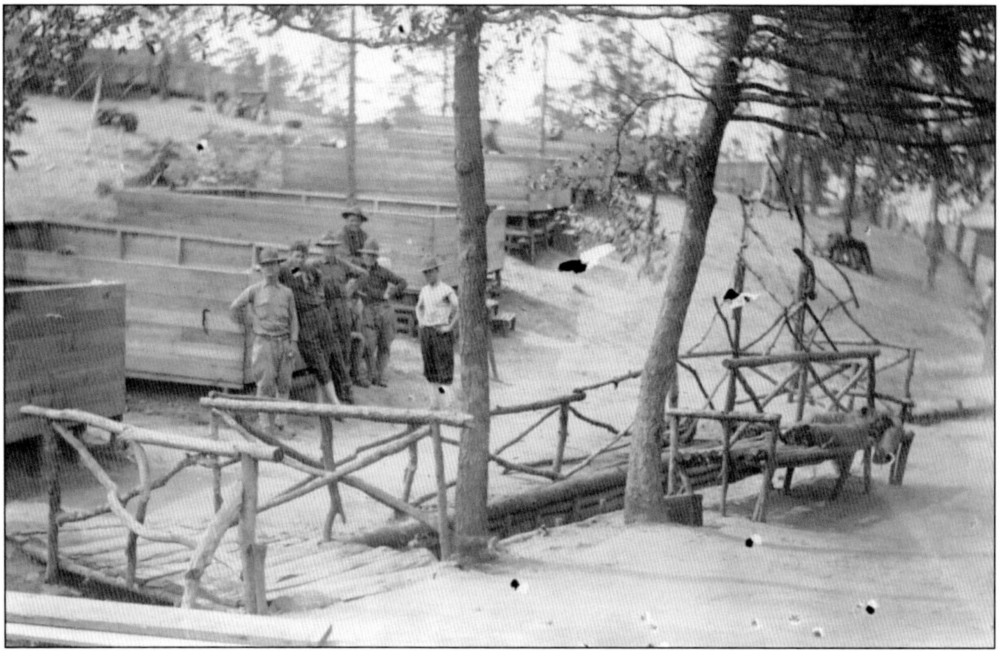

Work detail for the field camp at Amerige Field is pictured here. The image depicts in the foreground a rude bridge over a ditch and includes camp furniture constructed of tree logs. The area in the photograph is now a small hill near the present-day tennis courts.

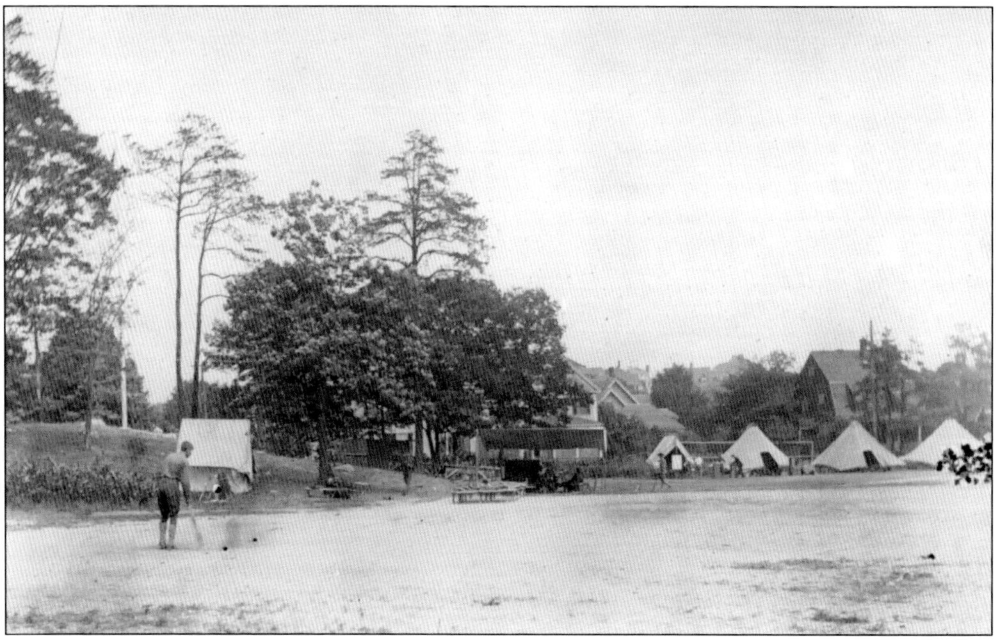

A view of the northern end of Camp Woodman is looking toward Pine Street. The man to the left is on a work detail, sweeping the grounds. Note the uniform puttees, which indicate an enlisted man since officers wore leather boots. The area is now a baseball field.

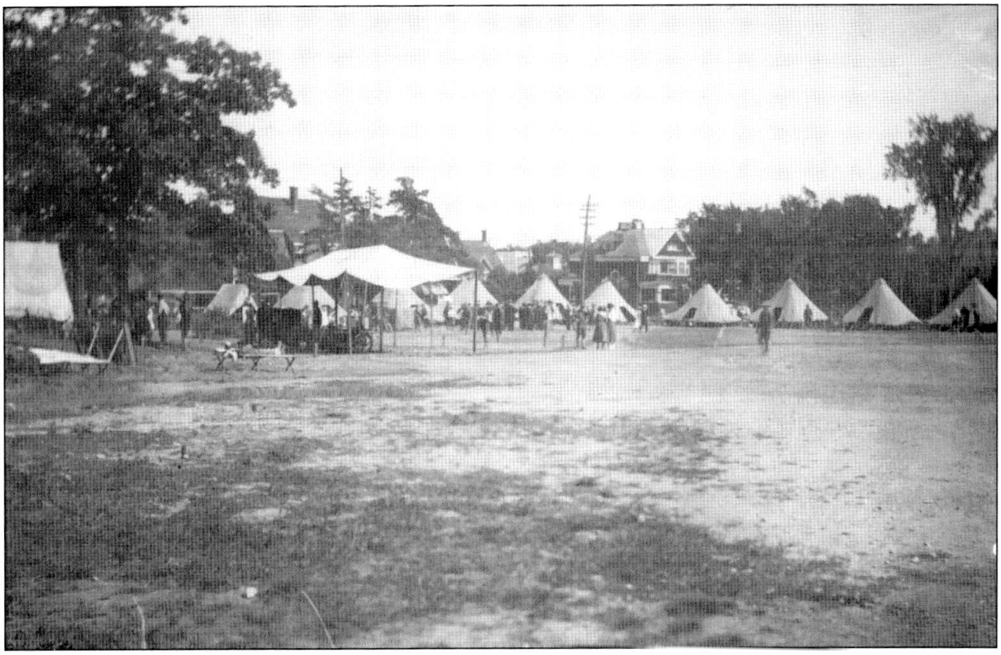

This image looks west to Savin Street and the Fells area of Malden. Shown in the background is a mess tent where the soldiers' food was prepared and served. Note the close proximity of the houses to the field here.

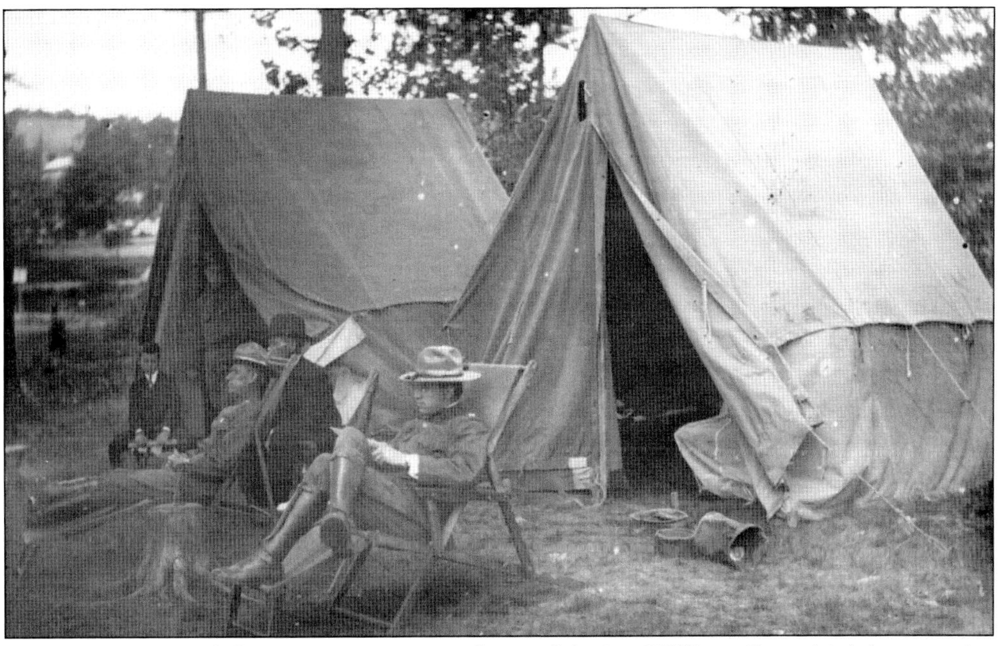

Capt. David Berg (left), company commander, and 1st Lt. William Oates (right), executive officer of Company L, are pictured relaxing before their respective field tents. The other men are unidentified.

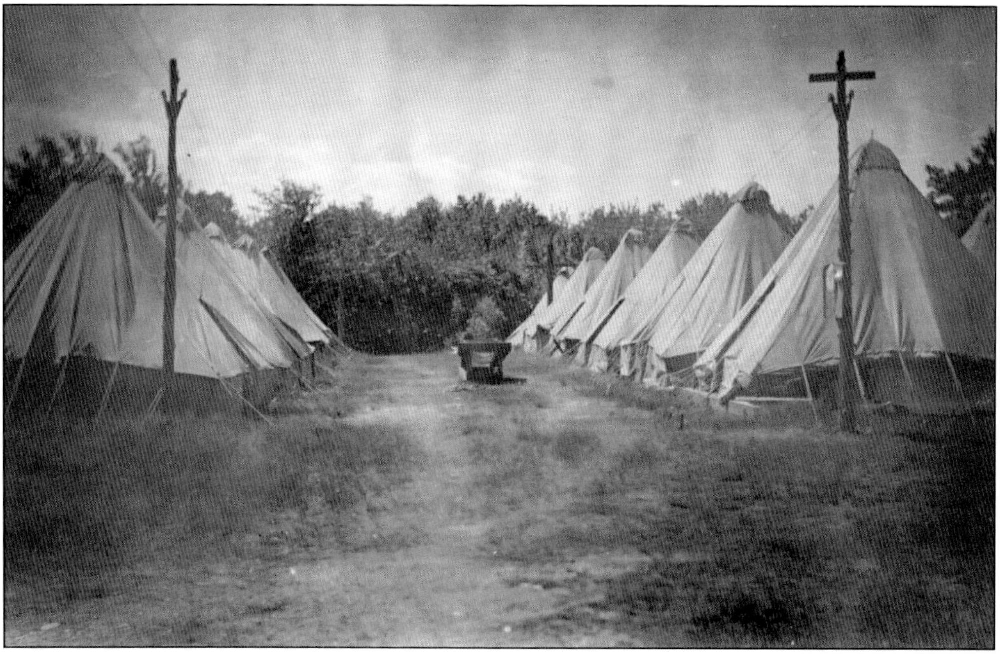

This view of the tents of two Company L platoons shows the accommodations afforded to the soldiers in the camp.

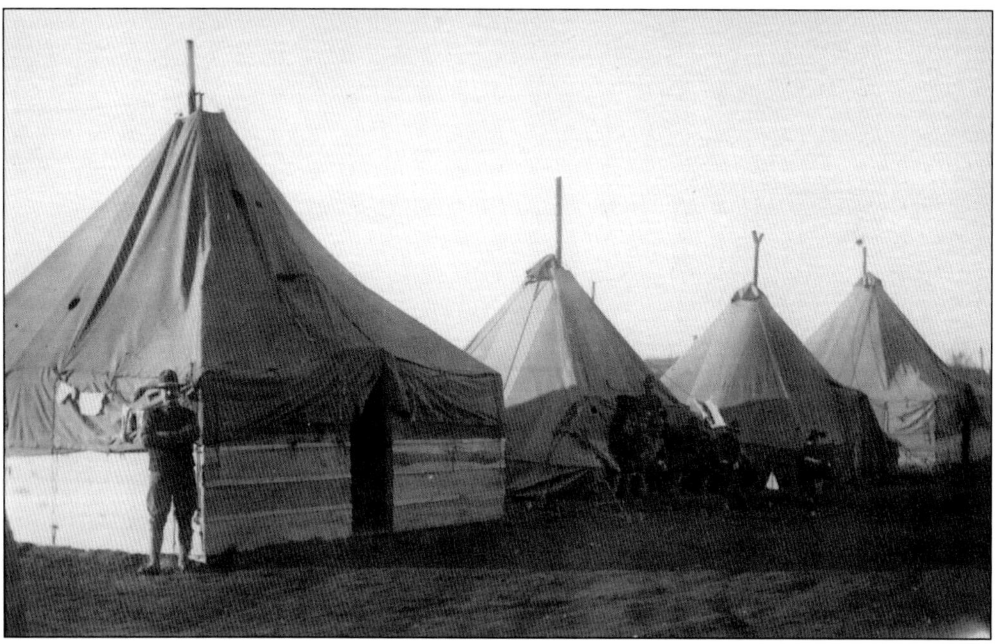

The field tents of the squad and platoon are braced with a wooden retaining wall to add stability and comfort.

Nine

Perry Pictures

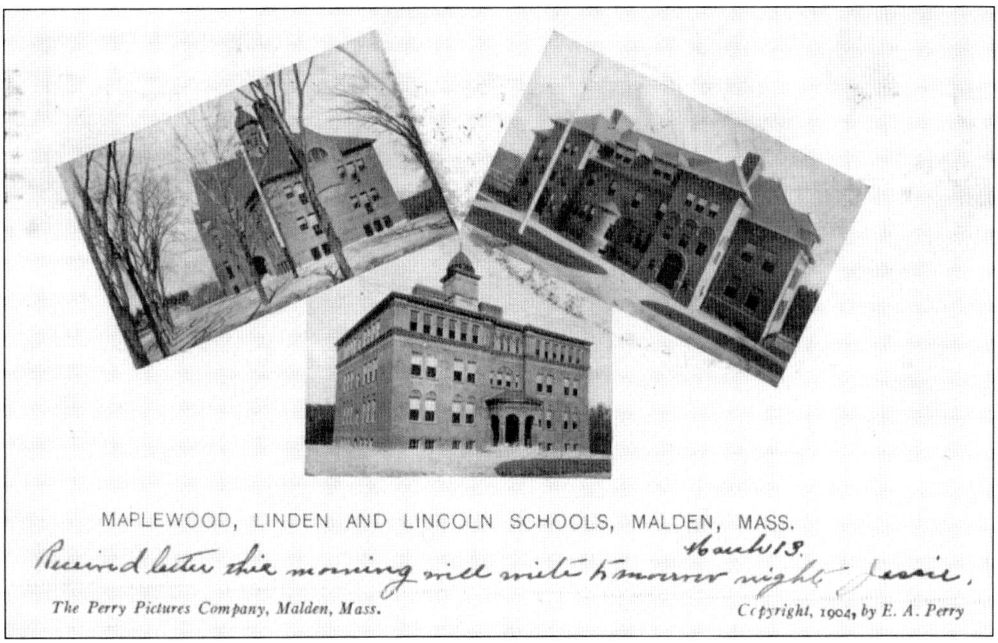

The Perry Pictures Company of Malden produced art studies of famous works for the use of students and to beautify homes throughout the United States. For many students, this was their introduction to art. Most people do not realize that the company also did other printing. This chapter reproduces some of the postcards of Malden produced by the Perry Pictures Company, all of them copyrighted in 1904. This postcard depicts three grammar schools as they appeared in the early 1900s. The Maplewood School was erected in 1886, and the Lincoln and Linden Schools were constructed in 1895, making them fairly new buildings at the time these pictures were taken.

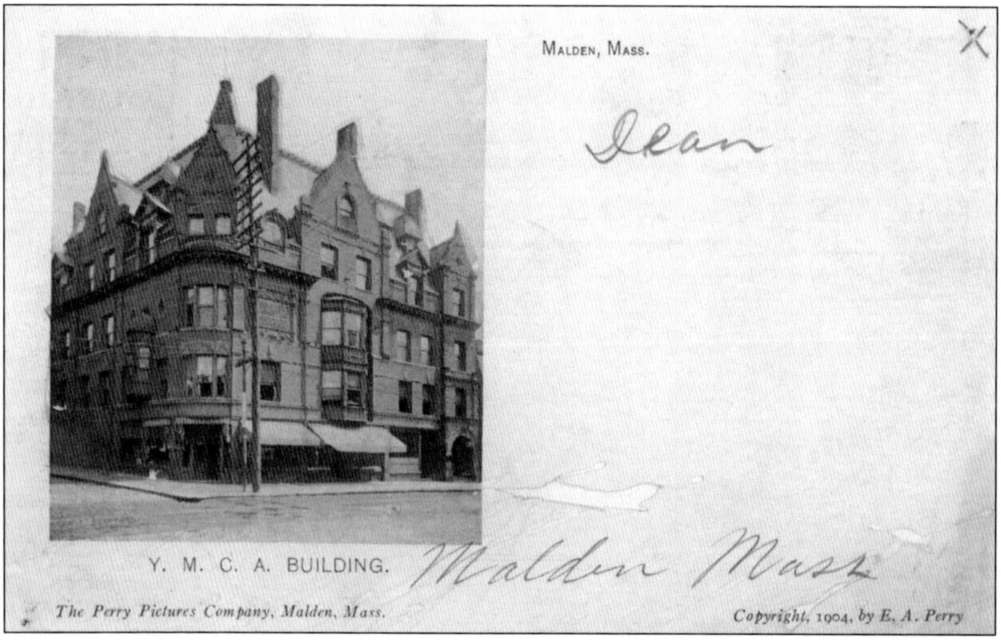

This view depicts the original YMCA building on Pleasant Street in Malden Square. The top two floors were remodeled at a later date (shown on page 58).

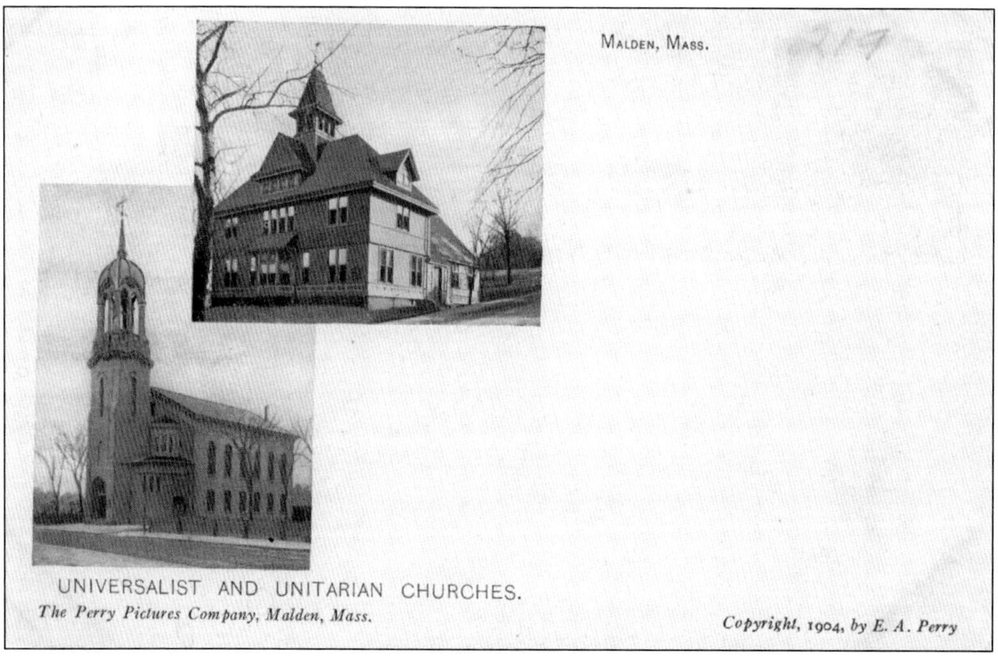

Two Malden churches are pictured. The Universalist Church was located on Main Street, near the corner of Centre Street, where Walgreens is now. The Unitarian Church was located at the corner of Hillside Avenue and Eastern Avenue.

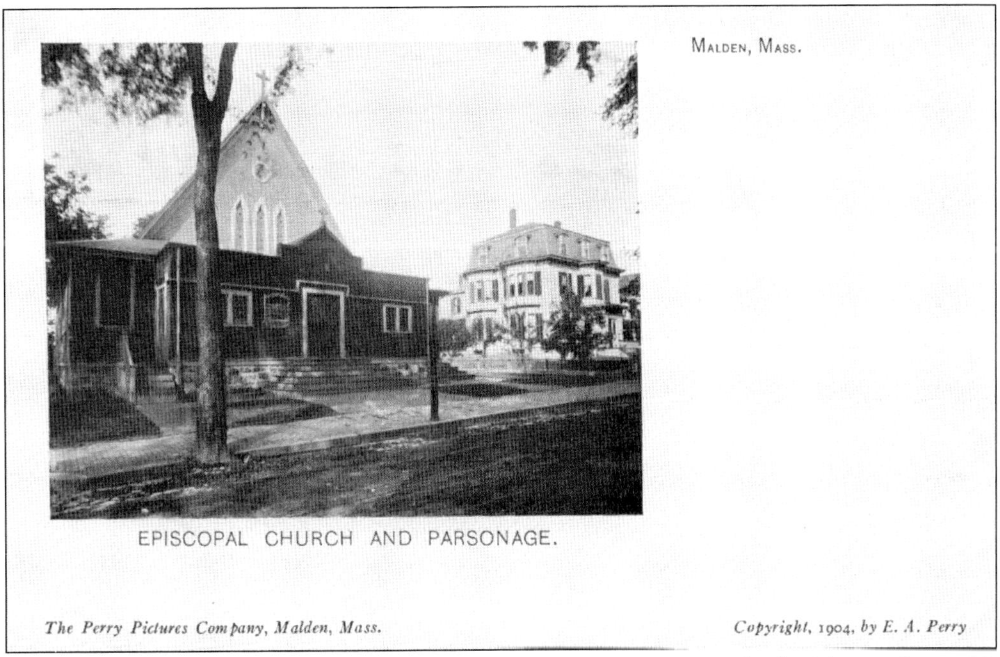

This view shows St. Paul's Episcopal Church on Washington Street. This building is the parish hall today, with some alteration.

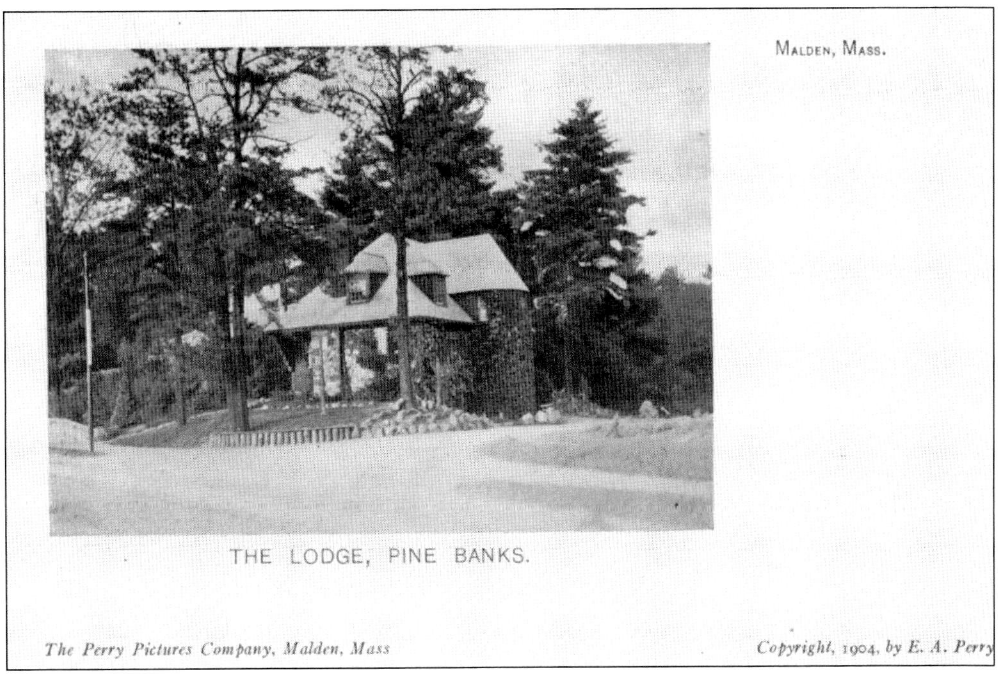

The Lodge at Pine Banks Park was originally a summer home used by Elisha Converse after he purchased what was formerly the Lynde family farm. Prior to 1905, Converse donated the land to the cities of Malden and Melrose for a park. The lodge now serves as the home of the park superintendent.

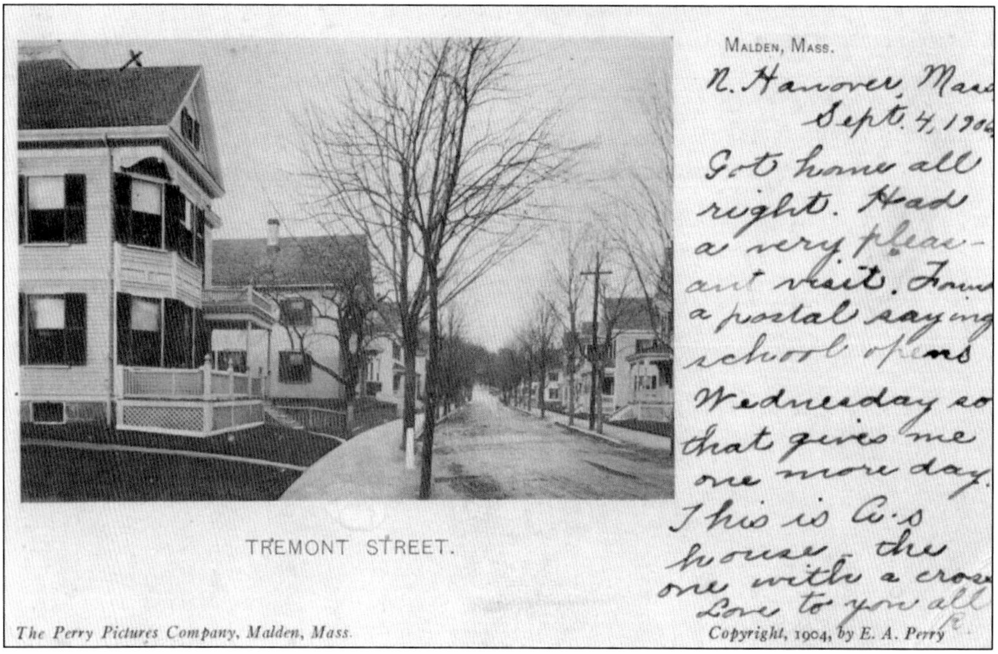

This view of Tremont Street, looking north from Salem Street, shows a number of single-family houses.

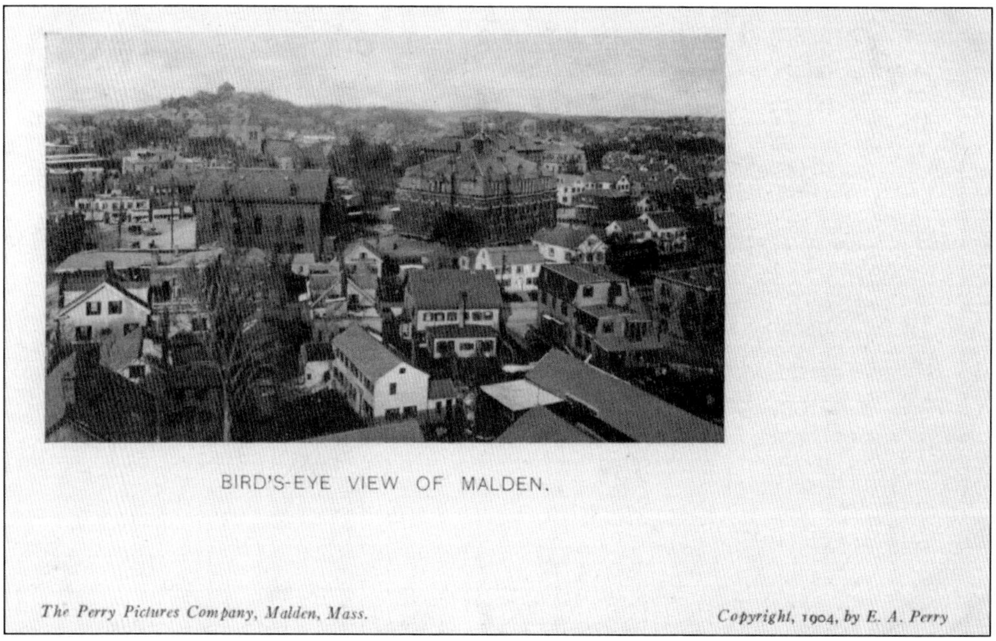

This image looks north from the Belmont Hill area of Malden. In the far distance is Waitt's Mount, on the top of which is a large water tower. To the left in the center is the city hall, built in 1857.

Ten

Advertising Postcards

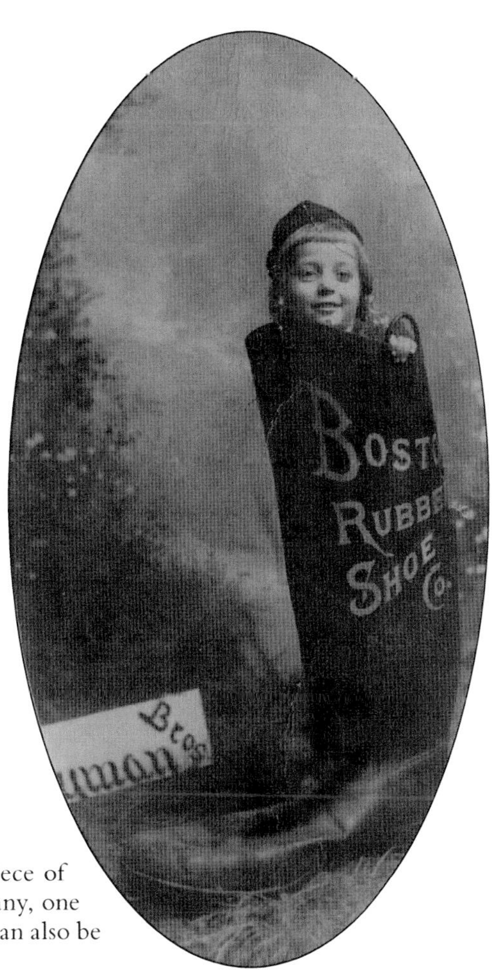

This very early postcard image was a clever piece of advertising by the Boston Rubber Shoe Company, one of Malden's largest manufacturers. This image can also be seen on trade cards of the period.

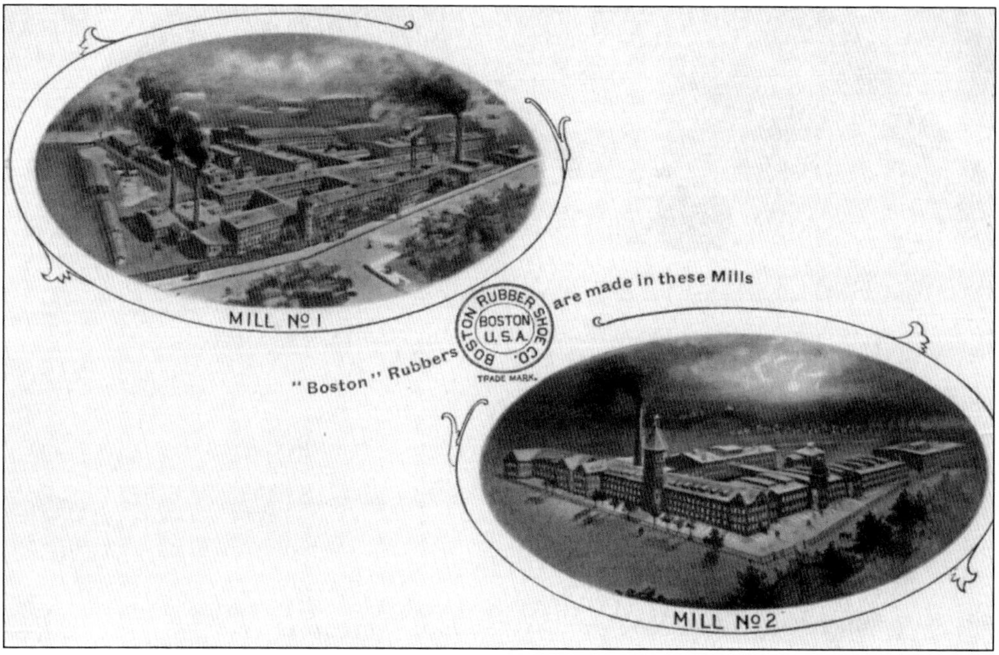

The Boston Rubber Shoe Company had two large factories by the late 19th century. Mill No. 1 was on Commercial Street in Edgeworth, and Mill No. 2 was on Washington Street, just over the line in Melrose.

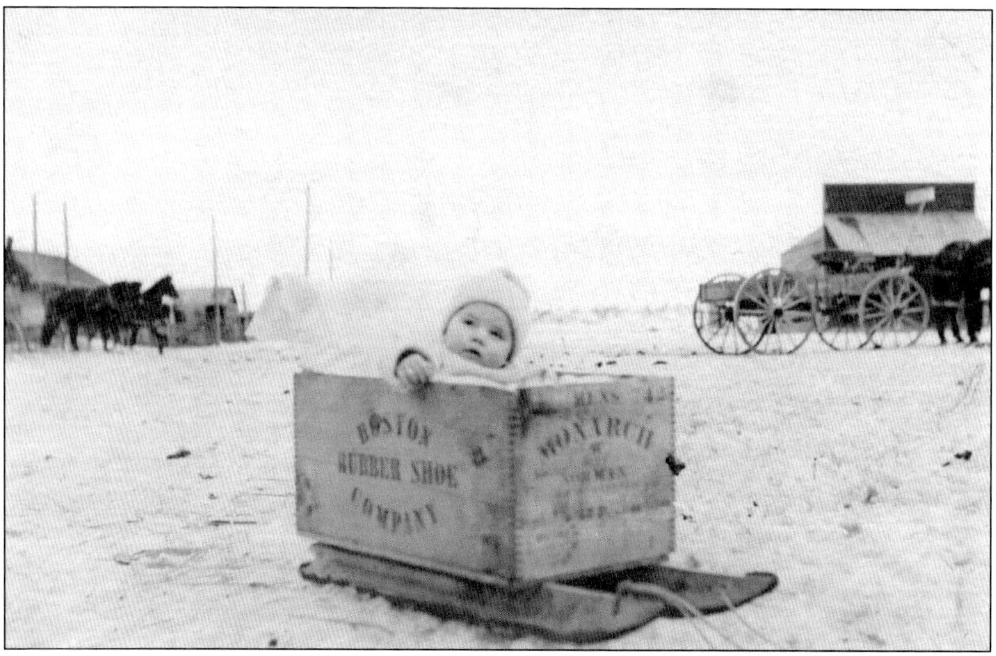

Another early advertising postcard of the Boston Rubber Shoe Company is pictured here. This one depicts a child on a improvised sled using a boot crate. Note the horse teams in the background.

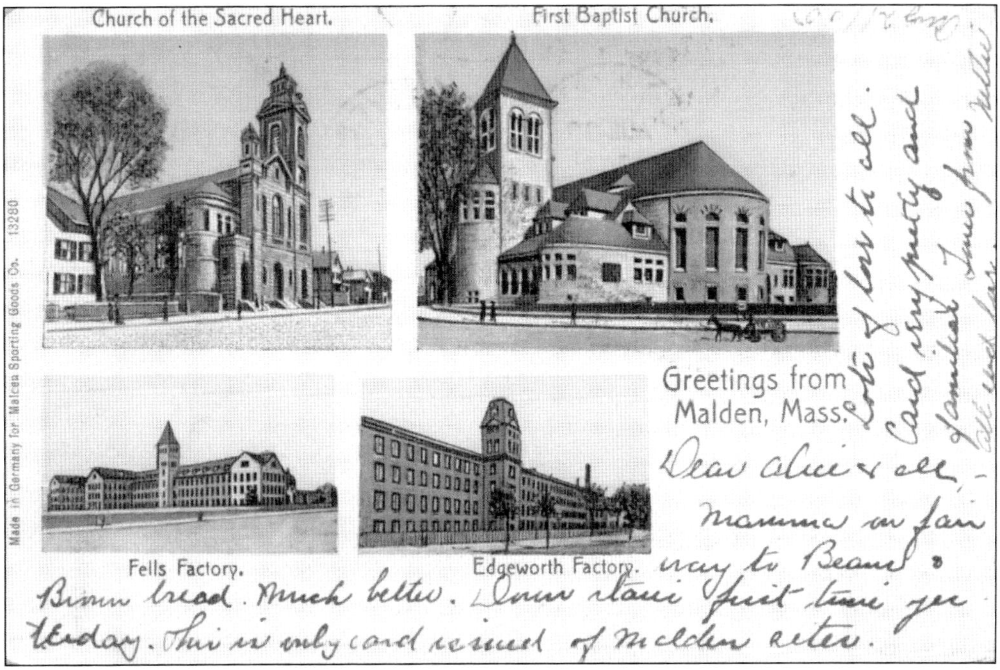

This multiple image card shows four Malden sites. The Sacred Hearts Church on Main Street in Malden Square and the First Baptist Church at the corner of Main and Salem Streets are shown at the top. The two lower images are another view of the Boston Rubber Shoe Company mills.

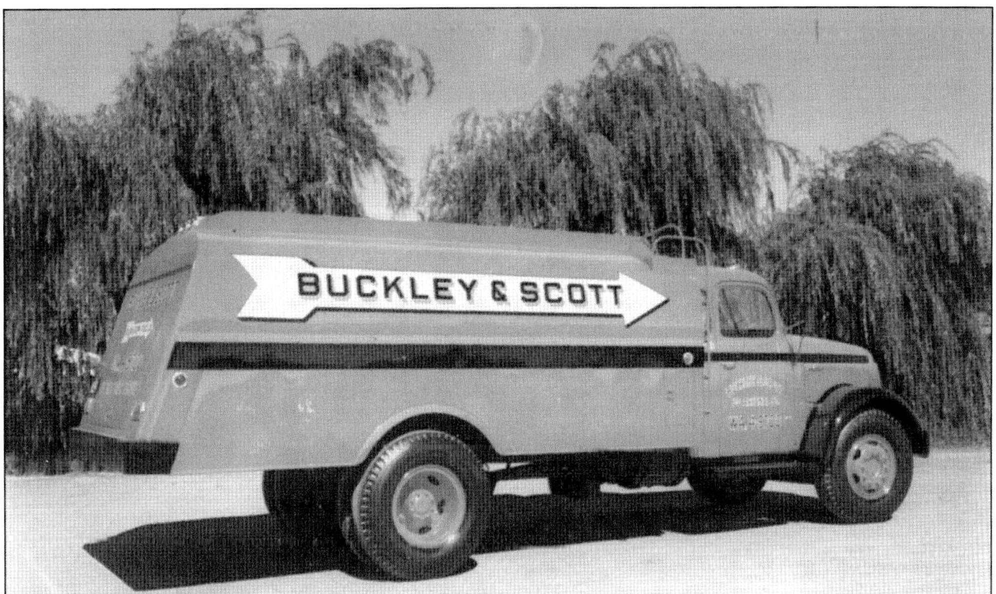

This photograph advertises the finished product of the Boston Steel and Manufacturing Company, located at Bryant Street and Eastern Avenue. The company specializes in making large fuel truck tanks.

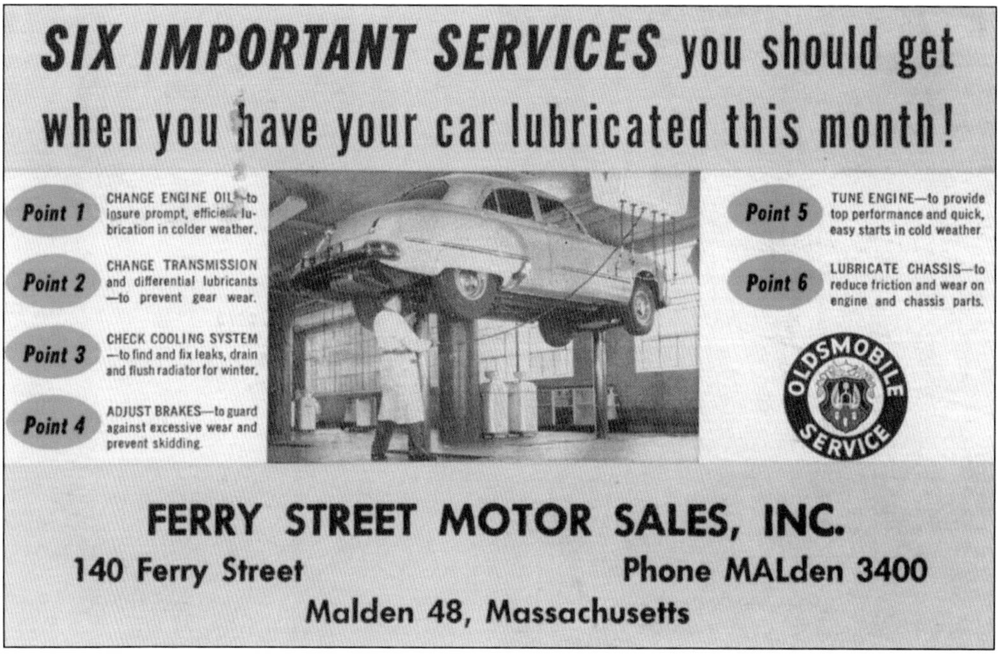

An advertising postcard from Ferry Street Motor Sales, located at 140 Ferry Street, depicts a 1950s Oldsmobile on a service lift. The card recommends a six-point lubrication and maintenance program. Many of these advertising cards show not only the product, but also the premises of the vendor. In many cases, both product and vendor have disappeared.

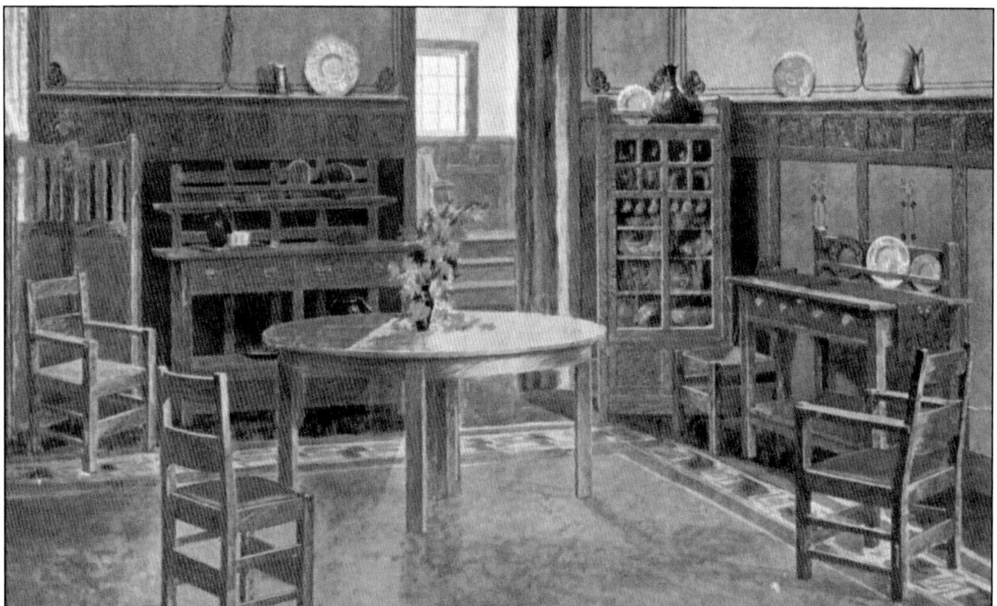

This c. 1911 postcard displays an artist's rendition of furniture for sale at the Caldwell Furniture Company at 130–134 Pleasant Street. The tables, chairs, cabinets, and other furniture shown are in the Mission or Arts and Crafts style of the period.

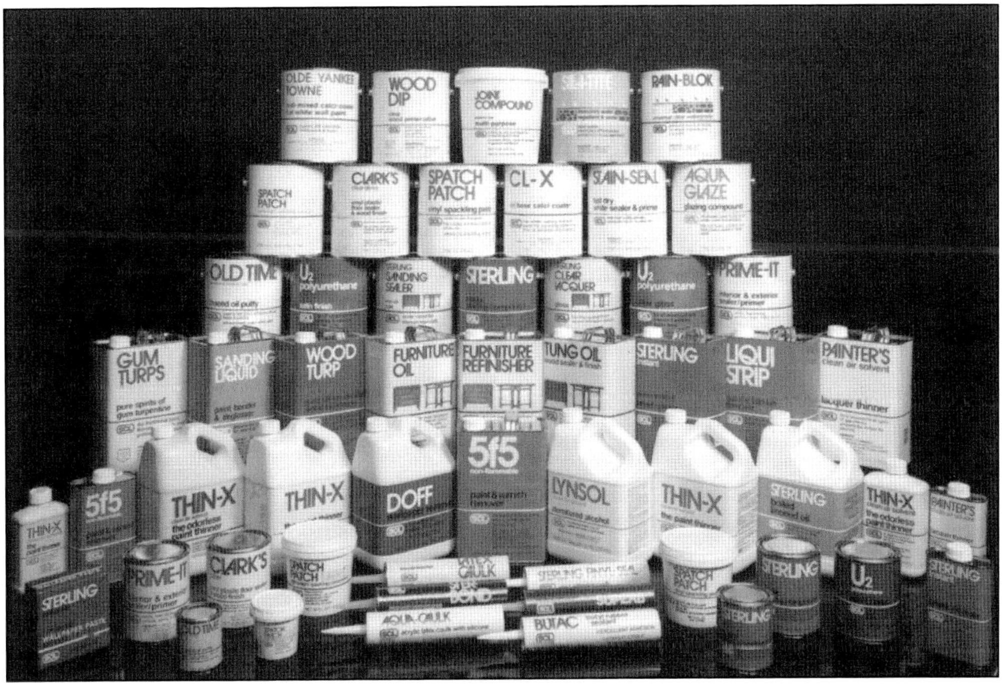

This photograph displays the large number of chemical products available from the Sterling-Clark-Lurton Corporation at 184 Commercial Street. At one time, Malden was the home of a number of chemical manufacturers.

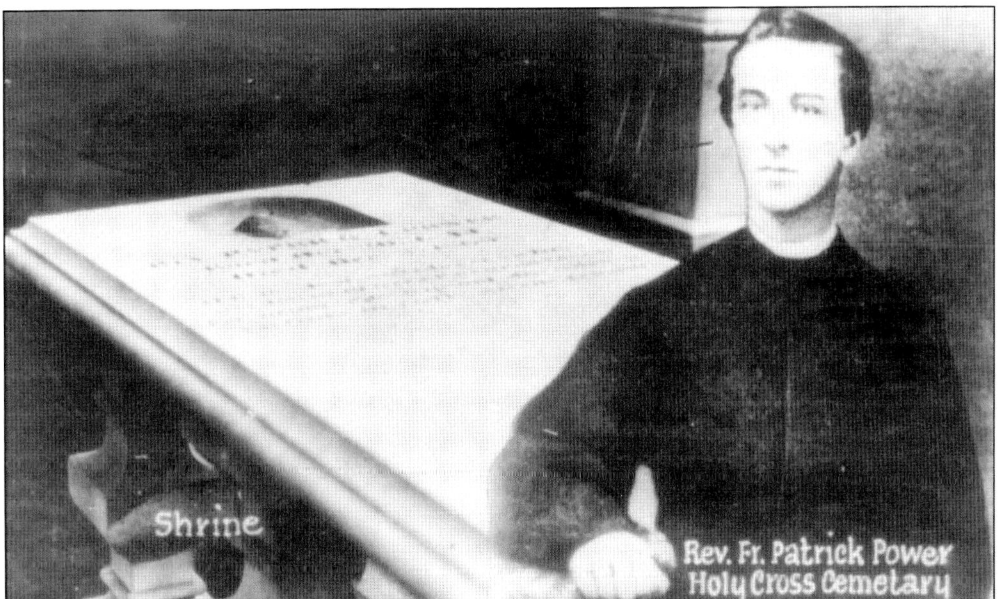

Fr. Patrick Power died in 1869 and was buried in Holy Cross Cemetery. In 1929, after miracle cures, such as sight being restored to the blind and the lame being able to walk, were reported at his grave, over a million people visited his gravesite. Many faithful still visit his grave to this day.

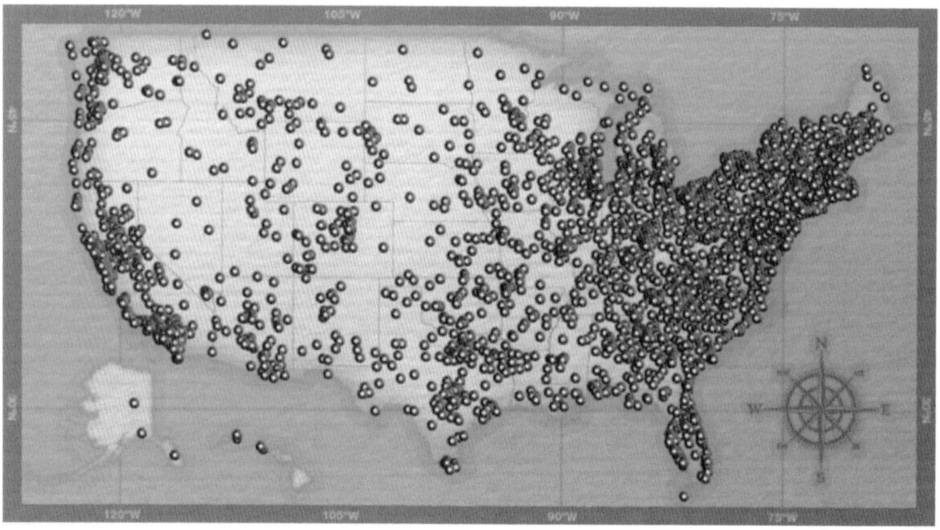